D0728322

To

_____

From

_____

Date

_____

365 Spirit-Lifting Devotions of Faith

ISBN-13: 978-0-8249-4524-4

Published by Guideposts
16 East 34th Street
New York, New York 10016
Guideposts.org

Distributed by Ideals Publications, a Guideposts company
2630 Elm Hill Pike, Suite 100
Nashville, TN 37214

Guideposts and *Ideals* are registered trademarks of Guideposts.

Acknowledgments
Every attempt has been made to credit the sources of copyrighted material used in this book. If any such acknowledgment has been inadvertently omitted or miscredited, receipt of such information would be appreciated.

Unless otherwise noted, Scripture references are from The Holy Bible, King James Version (KJV). Other Scriptures are taken from The Holy Bible, New International Version®, NIV®. Copyright © 1973, 1978, 1984, 2011 by Biblica, Inc.™ Used by permission of Zondervan. All rights reserved worldwide. The New King James Version (NKJV). Copyright © 1982 by Thomas Nelson, Inc. Used by permission. The New American Standard Bible® (NASB), Copyright © 1960, 1962, 1963, 1968, 1971, 1972, 1973, 1975, 1977, 1995 by The Lockman Foundation. Used by permission. *The Living Bible* (TLB) © 1971. Used by permission of Tyndale House Publishers, Inc., Wheaton, Illinois 60189. *The Message* (MSG). Copyright © 1993, 1994, 1995, 1996, 2000, 2001, 2002. Used by permission of NavPress Publishing Group. The New Revised Standard Version Bible (NRSV). Copyright © 1989, 1995, Division of Christian Education of the National Council of the Churches of Christ in the United States of America. Used by permission. Good News Translation® (GNT) Copyright © 1992 American Bible Society. All rights reserved.

Cover design, Interior design and typeset by Thinkpen Design, Inc.
www.thinkpendesign.com

Printed and bound in the United States of America

10 9 8 7 6 5 4 3 2 1

DAILY GUIDEPOSTS

365 SPIRIT-LIFTING DEVOTIONS

OF

Faith

Guideposts

INTRODUCTION

*F*aith is the beacon that lights the way along the road of our lifelong journey. It guides and protects us, enriching our lives with meaning and lifts us up with the knowledge that we are loved.

365 Spirit-Lifting Devotions of Faith will make the road easier to follow. This unique volume will keep you on course, no matter what life puts in your path. Each day offers a Scripture, a true-life story and a prayer that unites the devotion's theme. The devotions—one for every day of the year, including Leap Year—are by people from all walks of life who share their insights on how faith has touched their lives in everyday *and* extraordinary situations. Join them at work and on vacation, in good times and bad. Their stories will strengthen your own faith as you confront life's joys and challenges.

Meet Lindsey, the little walker-using ballerina who keeps up with the moves of other girls in her heart. Faith makes her a dancer too.

Vacation with Pam and David Kidd on the Isle of Vieques. There, trillions of microorganisms in the black-as-night water of Bioluminescence Bay reward visitors with a magical blue-green light—but only if they trust their guide and jump into the water.

Rejoice with Marion Bond West when her prayer for a terminally ill neighbor, "Lord, do something brand-new for E. J. today," is answered by a peaceful death in his favorite recliner.

Follow Brock Kidd's passage from despair to renewal as he comes to terms with his fiancée's decision to break their engagement and in the process gains a new understanding of his purposes in life.

Spend a week at the shore with Elizabeth Sherrill as her faith leads her to discover new wisdom in "words from the sea."

These and other faith-affirming stories make *365 Spirit-Lifting Devotions of Faith* a book to treasure and grow with, day after day and year after year. And because *365 Spirit-Lifting Devotions of Faith* is not bound to a particular year, you can start reading today and continue lifting your spirit in faith for years to come.

January

January 1

Make a joyful noise unto the Lord, all ye lands.
—Psalm 100:1

The "Rejoice" banner goes up on New Year's Day at my mom and dad's home. It usually hangs over the garage, the colorful letters on a white background reminding the neighbors to rejoice. Something of a historical artifact, it made its first appearance on January 1, 1983, carried by two Boy Scouts down Colorado Boulevard before a million people in Pasadena in that year's Rose Parade—what we always refer to as "Dad's parade."

That was when Dad was president of the Tournament of Roses, the volunteer organization that runs the Rose Parade and the Rose Bowl. He and Mom traveled across the country, meeting the bands that would march in the parade and the civic groups that would sponsor floats. They ate at pancake breakfast fund-raisers, shook hands with mayors and boosters, marched in other parades and cheered through Pac Ten/Big Ten football games. In preparation, Dad crowned a Rose queen and selected a grand marshal. But his biggest challenge was to come up with a theme for the parade.

I can remember some of the rejects: "Faith and Family," "Faith, Hope and Love," "Faith and Enterprise" (somehow I could never see that on a banner carried down Colorado Boulevard). Clearly Dad was trying to find the right message to help people celebrate the New Year. "It should have meaning for everybody," he said.

What Dad finally settled on was a simple verb, one that appears a couple of hundred times in the Bible. It was on the banner and the floats and in the band music, and it was the word he repeated that sunny morning as he waved from the horse-drawn, flower-covered carriage that led the parade.

"Rejoice."

What a way to greet the New Year!

Lord, on this New Year's Day, I rejoice in the world You made.
—Rick Hamlin

JANUARY 2

Sing to the Lord a new song.
—PSALM 96:1 (NRSV)

One New Year's day many years ago, worried over finances and an undiagnosed illness, I chose these words of Psalm 96 as my Bible verse for the year. Whenever I felt anxious, I decided, I'd learn a new hymn and replace the "what-ifs" with songs of faith.

The hymn I picked to launch the experiment was "Another Year Is Dawning" by Frances Havergal. Appropriate for the day, but also, given the unknowns I faced, faintly annoying. How could the author be so sure it would be "another year of gladness...of quiet, happy rest"? *Life in the nineteenth century*, I thought, *must have been a lot more placid than it is today!*

Several days later, spotting a book on hymn writers in our church library, I looked up this woman whose words I was singing. Frances Havergal's life, I quickly learned, was far from placid. I faced a potentially serious illness; Frances was ill all her life, never able to attend school, marry, have children. I worried about paying bills; Frances's father, an English clergyman, had scarcely started work in his first parish when he was thrown from a carriage and incapacitated.

Then when Frances was eleven, her mother died. In her grief, the girl turned to writing hymns of faith. Until her own death at age fifty-three, this frail woman never stopped composing verses that have given strength to others ever since.

I did have surgery when cancer was diagnosed that long-ago year; our family did struggle to make ends meet. But I had before me the example of a woman who faced her own unknown future with a high heart.

What will the new year bring? Frances Havergal knew only that when we turn to God with a song, it's sure to be filled with His presence "all the days."

Give me the songs again this year, Father, to make it "another year with Thee."
—ELIZABETH SHERRILL

January 3

"The one who believes in him will never be put to shame."
—Romans 9:33 (NIV)

*T*housands of Canada geese make their winter homes in Mississippi. The other day I watched a flock of them fly through the air and land on the surface of the water. I'd been having some difficulty adjusting to my new part-time role at work and I envied the geese; they seemed so carefree as they glided along. Then I remembered a song we had sung many times at our church:

Trust and obey, for there's no other way,
To be happy in Jesus, than to trust and obey.
Then in fellowship sweet we will sit at His feet.
Or we'll walk by His side in the way.
What He says we will do, where He sends we will go;
Never fear, only trust and obey.
(John H. Sammis, 1887)

As I looked at the geese and thought about my circumstances, I began to relax, knowing that the more I acknowledge that God is in charge, the more I can trust and obey Him. Can I be as carefree as the geese? I don't know. Can I be more carefree than I am and trust God more? The answer is a resounding yes!

Lord, help me to strive to trust You more.
—Dolphus Weary

JANUARY 4

The apostles said to the Lord, "Increase our faith!"
—LUKE 17:5 (NIV)

*I*ncreased faith was my prayer one New Year's Day twenty years ago. It wasn't a resolution—I knew how short-lived those were! Once I'd set out to memorize a Bible verse every day of the year; I kept at it until nearly February. Another time I resolved to start each day with a half-hour of praise. Sometimes I managed fifteen minutes.

It had been the same with efforts to muster the kind of faith I'd encountered working on people's stories for *Guideposts* magazine. People who gave away their livelihoods knowing that "God will provide." People confident of healing in the face of medical impossibility. People certain in bereavement that the loved one awaited them in heaven. How I longed for a faith like that!

Jesus' closest followers did too: "Increase our faith!"

Reading Jesus' reply to them—to me—I could almost see Him shaking His head. "You don't need great faith! Faith the size of a grain of mustard seed is enough!"

And so I stopped asking for the full-grown faith of the people I admired in *Guideposts*—maybe theirs started with little seeds too. Ever since then, I've kept a record of the everyday ways God invites me to fully trust Him. Invitations in such unlikely forms as a book of cartoons, an anonymous phone call, a crying child. Small gifts in day-sized doses, scaled to the need at hand.

And oddly enough, when I pray for seeds instead of flowers, my faith-life blossoms. Maybe it's the habit of looking each day for faith-builders so small they're easy to miss, but when I look back, sturdy little plants are pushing up in my garden here and there from those minuscule beginnings.

Faithful Lord, remind me again this coming year that it is not my faith
but Your great faithfulness that makes all things possible.
—ELIZABETH SHERRILL

JANUARY 5

After this, the word of the Lord came to Abram in a vision:
"Do not be afraid, Abram. I am your shield, your very great reward."
—GENESIS 15:1 (NIV)

*T*was peeling potatoes at the kitchen sink and listening to my four-year-old grandson Frank. He was in the next room, deep into one of the imaginative stories he loves to tell with his box of "people." This time Frank's people were in a snake-infested jungle. Wild animals were all around them. They were lost. "It was getting dark," he said in a stage whisper, "and they were very scared." There was a long pause, and I was all ears, wondering how Frank would get his people out of this mess. Finally, in a loud voice, he announced, "But God was with them."

I stopped, potato peeler in midair, wondering how God would bring the people out. But there was only silence. I tiptoed to the doorway and saw Frank putting the people back in the box. I don't know what was in Frank's mind or why the story ended there. *Perhaps he couldn't figure out an ending and so took the easy way out of leaving it with God*, I thought, smiling.

I went back to peeling potatoes and pondering a problem that seemed to have no solution. But Frank's unfinished ending kept going 'round and 'round in my head. "But God was with them." Finally I heard the truth of it.

Lord God, You Who are the Alpha and the Omega, the Beginning
and the End, help me to stay with You in the here and now.
—SHARI SMYTH

Then, opening their treasure-chests, they offered him
gifts of gold, frankincense, and myrrh.
—Matthew 2:11 (nrsv)

I collect Christmas books. Between Thanksgiving and Epiphany, I try to read them all. One is reserved for today. When I turn to the drawing accompanying the story, I'm distressed all over again. It's a stark pen-and-ink depiction of a bent old man riding on a camel. In the distance, three figures are hanging on crosses. The story is an ancient, heartrending legend about one of the wise men who visited the baby Jesus, the one who brought myrrh, a precious ointment for healing and anointing the dead. It takes place thirty years after his encounter with the newborn Child. In the prime of his life when he first found Jesus, he is now aged and crippled. He painfully dismounts at the foot of the cross to leave the same gift again: myrrh to anoint the dead and broken body of his King.

Though this story moves me to tears each year, it's the one I carry forward into the year with a determined joy. As the whirl and waiting of Christmas fades, I don't want to forget why Jesus was born. Following Him and His parents to Bethlehem is easy; following Him to Jerusalem, Gethsemane, Golgotha and the tomb is not so easy.

So where's the joy? The joy is in knowing what happens after. And each year, I imagine that the aged wise man, waiting at an inn for the strength to return home, stayed in Jerusalem long enough to learn the rest of the story.

Jesus, let me be always ready to give You the gift of myself: my heart,
my mind, my body, my actions, my prayers, my faith, my love.
—Marci Alborghetti

January 7

O LORD, Thou hast searched me, and known me. Thou knowest
my downsitting and mine uprising, Thou understandest my thought afar off.
—PSALM 139:1–2

*T*was twenty thousand feet in the air, my face pressed against the oval window of an airplane. Beyond, an infinite blueness blanketed the world with lonely space. My four-year-old son sat in my lap, his shaggy brown hair nestled against my shoulder.

The nose of the plane dipped. We began our descent. "In a moment we'll see a big city from the plane," I said.

We squeezed our faces into the little window and suddenly there it was, far, far below, gleaming in the sun like a child's miniature blocks. "Do you see the tiny people way down on the ground?" I asked. Bob nodded.

As he watched the ant-sized people, he asked, "Mama, is that what God sees when He looks down from heaven?"

A God's-eye view of the world? I thought of all the vastness God could see. A planet with four billion people, spinning in a universe with a hundred million galaxies. Suddenly, I felt small and insignificant...an ant-sized speck at the end of God's vision.

Bob tucked his head beneath my chin. His hair tickled my neck and some words of Jesus drifted to mind. "The very hairs of your head are all numbered" (Matthew 10:30, NIV). How could I forget? God deals up close and personally with every person. I turned to my son. "When God looks down on the world, He sees us so closely, He can count every hair on our heads. That's how special and near we are to Him."

"Wow!" Bob whispered, wide-eyed with wonder.

I smiled. That was my feeling, exactly.

When I feel tiny and insignificant, lost in the vastness
of everything, remind me that in Your eyes, I am special.
—SUE MONK KIDD

January 8

Pray without ceasing.
—I Thessalonians 5:17

or years I'd heard that drinking eight glasses of water a day would be good for my health, so I felt pretty noble when I finally made it my New Year's resolution. But as I walked into the kitchen one night, I was stunned to see my cat washing his face by scooping water out of my glass, dashing it on his face and circling his wet face with his paw. His bowl of water went untouched.

Just how long has he been doing this? Could I have caught some cat disease? I raced to the phone to call my vet, praying, *Please, God, let her answer right away. I could be seriously ill right now!* She answered on the first ring—*Thank You, God.*

"What's wrong with your cat?" she asked.

"Oh, it's not about Junior," I said. "It's about me. I just discovered he has been scooping out water from my drinking glass to wash his face. What should I do?"

There was a moment's pause and then she said, "Keep your water in the refrigerator." I could swear I heard her chuckle as she hung up the phone.

"What a waste of time and worry," I said to the vet when she was examining Junior during his next regular checkup.

"But not a waste of prayer," she commented. "Prayer is never wasted."

I've thought about what she said many times since then. Though it was something silly, that odd situation had led me to pray. If only I could stay as connected to God all the time. Now there's a subject for a resolution.

God, may I be inspired to pray more often, over big matters
and small, so I may become closer to You.

—Linda Neukrug

January 9

*O*n my drive to work I have to pass through an area of the highway called T-REX, which stands for Transportation Expansion Project. We're two years into the five years it's supposed to take the city to build a mass transit system right through the heart of Denver. To city officials, it's an exciting answer to our congested highways. To me, it's a nuisance.

I see it for what it is today; they see it for what it will be tomorrow. They have vision. And over and over, on television and in the newspapers and with signs along the highways, they try to communicate that vision to people like me. As I sit in bumper-to-bumper traffic, I need to know that the suffering is temporary and the best is yet to come.

God is the creator of vision. He Who knows the end from the beginning promises us over and over again that what's in store for us is to be in heaven with Him.

He keeps telling us the best is yet to come. So we should be encouraged while we endure disappointment or pain—or traffic snarls. God gives us His vision of heaven to hold in our hearts.

Father, help me to see Your vision, so I can look forward to what will be.

—Carol Kuykendall

JANUARY 10

Strength and beauty are in his sanctuary.
—PSALM 96:6 (NRSV)

*O*ne of my earliest memories is of sitting in St. Alban's Episcopal Church in McCook, Nebraska, gazing at the stained glass window above the altar. I must have been three or four years old and bored by a sermon I couldn't understand. That was when I started gazing at the colorful window. The sun was at exactly the right height to shine directly through the glass, radiating stunning blues, emerald greens and deep maroons onto the white choir robes and even onto my lap. The colors were so jewellike, they seemed magical to me.

Pulling on Mother's sleeve and pointing to the window, I said in a loud whisper, "Look! God is smiling at us from heaven!"

She put her finger to her lips and whispered, "No, dear. It's just the sun shining through the colored glass." But with preschool certainty, I was sure I was right. I had no doubt that those beautiful colors came from God and that He was smiling at me from heaven, just on the other side of the glass.

For the first of many times to come, I breathed in beauty and breathed out gratitude. Whether Mother knew it or not, I felt sure that beauty and the eyes with which to see it were special gifts from God—my favorite of all His presents.

Great Creator, thank You for painting our world with such heavenly colors.
—MARILYN MORGAN KING

January 11

I, even I, am he that comforteth you.
—Isaiah 51:12

*P*atricia, a member of our church, announced one Sunday that she had shingles and asked for prayers. I dutifully prayed and extended my sympathy when she said she was having a lot of pain.

But it wasn't until I got shingles myself that I understood the pain she'd been talking about. My shingles had advanced enough before I discovered them that our doctor wasn't sure we could get them stopped. But strong doses of an antiviral medication, plus the prayers of our church members, including Patricia, set me on the road to recovery.

When Patricia said to me during the worst of it, "I know what you're going through," I knew she did, and that was a comfort. When other members of our church who had never experienced shingles touched my hand and said, "I'm sorry," that was a comfort too. But the greatest comfort of all came from the Friend above, Who listened to my prayers and held my hand at night when I couldn't sleep.

Lord, help me reach out to someone today who is suffering,
even if I don't fully understand his or her pain.
—Madge Harrah

He provides food for those who fear him; he remembers his covenant forever.
—PSALM 111:5 (NIV)

*A*s a gymnastics coach I'm constantly lifting mats, moving equipment and helping children as they swing, climb and somersault through the air. When my husband and I found out I was pregnant, I asked the doctor about the potential dangers at work. "You don't have to worry right now," she said, "but the bigger you get, the more risk you'll have for back problems." I thought about leaving my job after my fifth month of pregnancy, but I was worried about our financial stability. "We'll be fine," my husband assured me, but I still had my doubts.

During a weekly Bible study, I explained my situation as we went around the room, sharing prayer requests. "I've never had to depend on someone else to take care of me," I admitted. "What if it's not enough?" Aliza, an older woman in the group, smiled at me and shook her head. "God is your provider. He always has been." She wrapped my hands in her own. "You can't depend on yourself or your husband. God will take care of your family, and it will always be enough." After her encouraging words I made a decision to leave after the fall semester. I didn't know how everything would work out, but I knew I could trust in the One Who had always taken care of me.

Then, just weeks after I gave my notice, I received an e-mail: A company was interested in some work I'd done years before. They wanted to give me a contract at three times the usual rate! When I calculated the income and the amount of time I'd be out of work, it was more than enough. I thanked the Lord, not just for the financial blessing and peace of mind, but for confirming Aliza's words so quickly.

> *Lord, You are my provider. You have always taken*
> *care of me, and it will always be enough.*

—KAREN VALENTIN

JANUARY 13

Whatever your hand finds to do, do it with all your might.
—ECCLESIASTES 9:10 (NIV)

*W*orking as a registered nurse with seniors in assisted-care homes, I found two types of residents. The angry ones didn't want to be there and, in a way, I didn't blame them. They'd lost so much: hard-earned homes and possessions, independence, privacy, good health. And then there were people like Mr. and Mrs. Epp, who radiated quiet acceptance. What secret had they found to keep discouragement at bay?

One morning before breakfast I entered their room with their medication. At first I didn't see the couple. They were sitting together at a small table sipping coffee from Royal Albert china cups. "Mugs from the home won't do," said Mrs. Epp, smoothing the lace tablecloth, "nor will the coffee from the dining hall."

Mr. Epp nodded. "This is how we've always done it," he said proudly.

There's comfort in our simple routines, in the ordinary tasks of life. When I feel frazzled, I consider the Epps and enjoy a hot cup of tea, take a stroll in the park or write a letter to someone I love. Sometimes the smallest things can make the whole day better.

Dear Lord, thank You for the familiar things that brighten my day.
—HELEN GRACE LESCHEID

January 14

He shall grow up before him as a tender plant,
and as a root out of a dry ground.
—Isaiah 53:2

There's an old patch of wood that we keep unpainted in our back room near the storage cabinets. The dates and names start at the bottom, a little more than three feet above the ground, in childish handwriting. The writing becomes more secure as the names rise higher, and it's positively mature well above five feet.

There's William on 9-12-99 and then William a foot higher on 5-10-03. Timothy seems to make the same rapid progress a little behind his older brother. Mom and Dad never seem to change. I never rise above five feet eleven inches, but the boys leapfrog over each other until you see them leap above their mother—a strong black line to mark the milestone—and then they rise above their father, leaving him in the dust.

Then the writing stops—no more updates; no need for more. But the old marks are still there, and I can glance at them when I'm getting down the gardening shears or looking for a screwdriver. My friend Tib reminds me that the one prayer God never answers is "Please, let nothing change."

When I cling too tightly to the past, I can look at this record of how the boys grew until they towered over me. So many answers to prayer in indelible ink. Someday we'll have to move from this home, but I hope the new owners can make their own marks of progress along the wood.

Lord, let me look forward, always remembering
the love that has been with me all along.
—Rick Hamlin

January 15

"So get to work, and may the Lord be with you!"
—I Chronicles 22:16 (TLB)

*A*fter Captain Chesley Sullenberger landed his commercial jet safely in the Hudson River a couple of years ago, he was interviewed by several reporters. One of them asked, "When you realized you were going down, did you pray?"

He hesitated. "I thought of nothing else but flying the plane."

At first I was surprised by his answer, but the more I thought about it, the more I appreciated his honesty. As a pilot myself, I understand how much concentration it takes to fly a plane, even when there's no emergency. When things go wrong, it's time for action, not conversation. Action is a kind of physical prayer, I think, and the airplane itself is a good example of how it works. On the ground, an airplane is the slowest and most awkward of creatures, hard to steer. But when it picks up speed and the wind hits the control surfaces, it suddenly becomes the most agile of all transports. You can steer it with the merest touch. Not until it gets into action can it be guided well.

Many kinds of prayer exist, all of them useful. There's a place for the all-nighter, with tears. There's a place for table graces and a time for the "flare prayer," when you cry out, "Dear God, help me!" But there's also a time for the wordless prayer, when you get up off your knees and get to work. When I do that, I can feel His wind beneath my wings.

Forgive me, Lord, but I can't talk right now. I have a plane to fly.
—Daniel Schantz

January 16

Open his eyes, that he may see.
—II Kings 6:17

*F*or hours I'd watched eight-year-old Alanzo wait patiently outside our makeshift clinic, an abandoned church with its interior divided by brightly colored sheets.

Every day that week, he had made the two-mile trek across the Belize countryside in hopes of finding relief from his headaches. Every day, he sat quietly while the doctors explained that the eyeglasses they had ordered for him had been delayed at customs and might not arrive until the next day.

On the final day of our two-week clinic the glasses arrived. Alanzo, always at the front of the line, eagerly waited as I fished out his prescription and quickly fitted him with a pair of too-large frames that he would eventually grow into. He looked up at me through the lenses, his dark eyes magnified by the prescription. His face lit up and he began pointing. "I see you!" he shouted. Running around the churchyard, he exclaimed, "I see you, rock! I see you, tree!" He turned, pointing to me, "I see you, lady!"

Laughing, I called him back over, holding up a mirror so he could examine himself. Looking into the glass, he drew in a slow breath and whispered, "I see me." That day he went home happy, calling out the names of sticks, buildings and friends as he passed.

I'm a long way from Belize now, but Alanzo's message has remained in my heart. There's a world of beauty all around me, if only I have eyes to see.

Lord, open my eyes to see Your glory in every flower and every face.
—Ashley Johnson

January 17

Our Father who art in heaven....
—Matthew 6:9 (NRSV)

*M*y father Harry J. Thorell served with the legendary 10th Mountain Division of the U. S. Army during World War II. In April 1945 he survived a perilous assault on Mt. Belvedere in the Italian Alps, thanks to fog, which obscured him and some of the other skiing soldiers who were resupplying ammunition. Dad escaped death, but some of his buddies did not.

Now, at age eighty-six, Dad was having a harder time dodging a new enemy—Alzheimer's disease. As the fog of forgetfulness blurred the present, Dad found himself transported more and more frequently behind enemy lines. Each time he wept for his lost comrades.

"I used to pray—how does it go?—'Our Father, Who art in heaven.... Our Father....'" He looked at me helplessly.

"Hallowed be thy name," I coaxed.

"Our Father, Who art...." Tears welled up in his eyes. I could give him the words, but he'd forget them again. What could I do to help? Then I spied a pen.

"Here, Dad." I grabbed the pen and printed the words of the Lord's Prayer on an index card. "The next time you want to pray, hold this card. The prayer is right here."

Dad looked at the card and then wiped his eyes. "Yeah...okay, I can do that." Then he tucked the prayer in his pocket and smiled.

Even if we forget our prayers, we won't forget You, God.
—Gail Thorell Schilling

JANUARY 18

*All Scripture is God-breathed and is useful for teaching,
rebuking, correcting and training in righteousness.*
—II Timothy 3:16 (NIV)

*L*ast year I took an intensive workshop training teachers to tutor people who have great difficulty reading or writing. One day we observed our instructor Kay work with a thirty-five-year-old man who read at a second-grade level. The birth of his first child had motivated him to try to learn to read.

"We don't get many adult students," Kay told us. "Imagine how much courage it takes for people to admit they can't read." Kay asked if anyone could guess the three main reasons adults will risk yet another humiliating experience of failure and seek instruction. We surmised correctly that the need to read job applications or newspaper employment ads would prompt someone to try to learn to read. To our amazement, however, the reason most frequently given by adults seeking help is "to be able to read the Bible."

How often I take for granted my ability—and my freedom—to read God's Word. I know an Orthodox monk who traveled in the former Soviet Union during the years Christians were persecuted there. An elderly woman approached him and asked if he could give her a Bible. Anticipating such requests, he had brought Bibles with him and managed to give her one when his official guides weren't looking. Tears streaming down her face, she took the book from him and kissed it. Clutching it to her chest, she whispered, "Spasiba, spasiba" ("Thank you, thank you").

*Lord, please remind me not to neglect the precious gift
of Your Word, but to open it each day and make it my own.*
—Mary Brown

Calling the Twelve to him, he began to send them out two by two.
—MARK 6:7 (NIV)

I sat on a splintery packing crate, struggling to get my feet into the hip boots our host Janet had just handed me. Janet had lived on this New Zealand oyster farm all her life; she'd put on both her boots by the time I'd wiggled and stamped my foot halfway into one. Stretching out before us in the shallows of the bay were rows of oyster frames perched on posts. Between some of the posts Janet had strung fishnets. My boots on at last, we set out to see what the nets had caught for our dinner. The first part of the journey was easy, but with each step it got harder to lift my feet out of the clinging muck. Soon Janet was far ahead.

Don't fall, I kept telling myself as I wrestled one leg after the other from the deepening sludge. I didn't know how I'd ever get up, and the tide was coming in. Janet was still striding forward, but the mud was now almost knee-deep, and with every tugging step I came close to overbalancing. And then, of course, it happened. I toppled backward in slow motion until I was sitting chest-deep in the rising water. Fighting down my pride, I called for help. Janet turned, hurried back, gripped my hands and braced herself as I pulled myself up. She steadied me, too, all the slithery way back to the shore. While I showered in the farmhouse Janet returned to her nets to bring in our dinner.

That evening I lay in the guest-room bed thinking that, in an age that exalts independence, I'd discovered why Jesus sent His disciples out "two by two." There's a lot of mud out there, waiting to catch any one of us and hold us captive, unable to get up by our own strength. But two by two—that's a very different story.

Grant me grace today, Lord, to ask without shame for the help I need.
—JOHN SHERRILL

JANUARY 20

Yours, O Lord, are the greatness, the power, the glory, the victory,
and the majesty; for all that is in the heavens and on the earth is yours;
yours is the kingdom, O Lord, and you are exalted as head above all.
—I CHRONICLES 29:11 (NRSV)

W hen I first moved to Vermont a dozen years ago, people said to me, "Be careful when you drive at night—you sure don't want to hit a moose!" I'd reply by asking how common an occurrence this was, and they would invariably say something like, "It happens. And believe me, you don't want it to happen to you!"

Four years went by before I ever saw a moose. I was driving home from work in the early winter darkness. The moose was a teenager, so to speak, and yet it must have been seven feet tall. I had never seen anything like him outside a zoo. It was standing in the middle of the road, and I couldn't get around him. So I honked the horn. Big mistake. The enormous creature did not run away like a deer; it came toward me, so close that when it snorted, I was sure I felt it. I've seen three or four moose since that first day, and the sight of each one reminds me to be respectful.

God is far mightier than any moose, and even though I don't feel God's power breathing on my neck, I know it through His acts recounted in Scripture. What I read in the Bible reminds me to give Him my respect—in how I think, in what I say and in my actions—as well as my love. Holy and Powerful One, help me keep close to You today.

Whatever strength I possess comes from You.
—JON SWEENEY

The Lord sustains them on their sickbed
and restores them from their bed of illness.
—PSALM 41:3 (NIV)

Queasy stomach. Headache. Chills. I'm sick.

Why today, Lord? I felt like a million bucks when I went to bed. I've been taking vitamins by the handfuls and eating right. I have a million things to do and getting sick wasn't on my list. The best thing is just to pretend it's not happening. *Sick? I'm not sick.*

Uh-oh. It's worse when I stand. Let me just take a minute. I need to pull myself together. I'm sure I'll feel better after I take a shower and grab something to eat.

Ugh. The thought of food...maybe I can get some liquid into me. I might be able to handle that. But just a couple of sips. I feel...awful.

How am I going to get through this day? Meetings. Deadlines. E-mails. Maybe I can work from home, do it all online. But the thought of even logging on makes me want to crawl back under the covers.

Now my head is really pounding. My stomach is doing cartwheels. My wife Julee takes a look at me. "Not good," she says and points me back toward the bed, which appears to be my one and only destination today. I collapse facedown on the sheets.

Lord, this is not fair. The last thing I need is to be sick. Surely You know that. Why today? What will people think?

They'll think you're sick, the answer comes to me. *And that's okay.*

Is it? I think about this and suddenly feel the nearness of God. I sense I will be praying a lot today. I will not be separated from Him by PowerPoint presentations or strategy sessions or budget meetings. I will give myself up to His care, hard as that is for me to do sometimes.

Funny, getting closer to God wasn't on my list today.

Teach me, Lord, to find every opportunity,
even in sickness, to draw nearer to You.
—EDWARD GRINNAN

All things work together for good to them that love God,
to them who are the called according to his purpose.
—ROMANS 8:28

My wife Nicole and I had been trying to decide if I should go into business for myself, weighing the security of a full-time job against the excitement and risk of a life lived without a safety net. I'd been attracted to the idea of being my own boss, but having been an employee for my entire adult life, I was reluctant to carry all the financial burden myself.

One evening, on a whim, I attended a Bible study I'd never been to before. The study guide contained this fill-in-the-blank question: "Christianity affords you a life of _____." A column below listed some of the possible answers: forgiveness, sanctification, grace, things I might have expected. But about twenty words down came one I didn't expect: risk.

I just couldn't stop staring at that word. To me, risk had always seemed so… risky. But the more I thought about it, the more I felt that risk was indeed a part of the Christian life. The Lord wants us to live in freedom, and that includes having the faith to take risks sometimes, to make room for Him to be God.

Right then and there, it was settled: I would go into business for myself. Would I live an uncertain life? Yes. Was I relying on God to do all the things I couldn't? Absolutely. Was I giving up control to God? Without a doubt. But that, I thought, was the whole point.

Lord, when I'm anxious and uncertain,
help me to trust in Your plan for my life.
—DAVE FRANCO

JANUARY 23

No one has ever seen God; but if we love one another,
God lives in us and his love is made complete in us.
—I JOHN 4:12 (NIV)

*W*hen I was a teenager and a new immigrant to Canada, I often felt friendless and unloved. At the time, my family attended a small Sunday school in a community hall in Surrey, British Columbia, conducted by a mail carrier and his wife.

We older children would arrive early to help Mr. McGladdery shove the benches in place. His wife would deposit her baby on the lap of her oldest daughter and hurry to the dilapidated piano. Then her husband would go to the front of the room, rake his fingers through his hair and announce the first hymn. After we'd sung a few songs, he would give a Bible lesson using simple English words that even we, who struggled with the language, could understand.

"For God so loved the world, that he gave his only begotten Son, that whosoever believeth in him should not perish, but have everlasting life" (John 3:16), he read. Then he said, "Put your name where it says 'the world' and 'whosoever.' God loves each one of you individually, personally."

On Sunday afternoon, my sister and I would often visit the McGladderys. More than once we disturbed their afternoon nap. No matter, they urged us to "come on in." If it was supper time, Mrs. McGladdery would put two more plates on the table and invite us to eat with them. And always, they treated us warmly, as if we were family.

Knowing Mr. and Mrs. McGladdery did more for me than help me find my way in a strange new world. Experiencing their unconditional love on Sunday afternoon made the love of God they proclaimed on Sunday morning all the more real.

Father, I marvel at Your unconditional love, which accepts me
as I am. I want to grow in this love and pass it on to others.
—HELEN GRACE LESCHEID

However, our God turned the curse into a blessing.
—NEHEMIAH 13:2 (NKJV)

*S*aturday was my parents' sixtieth wedding anniversary. My four siblings and I reserved the fellowship hall at their former church in Dallas for a come-and-go reception in their honor.

I prayed it would be more than a nice little reception. Since moving from Dallas to east Texas, Mother and Daddy had suffered several years of serious health problems in a new town with few friends. Mother deeply needed to reconnect with her old ones.

Unfortunately, that Friday our plans came unraveled. An ambulance ushered my father to a hospital fifteen miles away, and clouds threatened a rare snowstorm. *How can we go on with it?* I thought. Yet how could we not? Family members were already en route from five hundred miles away.

So not only did I talk to God about the snowstorm, I talked to the storm itself. I took authority over it; I rebuked it; I spoke peace to it in the name of Jesus. After all, He calmed a storm and He did say believers would do greater works than He did.

You can probably guess what happened.

It snowed all Friday night and most of Saturday—four inches. Mixed with my discouragement was this one mental reminder from God: *Trust Me. I know how to bless My children.*

We decided to go on with the reception without Dad and hoped somebody would show up. Amazingly, almost seventy people did! Our come-and-go turned into a come-and-stay; for three and a half hours friends and family ate, talked, laughed, hugged my mom and wrote notes to Daddy in the hospital.

God, indeed, knew how to bless His children. The glow of the evening stayed with Mother longer than the flowers they received. And the snow was a bonus that will continue to bless her every time she remembers how people loved them enough to come in spite of it.

Father, help me to trust that You know best how to bless Your children.
—LUCILE ALLEN

Be careful for nothing; but in every thing by prayer and supplication
with thanksgiving let your requests be made known unto God.
—PHILIPPIANS 4:6

"Mom, ready for dominoes?"

"When I finish," I say, quickly looking up from the computer. I read the prayer submitted to OurPrayer.org and click the Approve button so it posts on the site. OurPrayer.org is a Guideposts website where I blog, edit inspiring stories and review prayers.

"Now?" Solomon taps the domino box on the computer table. I nod. As a work-from-home mom, finding a happy balance between work and play is an ongoing challenge. The kettle whistles, and I pour myself a cup of chamomile tea and grab a juice box for Solomon. This time of day, while Henry naps, is what Solomon calls SMT: Special Mommy Time.

Solomon rests his chin on the table as we select our dominoes. One by one the tiles turn into a long snake of black dominoes and white dots. As Solomon thinks over his next move, my thoughts drift to a prayer that's submitted every day by the same OurPrayer member: "Dear God, thank You for today." More than a decade ago, when I worked for a company that helped launch websites, we brainstormed the ways we thought the Internet would change the world. We spoke of advancements in entertainment and commerce; we never imagined people reaching out to each other online with love and support, one prayer at a time.

Sitting in a patch of sunlight with Solomon, I say a prayer of thanksgiving for the blessings in my life and for that special OurPrayer visitor who reminds me every day that today is a gift to cherish.

Dear God, thank You for today.
—SABRA CIANCANELLI

JANUARY 26

*And because ye are sons, God hath sent forth the Spirit
of his Son into your hearts, crying, Abba, Father.*
—GALATIANS 4:6

*J*ulia and I were tired last night. We'd had a hectic weekend of ballet recitals, museum visits and soaking rain, and the workweek had been a busy one. We were desperate for sleep; fifteen-month-old Stephen was not. He climbed up into our bed, lay down next to me and patted me with his hand. "Daddy!" he said.

"Yes, it's Daddy," I mumbled. "I'm right here. Go to sleep."

Stephen smiled. "Daddy!" he said and patted me again.

"Night-night, Stevie," I said, putting my head back on the pillow.

"Daddy!" he said, as if he had discovered something wonderful. "Daddy! Daddy! Daddy! Daddy!"

I turned toward him, looked into his eyes and stroked his cheek. Suddenly I didn't feel so tired.

Stephen didn't want me to play with him or read him a board book. All he wanted was to be with me and to let me know how happy that made him.

It made me happy too. And it made me think: Usually I come to my heavenly Father burdened with needs—for forgiveness, for healing, for strength. And it's good that I do that. But how often do I just let myself rest in His presence and tell Him I love Him?

I turned out the light, and Stephen settled down. As sleep came, I prayed:

Abba, Father! Daddy! Daddy! Daddy!
—ANDREW ATTAWAY

January 27

All...fall short of the glory of God.
—Romans 3:23 (NRSV)

When composing, Wolfgang Amadeus Mozart would sometimes whistle random phrases from the music he was working on. One day in the spring of 1784, he visited his favorite Viennese pet shop to discover that the store owner had taught a young bird, a Vienna starling, to mimic snatches of a song popular at the time. Mozart tried whistling a phrase from his current work-in-progress. To the composer's delight the bird repeated the melody. Mozart immediately bought the young starling, recording the purchase in his Notebook of Expenses.

In time Mozart and the bird became fast friends, his pet often sitting on his shoulder while he worked and whistling along with him. There was one disappointment though: No matter how hard he tried, Mozart was never able to train the bird to get intervals exactly right. Always one or more of the notes was off pitch.

One day his pet flitted over and began to sing a phrase of a new concerto, singing a G-sharp instead of the G-natural Mozart had written and also missing other notes. I like to imagine that Mozart smiled. What we do know is that he took out new manuscript paper and simply rewrote the music, building the bird's imperfections into the Piano Concerto in G Major we've enjoyed ever since.

These days, when once again I fall short of an ideal I've aimed for, I remember Mozart's starling. Doesn't God do exactly what Mozart did? Rewrite our "music" so that in His hands even our shortcomings become part of His harmony?

> *Father, help me to appreciate more and more every day*
> *what a privilege it is to sing with You.*
> —John Sherrill

*Let us not become weary in doing good, for at the proper time
we will reap a harvest if we do not give up.*
—GALATIANS 6:9 (NIV)

*I*t never dawned on me when we bought our home in Poughquag, New York, that living on the slope of what was once pastureland would be a landscaping challenge, but it certainly was.

After a futile attempt to persuade grass to grow on the steep incline directly behind our back deck, we created a garden of Russian olive, rug junipers, variegated barberries and potentillas. Over the years our garden has improved dramatically. Pine bark nuggets have become mulch, earthworms have gone where no spade at one time could penetrate, and seasons of working the rocky terrain have made this once inhospitable hillside quite lovely.

This year my wife and I decided to plant a few dozen perennials in our garden. Kathy laid out a design, and we began digging. The anchor trio of plantings needed to be done first. With two down and one to go, I—clink!—hit what I thought had to be the backside of the Rock of Gibraltar. I approached it from a different angle and—clink! I tried digging from the other side of the planned hole and—clink! I used a hoe instead of the shovel and—you guessed it—clink! "Kathy, we've got a problem," I said. "This isn't going to work."

Kathy took the hoe from me, and I went to get an iced tea. When I came back, she handed me a palm-sized flat stone, my Rock of Gibraltar.

"How'd you do that?" I asked her.

She smiled. "Let me give you a life lesson," she said. "Like most problems, this one wasn't as large as you'd imagined. Because your first attempts didn't solve it, I worked around it and enlarged the diameter of the hole until the edge of the problem appeared. The rest was easy. Problem solved."

Life lesson, indeed.

*Father, thank You for our beautiful garden and for a life lesson
in perseverance for an easily frustrated gardener.*
—TED NACE

JANUARY 29

For when I am weak, then am I strong.
—II CORINTHIANS 12:10

A little more than a year ago my husband Lynn suffered massive bleeding in his brain. He survived two critical surgeries and spent nearly two weeks on life support in ICU. At first the doctors didn't give us much hope for his recovery—or even survival. In spite of that prognosis Lynn has made a miraculous recovery and is now back at work in his law office.

I'm not sure my recovery has been as good. During that critical time a fear was born within me that I kept stuffing down to a hidden place deep within my soul, refusing to acknowledge its continuing presence. That fear has grown and spread, and it keeps bubbling to the surface when Lynn doesn't get home at his usual time, or when he disappears into another part of the house and is silent for too long, or when I can't reach him on the telephone.

Over and over the Bible tells us we aren't supposed to worry, so admitting that I still face fears in spite of Lynn's recovery makes me feel unfaithful and weak. But acknowledging that weakness also makes me aware of my dependence on God. One by one, as I acknowledge these fears, I remember God is in control... and is loving...and is always with me.

Lord, in my weakness, I am totally dependent upon Your strength.
—CAROL KUYKENDALL

*Present yourselves to God as those who have been brought from death to life,
and present your members to God as instruments of righteousness.*
—ROMANS 6:13 (NRSV)

I like to pray in different ways and in unusual places. Sometimes I try to incorporate movement and imagination into my prayers. So when I feel helpless, confused or in need of comfort, I envision the Lord cradling me as He would cradle an infant. If I'm praying for my marriage, I picture Him walking with Charlie and me, arm in arm, or holding our hands as we all walk together. When I pray for someone who's ill, I imagine the Lord holding that person or raining a healing light down upon him or her. And when I pray for healing or forgiveness for myself, I throw my arms up into the air and ask Him to pour out His forgiveness and healing on me.

I was praying this way recently when it occurred to me that I might have it all backward. I'd opened my arms to the Lord, praying He would pour His forgiveness and healing over me, but wasn't I missing a step? Shouldn't I be opening my arms to the Lord first to acknowledge and release the sin and the sickness I needed Him to forgive and heal? Only after I'd willingly relinquished these maladies of the soul and body to God, trusting He would remove them, could I sincerely ask for the forgiveness and healing I sought.

*Jesus, You know my flaws and frailties. As I pray in Your name,
give me the courage to trust them to Your healing Spirit.*
—MARCI ALBORGHETTI

January 31

When calamity overtakes you like a storm,
when disaster sweeps over you like a whirlwind....
—Proverbs 1:27 (NIV)

*I*t came on our family like a tsunami, a series of events that left us gasping for respite.

The first wave began on November 22. In the morning our son Peter called to say he had just been given the stay-behind slot as his reserve unit left for Iraq, and a photographer from *Sports Illustrated* came to my mom's assisted-care facility to photograph the two of us for an upcoming story on Red Sox fans. These were grand things. But late that night I sensed the first rumble: "Mom," our son Tom said when I answered the phone, "Susan was carjacked at gunpoint this evening."

As it turned out, November 22 was to be Mom's last day up. On December 10, she died, after thoroughly enjoying her "fifteen minutes of fame." On January 5, Susan, six-and-a-half months pregnant with our first grandchild, was admitted to the hospital, her contractions growing. On January 8, our son John's wife of barely a year moved out, leaving us all devastated. On January 11, Tom called us just before midnight: "Congratulations, you have a grandson! We've named him William John Rogers and nicknamed him Jack. He weighs three pounds, nine ounces. He cried when he was born, which is a great sign. He's off to a good start." Then, on January 30, Bill and I arrived at his mother's assisted-care facility to be told she had died just a few minutes before. The last wave had crashed.

But in the losses and worries, we began to find treasures—the greatest of them were people, both known and unknown to us, who would pray us all the way through into calmer waters.

Thank You, Lord, for the living strength of prayer and the love that sustains us in times of crisis. I think of _____,
who desperately needs Your touch right now.
—Roberta Rogers

February

FEBRUARY 1

Thy will be done.
—MATTHEW 6:10

*O*ur grandson Mark was almost two when he and his parents Paul and Marilynne came for dinner one Sunday.

While we were saying grace, chubby-legged Mark, curious about all the goodies on the table, stood up in his high chair to have a look. "Mark, sit down," his father told him.

Mark continued to stand, his eyes on the fried chicken.

"Marcus, sit down!" Paul repeated.

Looking at his father with determined blue eyes, he said, "I don't!"

Paul rose from his chair and started toward his son, but by the time he reached the high chair it had a quickly seated occupant.

Paul smiled and whispered to us, "He's still standing up inside."

At the time I was inwardly smiling, but Paul's remark has stayed with me ever since. Sometimes when I'm reluctantly doing what I know God wants me to do, I too—in secret rebellion—am "standing up inside."

Jesus, You taught us to pray "Thy will be done." Help me
to be obedient to that will...inwardly and outwardly.
—ZONA B. DAVIS

FEBRUARY 2

*We have also a more sure word of prophecy; whereunto ye do well
that ye take heed, as unto a light that shineth in a dark place,
until the day dawn, and the day star arise in your hearts.*
—II PETER 1:19

*M*y sister collected owls: owl pictures, owl ornaments, owl jewelry. After she passed away, I hung one of her Austrian crystal owls in a window where it would catch the rays of the rising sun. One morning while relegated to an easy chair because of back problems, I watched that tiny owl spin ever so slowly in the current of warm air filtering out of the radiator beneath it. At first, the crystal reflected only the dim light of the early dawn. But as the sun rose higher and higher, the crystal caught its rays, refracting them into dozens of tiny rainbows revolving about the room, their colors becoming more and more intense.

Sometimes in the darker moments of life, I tend to lose sight of what God promises for the future, yet I believe He has plans for this world, even though I can't see them. In the revealing light of Scripture and historical hindsight, however, dozens of His fulfilled prophecies shine out more and more, like tiny rainbows to give me hope.

*Lord, help me hang Your promises in the window of my soul and let
the light of Your Spirit shining on them give me courage day after day.*
—ALMA BARKMAN

For unto us a child is born, unto us a son is given.
—ISAIAH 9:6

O kay, I admit it. It's February and I still have Christmas music in my car's CD player. Why? Maybe because I can't remember where the CD cases are. Or because I'm too lazy to haul another handful of CDs out to the car and do the great switch-over. Or perhaps it's because I'm mostly a radio kind of girl when I'm in the car. Or maybe it's because listening to Christmas music in February is a very good thing to do.

Today I was driving home from work, surrounded by the bleakness this time of year always brings to my part of the country: gray skies, gray tree branches, gray snowbanks, icy gray highways. But into the midst of that came a hundred-voice choir singing "Emmanuel, God is with us!" And I realized it was true. Not just in the fir-decked, red-bow days of December, but all year long. In the nitty-gritty, day-in-day-out routine of life, God is with us! So why pack away the wonder and joy of Christmas with the jingle bells and holly berries? "Oh come, let us adore him—Christ the Lord!" It seemed the perfect thing to do on a chilly February afternoon.

When I got home, I kissed my husband on the cheek and said, "Merry Christmas!" Gary—who has known me a very long time—didn't even seem surprised.

Holy Christ Child, be Lord of my life 365 days a year!
—MARY LOU CARNEY

*My flesh and my heart may fail, but God is the strength
of my heart and my portion forever.*
—PSALM 73:26 (NIV)

*O*ur sons were all born with a rare blood disorder. Ryan and Joel barely survived it, but by the time of our third son's birth, a machine was available that would cleanse Kathy's blood of antibodies so it could be given to the baby and prevent the severe reactions Ryan and Joel had suffered. The doctor set a definite date for the procedure—the baby would be delivered by C-section—and assembled an expert medical team.

But Kathy's labor pains began on a holiday weekend. She called the doctor, who was dismayed: Except for the technician who operated the blood-cleansing machine, the members of the team were all away for the holiday. The hospital staff was tense, and so were we.

Everything seemed to be going well until it was time to begin the blood-cleansing. The technician couldn't get the machine started. She tried a few times, with no success. At that point even Kathy, the most positive thinker I know, began to look frightened and her blood pressure began to rise.

"Aren't you a pastor?" asked the technician. "Let's pray for God's help."

I prayed. And after our prayer, the machine began its work and soon a healthy Kyle Vincent Nace was in his mother's arms.

*Father God, I know my weakness. I depend
on Your strength to make my life a joy.*
—TED NACE

Enter his gates with thanksgiving, and his courts with praise.
Give thanks to him, bless his name. For the Lord is good; his steadfast love
endures for ever, and his faithfulness to all generations.
—PSALM 100:4–5 (NRSV)

On a bleak windy morning I switch on my iPod to block out the noise of the city. It does, but increasingly I'm not sure I can. Life drags with every footstep. One of the things the iPod can do is "shuffle"—the little guy inside picks out song after song in random succession. I shuffle, and Mr. Shuffle lights on a track from Peter, Paul and Mary: "Take my hand, my son," they sing, "all will be well when the day is done." Their song speaks to daughters as well as to sons. The strong hand of God slips under my elbow, and my steps get a little faster and a little steadier.

We faithful readers of the Bible talk a lot about miracles, but do we notice the small miracles that happen to each of us when doing the dishes or walking home from work? I have nine hundred fifty songs on my iPod. That in itself seems like a miracle. How does all that music tuck itself into a tiny plastic box that fits in the palm of my hand? Miracles wear many different faces, making different sounds and offering different kinds of help. This one was just a song from a small piece of plastic, but it was one to treasure and for which to thank God.

May I watch for life's miracles, great and small, share them
with others and always give You thanks, Lord.
—BRIGITTE WEEKS

FEBRUARY 6

Thou didst cleave the earth with rivers.
—HABAKKUK 3:9

I'm a fan of the TV show *Jeopardy*, from way back when Guideposts's friend Art Fleming was the host. On a recent show, the contestants were given the answer "China's Yangtze River." The question they were being asked to provide was "What is the third longest river in the world?" I'd have thought the Mississippi was the answer, but at 2,348 miles, it's only the longest river in the United States.

The Nile is the longest river in the world, measuring 4,160 miles; the Amazon second longest at almost 4,000 miles. I've boated on all three and find it hard to believe anything is bigger than the Amazon; more water flows through it than the Nile, Mississippi and Yangtze combined, it's that humongous. My memory of the Amazon is of fishing for piranhas that would bite on anything that moved. "Don't put your finger in the water," our guide joked.

There are important rivers in the lands of the Bible too, such as the River Jordan, which flows through the Sea of Galilee into the Dead Sea. And two rivers, the Tigris and Euphrates, are important in biblical history for Babylon and Nebuchadnezzar, Nineveh, possibly the Garden of Eden, and the land of Ur, the birthplace of Abraham, the common patriarch who defines the faith for half the world—Jews, Christians and Muslims.

For me, Abraham personifies obedience to God. When the Lord told him to leave his home and go "unto a land that I will shew thee" (Genesis 12:1), Abraham didn't say, "But I'm seventy-five years old," or "How about next year?" No, Abraham and Sarah obeyed, taking all their possessions out of Haran, in today's Turkey, and headed south, no doubt along the Euphrates and Jordan Rivers. They and the sheep and goats they probably took with them needed water to survive, and God provided. He always does to those who are faithful.

Teach us, God, both to listen and lace up our shoes,
to obey all Your orders, not pick and choose.
—FRED BAUER

FEBRUARY 7

And in Christ you have been brought to fullness.
He is the head over every power and authority.
—COLOSSIANS 2:10 (NIV)

*M*y friend Joanna leads a girls' Bible study at our church. She tries to keep things light and uplifting, giving the dozen or so teenagers a brief respite from their daily stresses by studying God's Word. When the class began, Joanna gave the girls an assignment. "At the next meeting, I want you to introduce yourself to the group." She wasn't looking for names and club affiliations, but for insight into how the girls saw themselves.

Joanna called me to talk about the assignment and asked me to do the exercise. She planned to read it to the girls at the start of the class to get the discussion moving. "Sure," I said. Certainly I knew myself well enough to write a few paragraphs.

"Who I Am; Ashley 101," I wrote quickly. Then nothing. I stared at the blank page in front of me, thinking of all the things I thought I might be expected to say. "I love Jesus. I am a Christian," I wrote. It was true, but somehow it felt forced. I scratched it out. Page after page lay crumpled around my bedroom. "Why is this so hard?" I said to no one in general and God in particular.

Then it dawned on me. I kept trying to make a list that had God as the first priority. It felt forced because He wasn't the first priority—He was so much more than that. He wasn't a bullet point on my list; He was the paper the list was written on, the foundation for everything I wanted to be and to do. Suddenly, writing about who I am and what I value became much easier.

Lord, help me remember that You are in everything I do, say, see and experience.
—ASHLEY JOHNSON

FEBRUARY 8

We do not have a high priest who is unable to empathize with our weaknesses, but we have one who has been tempted in every way, just as we are.
—HEBREWS 4:15 (NIV)

*S*low down," my doctor said. "You're not Superman, you know."

I'd been complaining to him about a nagging summer cold. I hoped he'd whip out his trusty prescription pad or give me a shot of something miraculous. Instead he went into Marcus Welby mode.

"When we get older, it can take more time to recover from a bad cold or infection. We're more vulnerable."

That word *vulnerable*—I'd come across it just recently in another context, something Catherine Marshall had written about "the vulnerable Jesus." Christ, in His years on earth, thirsted, got tired, wept. Presumably He caught colds; perhaps He had sinus problems, bad vision or sore joints—the dreary commonplace ills that dampen folks' spirits everywhere. And when He hung on the cross, He suffered as any of us would under such torment.

Yet I resist admitting my own vulnerability. I always have. Vulnerability equals weakness, doesn't it? Oh, I don't really believe that, or at least I think I know better than to buy into that old masculine stereotype. But stereotypes die hard, and recognizing my inherent human vulnerability is not so easy for me.

Still, this is what Christ's life taught us: that in our weakness we are made strong, that in obedience we find freedom, that in surrender we embrace victory. And what better way to give proof to this than by taking on our humanity and living as we do, with all of our frailty. Jesus showed us not just the nature of God but also our own.

Lord, help me to see that in my search for myself, I will always find You.
—EDWARD GRINNAN

February 9

"I will settle them in their homes," declares the Lord.
—Hosea 11:11 (niv)

*M*y wife Rosie and I attended a house dedication outside of Mendenhall, Mississippi. A lady called Mama Buckley had built a new house after a fire had burned down her old one. I wondered why she'd gone to all the trouble at her age when she could easily have moved in with one of her children.

Mama Buckley greeted us with a big hug, her eyes filled with excitement. She insisted on giving us the grand tour. She showed off her bedroom closet; this was the first time in her life she'd had one to hang her clothes in. Now she had closet space for towels too, and carpet on the floor, and a room where she could wash and iron. Insurance money had covered the materials and, with the help of her children and their friends as well as volunteers from church, she was able to have the house built without going into debt.

At age eighty-seven, Mama Buckley still believes that God is faithful. She'll live in her new earthly home with joy until God takes her to her eternal home in heaven. What a great way to enjoy the blessings of God!

Lord, help me understand that no matter how old I am,
I can still trust in Your faithfulness.
—Dolphus Weary

"And lo, I am with you always, even to the end of the age."
—MATTHEW 28:20 (NASB)

*W*hen I was a teenager, my brother and sister and I liked to gather around my five-foot-three mother. We'd look around as if searching for her and ask in jest, "Hey, have you seen Mom? Where's Mom?"

Poor Mom. And soon, poor me. My days of towering over my children are numbered. Elizabeth has stabilized at about my mother's height, but John and Mary are already there and they still have a long way to grow. Maggie's always been an Amazon and towers over her peers. Only little Stephen (who's still in size four) is likely to be looking up to me for a while.

Suddenly, I'm a mom of big kids. My conversations are no longer punctuated by dashes after a two-year-old. I don't have a baby for whom I need to carry a set of clean clothes. My shoulder bag is lighter; the stains on the laundry are fewer. Instead of having toddlers with ten short meltdowns a day, I have teenagers who condense their angst into occasional three-hour marathons. Life is different; I'm different too. I've grown more understanding in some ways and crankier in others. I listen more and talk less. I have less energy. I have more time to myself. And as I reach middle age, I wonder, *Do I know God better than I did a decade ago? If I could go back in time for an afternoon, would my faith back then be richer or poorer than it is now?*

I ponder this (I ponder more nowadays) and conclude that perhaps I'm asking the wrong question. I've grown up with God, walked and talked with Him all these years. Most likely, faith has its own flavor and texture over time, in the way that being a mother of toddlers is different from being a mother of teens.

Jesus, thank You for being beside me all these years.
Help me love You more, always more.

—JULIA ATTAWAY

"Come to me, all you who are weary and burdened, and I will give you rest."
—MATTHEW 11:28 (NIV)

King is a catfish. He lives on the bottom of my 130-gallon aquarium. At night he patrols the quiet waters like a pewter submarine, his stringy antennae sweeping the gravel for leftovers. The little fish know to stay out of his way.

During the day, he reclines in his slate cave, his antennae guarding the entrance. At feeding time, he shoots out of his cave like a rocket, muscling in on the shrimp pellets and bloodworms while keeping an eye on his cave.

Meanwhile, my timid red hooks swim in a school for safety. These shiny silver fish that look like flying saucers with red handles stick with the crowd. If I kept just one or two, they'd huddle in a corner, banging their noses raw to get to their reflections in the glass.

The bottom-line truth is that King will never share his cave and a red hook will always be in a group. Survival instincts shape and rule these creatures. I can't change them. I can only stock the tank and arrange their environment to help them be what they are.

Mirrored in this little fish story is a larger, humbling truth—where it counts, I can't change myself. I can change my environment, my appearance and even my behavior. But for honest-to-goodness, liberating, inner-peace-bringing wholeness, I am as powerless as a red hook beating its nose against the glass. I must surrender to a Power greater than myself, believing that He is willing and able to change me.

In the good news of the Gospel, I can be free, one day at a time, by turning my unmanageable self over to Jesus.

Lord Jesus, a new day, a clean page of my life, is dawning. Write Your will on it.
—SHARI SMYTH

They that wait upon the Lord shall renew their strength;
they shall mount up with wings as eagles; they shall run,
and not be weary; and they shall walk, and not faint.
—ISAIAH 40:31

I was tired: tired of winter, tired of the cold, and sore and stiff from shoveling the previous day's snow out of my driveway. As I walked to my office at the Peale Center for Christian Living, trying hard not to let my tiredness show, Angela sped by me.

Angela works in our prayer department, and today she was walking with extra energy and enthusiasm. "Angela," I called to her, "slow down a minute and tell me why you're so lively today! You don't seem to be suffering from the winter blahs."

Angela stopped and waited for me to catch up with her. "Well," she said, "I try to get my energy flowing every day. I focus on a simple thought, and it seems to get me going, even when I really don't want to."

"What's the thought?" I asked. "I certainly could use a boost today."

"Every day," Angela said, "I say to myself, 'Angela, put more pep in your step.'"

Well, that didn't sound very inspiring to me. In fact, it sounded kind of silly. But I really needed help getting my day going, so I stood up as straight as I could and said, "Ted, you're flatter than a day-old glass of seltzer. Put more pep in your step!"

For a few minutes I followed Angela around the building, trying to catch her stride. And as I did, I could feel the energy flowing. I pulled even with Angela, gave her a wave and a thank-you, and headed for my office. I couldn't wait to start the day's work.

Lord, when those February blues have got me down,
give me a positive attitude and put more pep in my step.
—TED NACE

What time I am afraid, I will trust in thee.
—PSALM 56:3

*W*hat were the chances of our friend Dan's phoning the very day we learned that our son had to undergo surgery? We'd had a warm but brief relationship with Dan Montgomery years earlier; it had been a decade and more since there'd been any communication at all between us.

But here was his voice, cheerful and caring, and because I know Dan is a psychologist with long experience counseling people in crisis, I poured out my anxiety. We lived so far away from our son, we had so few details, I could get no answer either on his home phone or at the office—"Walk right now to the wall nearest your phone," Dan broke into this outburst.

Surprised and puzzled, I took a couple of steps to the wall next to my desk.

"Stand a foot or so out from the wall," the instructions continued. "Now lean against it. Be far enough away that if the wall weren't there you'd fall."

I moved out from the wall and let my weight rest against it.

"Now," Dan said, "relax your muscles. Let the feeling of trusting the wall spread all through you. Feel how effortlessly the wall upholds you. See how you can rest, even though you yourself are off balance."

It was true. Leaning on the wall, I gradually released the tension in my shoulders...my arms...my stomach.

"In a time of crisis," Dan said, "we can learn to lean on God the way you're leaning on that wall. It's when we learn the difference between believing in God and trusting Him."

Two good gifts came with that phone call: a reminder to lean on God through the anxious days of our son's surgery and slow recovery and, for any time, a faith-builder that's as close as the nearest wall.

Faithful Lord, let me notice walls today—and
remember that the walls of Your city stand forever.
—ELIZABETH SHERRILL

And be not conformed to this world: but be ye transformed
by the renewing of your mind, that ye may prove what is that good,
and acceptable, and perfect, will of God.

—ROMANS 12:2

*J*esus' first disciples, Peter and Andrew, would probably have smiled at the bumper sticker I saw the other day. I'D RATHER BE FISHING, it said. You'll recall what Jesus said to the two when He saw them casting their nets: "Follow me, and I will make you fishers of men" (Matthew 4:19).

Legends that people put on their cars or the imprints on their T-shirts say a lot about what's on their minds. Some things are funny, some gross, some political, some organizational, some religious, like WWJD—What Would Jesus Do? The Gospels give us a good idea about the answer, most of the time. But on some issues, people disagree.

Abraham Lincoln noted that knowing where God is on some issues takes a good deal of cogitating. During the Civil War, an opponent of the president suggested that God was not on Lincoln's side. Lincoln's answer: "My concern is to be on God's side, for God is always right."

How can we ascertain God's will? I've always been told to discuss issues with others, to study the Bible and to pray for God's guidance. My difficult questions are usually resolved that way.

Direct us, God, when we face a tough decision,
Give us wisdom, give us courage, give us vision.
—FRED BAUER

FEBRUARY 15

Let us therefore approach the throne of grace with boldness,
that we may receive mercy and find grace to help in time of need.
—HEBREWS 4:16 (NRSV)

*T*live in a townhouse. This means just a wall separates me from my neighbor, an older woman who isn't as strong or steady as she used to be. I'm her Lifeline® contact person; I try to watch out for her and listen for any calls of distress. So I was surprised at her report at noon one Saturday, when I knocked on her door, delivering a taste of my cooking: "I fell off a chair this morning. I didn't hurt myself, but it took me an hour to scootch across the room and pull myself up."

"What? Why didn't you yell or bang on the wall?" I asked.

"Well, I didn't want to bother you."

"It's not a bother. You were in trouble," I said.

"Well, I didn't think you'd hear me—if you were in the kitchen or upstairs or..."

"Why didn't you push the Lifeline button, so I'd get an emergency call?"

"Well, I know I gave you a key, but..." She hesitated before continuing. "Do you really know where it is? I figured you wouldn't be able to find it."

"Yes, I know where it is." I smiled and tried to make light of the situation. "Next time give me a chance. Holler!"

As I recall this conversation, I hear myself as the one who is weak or has fallen but finds an excuse—my independent spirit, my lack of confidence—for not asking God for help. And then I hear God having the last word: "Next time give Me a chance. Pray!"

Lord, in my time of need, give me confidence in Your ability
to hear my prayer and Your willingness to grant mercy and grace.
—EVELYN BENCE

"He is not far from each one of us."
—ACTS 17:27 (NRSV)

*T*hadn't wanted to go to church that Sunday; it was a long time since I'd felt close to God. Simply out of habit, I dragged myself to the ten o'clock service anyway—only to find myself sitting in front of a crying child.

Crying? Howling was more like it, a din that drowned out the opening prayer, the announcements and the first hymn. At last, the mother took the sobbing child out—a little boy about four years old, I saw as they passed my pew. The damage was done, though; whatever chance I'd had to feel God's presence was thoroughly squashed.

Nor did the sermon help. The regular minister was away and a lay preacher droned through a printed dry-as-dust lecture. I went to the coffee hour (the coffee was lukewarm) in a grumpier mood than when I'd arrived.

The four-year-old was there, a cookie in each hand, screaming fit over. "I'm so sorry for the racket," his mother apologized to the group around the coffee urn.

It had taken her a long time, she went on, to calm him down enough to learn what the trouble was. "He kept saying, 'God's gone!'" Finally his mother realized it was because the minister wasn't there. "We've told him this is God's house, and he must have thought the minister in his robe was God."

All of us chuckled at a four-year-old's mistaking a man for God. And yet, I thought as I drove home, wasn't I doing something just as foolish? Mistaking my own absent faith for the absence of God Almighty? My mood—uplifted or downcast, attentive or bored—what did it have to do with the changeless reality in Whom "we live and move and have our being" (Acts 17:28, NRSV)?

Faithful Lord, help me seek You in fact and not in feeling.
—ELIZABETH SHERRILL

FEBRUARY 17

"Let me tell you why you are here. You're here to be salt-seasoning that brings out the God-flavors of this earth."
—MATTHEW 5:13 (MSG)

*Y*ears ago I looked for a way to serve God on the front line. Some people told me the main thing was sharing the good news. Others said the best witness was to do such things as visiting prisoners and feeding the hungry. Wanting to discover God's will for me, I dove into the Bible. I was stunned to read that Jesus told His disciples to consider themselves blessed when "you're at the end of your rope," when "you've lost what is most dear" (Matthew 5:3–4, MSG), as if these tragedies were actually God's delivery vehicles for sending us His blessings. Ridiculous! I'd already lost a lot and had been at the end of my rope!

"Lord," I finally said, "just tell me straight: What good news do I have to share? Why am I even here?" My eye caught Jesus' next sentence: "Let me tell you why you are here. You're here to be salt-seasoning that brings out the God-flavors of this earth."

My world changed. Maybe the best news I could bring was this: As I surrender my life to the Lord, He offers me the courage, honesty and willingness to face and walk through the most difficult problems with my eyes wide open! And for me, that's very good news.

Lord, Your blessings are good news indeed when it comes to spiritual maturity, even if they sometimes feel a little like sandpaper. Amen.
—KEITH MILLER

FEBRUARY 18

My help cometh from the Lord, which made heaven and earth.
—PSALM 121:2

*I*n all the years I've been at Guideposts (some fifty-two of them), there have been a few special moments when I was certain God was speaking to me. One of them was at a family dinner table in Sherman Oaks, California.

I was there covering the story of the horrible accident in which Anne Shelly's left arm was severed by a Cessna airplane's propeller. The story won fifteen-year-old Anne a prize in the Guideposts Youth Writing Contest for 1973.

Anne trusted God—completely. From the moment she lay on the tarmac of the airport at Van Nuys, she asked God to give her back her arm. And He did. When I saw her a year later, she could swim, dance, knit and hug her family and friends.

I ran down in my mind the unusual events, when every passing minute had been crucial: that a young man who heard the accident came running in the dusk, dashed for a telephone; that he called the fire department and explained the trouble so specifically that attendants came prepared to minister to Anne; that the doctor at the hospital's admissions desk, who was there only by chance, should be the very man who knew the surgeons who had performed this type of rare orthopedic surgery; that those surgeons in a peak vacation period should be available and there within the hour.

"What a collection of coincidences," I said at the dining table.

Anne's mother didn't hesitate to speak the words that have stayed with me since. While passing the butter she said matter-of-factly, "There are no coincidences."

I try to remember those words, Father.
—VAN VARNER

FEBRUARY 19

Let each one do just as he has purposed in his heart;
not grudgingly or under compulsion; for God loves a cheerful giver.
—II CORINTHIANS 9:7 (NASB)

A few days ago I attended a Bible study taught by my friend Todd Still, a New Testament scholar as fluent in Greek as he is in English. As we read from Paul's letters to the church in Corinth, we focused on the familiar phrase "God loves a cheerful giver."

"The most literal translation," Todd said, "is 'God loves a hilarious giver.' Cheerful is the most common translation. But that word is mild. The most literal interpretation of the Greek adjective is 'hilarious.' And that word is extreme."

I jotted down this bit of knowledge in my notebook and quickly forgot about it. A few weeks later I received a letter reminding me that the pledge I'd made to a worthy cause was due. The day before, I had paid my son's college fees and expenses, and when I consulted my checkbook, I discovered that I was almost broke.

Suddenly I recalled Todd saying, "God loves a hilarious giver." Sitting down at my desk, I wrote the check. And then I began to laugh. I laughed at myself, old grouch and tightwad that I am. I laughed at the smallness of the check amidst the immensity of God's love and provision. I laughed from a joy that can only come from giving "not grudgingly or under compulsion," but out of a hilarious and ridiculous freedom.

God, bless me with the laughter that only comes from giving. Amen.
—SCOTT WALKER

FEBRUARY 20

Now it is required that those who have been given a trust must prove faithful.
—I CORINTHIANS 4:2 (NIV)

*W*hen I was twenty years old, I moved away from my home in Ohio and found work in Colorado. What I lacked in experience, I tried to make up for in dependability. I saved enough money for tuition and went to college, but I always returned to the same job. I didn't miss a day of work until my third year with the company. I got some kind of flu over the weekend and had to call in sick. My boss said, "It figures. Most workers tend to get sick on a Monday." His remark inspired me to find another job.

I thought about that old boss of mine the other day when I read a letter the sixty-five-year-old George Washington wrote describing his daily routine: "I begin with the sun.... If my hirelings are not in their places at that time, I send them messages expressive of my sorrow for their indisposition." He didn't accuse them of playing sick.

Much has been written about Washington's leadership qualities, but I think kindness and trust are two of his most overlooked traits. I imagine that Washington showed the same kindness and trust to his wife, his wife's children, his troops, his colleagues and his constituents. He trusted them, and the people he trusted proved faithful.

Dear Lord, thank You for giving us great leaders
to follow so we might learn to lead those who follow us.
—TIM WILLIAMS

This is too glorious, too wonderful to believe! I can never be lost to your Spirit!
—PSALM 139:6–7 (TLB)

*T*suppose I knew God cared about me, but I didn't feel He did. That all-important truth of not relying on feelings had somehow escaped me. *Who am I, anyway, that God should really care about me?*

My daughter Julie phoned later that day, and I asked about my grandchildren as usual. "Thomas did something you won't believe," she said. "He's going to be like you about books, I suppose." When I inquired what he'd done, she explained.

"He ran into the house yesterday bellowing for me. He almost ran into me in the kitchen. Out of breath, he gasped, 'Is it true, Mama? Is it really true? Can an eight-year-old boy like me get his own library card?' When I said he could, he begged me to take him to the library right at that moment. Because it seemed so important to him, I did. He told me to wait in a corner while he walked up to the counter all alone. He was a bit uneasy, but he did it. Mother, he had tears in his eyes when we left! He showed me his library card and couldn't stop smiling! What kind of child do I have?"

I don't remember my answer. Julie's story had a message for me, and I listened to the silent voice in my heart. *It's true, Marion. A grandmother like you can have My full attention and care whenever you desire it. Just ask.* After we hung up, I ignored my feelings of fear and doubt and approached the Throne of Grace. I didn't even know what to say.

I've been missing you, child. God reached His loving arms toward me.

Oh, Father, it's true, it's really true! You know me and love me!
—MARION BOND WEST

*Immediately Jesus, perceiving in Himself that the power
proceeding from Him had gone forth, turned around
in the crowd and said, "Who touched My garments?"*
—MARK 5:30 (NASB)

When Jesus asked who had touched Him in the crowded street, a woman fell trembling at His feet and confessed. For twelve years she'd suffered a worsening health condition, going broke paying physicians. She had pretty much given up until she heard about Jesus. She thought if she could get close enough to touch just the fringe of His cloak, she would be made well.

Her plan was to sneak up behind Jesus in the press of people, reach out with a quick furtive touch and then disappear in the crowd. It almost worked. Only Jesus felt power go out from Him at the same instant the woman felt in her body that she was well. Her reach and Jesus' response met in a miraculous healing.

The Bible doesn't give her name, but I call her the fringe lady—*faith reaching in God expectation*. Jesus' parting words, "Go in peace and be healed of your affliction" (Mark 5:34, NASB), must have been a soothing salve for all of her remaining years.

I find real hope in this story. The fringe lady's faith was desperate, even frightened—the way my faith gets when my best efforts have failed and I think I'm out of options. Yet Jesus commended her, saying, "Daughter, your faith has made you well" (Mark 5:34, NASB). Wherever I am—however alone or exhausted or distraught—when I sincerely reach for Jesus, I know He will respond to the barest touch.

*Holy Spirit, when I'm out of answers, help me
to summon the faith to reach out for Jesus.*
—CAROL KNAPP

FEBRUARY 23

And the pleasure of the Lord shall prosper in His hand.
—ISAIAH 53:10 (NKJV)

Hugh Hudson's 1981 movie masterpiece *Chariots of Fire* tells the story of Eric Liddell, a runner in the 1924 Olympics who refuses to run on Sunday out of respect for God's Word. Because of his refusal to run on Sunday, Eric is forced to run in a longer race, the four-hundred meter, for which he hasn't trained. But he flies like a rocket and breaks the tape in a thrilling victory.

What could inspire a man to such a feat? I wondered. I think the answer is in his conversation with his sister Jenny before the race. She thinks running is frivolous for a man who is going to become a missionary.

"God made me for a purpose," Eric explains. "He also made me fast. When I run, I feel His pleasure. To give it up would be to hold Him in contempt. To win is to honor Him." Jenny is satisfied with his answer. Just before the race, she hands him a note on which she has written I Samuel 2:30 (NRSV): "For those who honor me I will honor."

To do what God designed me to do is to feel His approval. When I'm writing on the chalkboard of my classroom, hoeing in my garden or fixing a student's car, I can feel God's pleasure flowing through my hands. Everyone has gifts from God. To develop those gifts and to use them for others makes one a conduit for the power of God. You can almost hear Him say, "Well done, good and faithful servant."

Help me to win the race of life for Your honor, Lord.
—DANIEL SCHANTZ

FEBRUARY 24

Thou, O Lord, art a God full of compassion, and gracious....
—PSALM 86:15

Some time back two people in our church wrote a long list of all my husband David's and my real and imagined failings and put it in all the mailboxes in the church office. Although our church's ruling elders demanded an apology from the writers, none was offered.

Church had always been my refuge and now it was torture to make myself go. And then one Sunday, sitting in church, I was sure I heard God speaking to me: *I want you to write those people a letter in the spirit of forgiveness.*

The mere suggestion was incredible to me. *Surely You're kidding, God!* But the words stuck in my head and refused to budge.

Two days later I sat down at my computer just to get rid of the wild notion that God wanted me to write the letter. But when I raised my hands over the keyboard, they shook so much I couldn't type. *Okay, God, if You really want me to do this, I'm going to need Your help.* This time when I raised my hands, I typed away.

The letter was short, to the point and written in the spirit of forgiveness just as God had asked. I dropped it in the mail and let it go.

The next Sunday my chief critic approached me at the coffee machine. He hinted that I'd written just to ingratiate myself to him, and then he turned and left. It was clear my letter had missed its mark.

That's when a miracle happened: A perfect peace descended around me; my fear was gone. Church was beginning to feel like home again. God hadn't really meant the letter for my critics; He'd meant it for me. I was free.

Father, help me always to be a messenger of Your grace.
—PAM KIDD

57

FEBRUARY 25

O Lord, how long shall I cry, And You will not hear?
—HABAKKUK 1:2 (NKJV)

*J*ust once in my life, Lord, I'd like to have a conversation with You. Sure, I'm glad You hear our prayers, but it's really hard to have a relationship with someone who never responds, You know? It would be really great if just once we could have a back-and-forth, where I say something like, 'How are things in heaven?' And then You say, 'Things are always fine in heaven.' And then I say, 'Well, things are not so fine down here. Our friend has cancer, and all summer we've had floods. Do You have anything to say about that?'"

"Have you read my book Habakkuk?"

"Habba what? Is that in the Old Testament?"

"So you haven't read the things I've already said?"

"You got me, but I would just like to hear the sound of Your voice and see the expressions on Your face. You know...body language."

"Do you like thunder? My voice is like that. Can you stare at the sun? I dwell in unapproachable light."

"But if You could sort of disguise Yourself as a man and come down here for a visit..."

"I did that long ago. I went to weddings and funerals. I taught in the marketplace and schools. I played with children. But not everybody liked Me. Remember, I hear every prayer you utter and I think of you every day. I look forward to visiting with you in heaven even more than you do."

It's so hard to live by faith, Lord, and not by sight. Give me patience!
—DANIEL SCHANTZ

For your steadfast love is before my eyes.
—PSALM 26:3 (NRSV)

The morning news was filled with tragedies, arthritis pain had kept me awake all night, and I was feeling that the universe was a pretty unfriendly place. That's when God reminded me of an eleven-year-old girl who had felt the same way.

I was that girl, and I didn't have a single friend in ballet class. When we did a pas de deux, everyone seemed to have chosen a partner already and I'd have to do the routine alone. Between lessons we were supposed to get together in smaller groups to practice, but every group was full when I tried to join. After the Christmas show, I dropped out.

It was nearly two years later that I became friends with one of the girls from that class. "We all used to think you were so stuck up," Ann said as we walked home from school one day. "You'd never wave or smile back."

"What do you mean?" I said.

"I mean you'd be all friendly with me one day and the next you'd walk right by as though you didn't see me."

As though you didn't see...

It was a light going on in the dark place where I'd kept the hurt and rejection. I was twelve when my poor eyesight had at last been detected, glasses had been prescribed and a bright, sharp world had come into focus.

Before, people had smiled at me but I hadn't seen!

The memory of that walk with Ann leapt across the years. "Do I seem uncaring?" God said. "Come closer and look again."

Faithful Lord, remind me that when I cannot see Your smile,
it is my sight and not Your love that is limited.
—ELIZABETH SHERRILL

February 27

Let not your heart be troubled, neither let it be afraid.
—John 14:27

*T*he icy wind bit my cheeks as I pulled the blue plastic sled, loaded down with hay, into the corral. I shooed my three horses and two mules away from me so I wouldn't get kicked while they fought over the hay. My mind buzzed with problems from work; I'm a lumber broker, and I sell truckloads of lumber to customers all over the United States.

Today I'd gotten a call from one of my Amish customers in Pennsylvania: "Rebecca, the wrong lumber is on the truck." The mill—in Arkansas, twelve hundred miles away—had misloaded the truck, but it was my responsibility to sell the lumber anyway. And I didn't know anyone else in Pennsylvania, much less anyone who wanted a whole truckload of lumber!

I tossed the hay into the last wooden feeder, and as I walked away, Little Girl, one of my mules, followed me. I slid the chain off the gate and felt Little Girl's warm breath on my neck. Then she gently placed her black fuzzy head on my shoulder. "I'm sorry, Little Girl." I turned around and stroked her face. "I was so caught up with my problems that I never even gave you a heart check." My nightly routine is to walk up to each horse and mule and wrap one arm over its withers (shoulders) and the other arm under its neck. I hold the hug, with our hearts beating side by side, until the animal sighs.

I wrapped my arms around Little Girl. As I held her for a moment, she sighed as if she just unloaded all her problems. I sighed too, and when I did, it was as if God was telling me, *Why don't you let Me wrap My arms around you? I'll take your troubles.* "Okay, Lord," I said with a chuckle, "I might not know anyone in Pennsylvania, but You know everyone there."

Lord, thank You for teaching me to do heart checks with You.
—Rebecca Ondov

FEBRUARY 28

Be silent before the Lord God!
—ZEPHANIAH 1:7 (NRSV)

*M*y sister Betsy stayed silent for an entire week when we were young. She was perhaps twenty years old, a student of spirituality. I was thirteen, a student of surliness. She announced she would be silent for a week and then commenced to do so.

My parents were graceful about it. "Seems like there's more room in the house," said my dad.

"We should applaud this form of prayer," said my mom.

"Is this permanent?" said my brothers.

Eventually my sister spoke again—to yell at me, as I recall—but I never forgot that week. I was reminded of it recently when she emerged from a whole summer's silence at the monastery where she now lives. I asked her what her first words were when she emerged from her silent retreat, and she grinned and said, "Pass the butter," which I did, which made her laugh, because those actually were her first words after the retreat.

"Is it hard to be silent?" I asked.

"In the beginning it is," she said. "Then it becomes a prayer."

This morning, thinking of my sister, I rise very early and sit silently over my reading, and men talk to me of silence. "All profound things and emotions of things are preceded and attended by Silence," says Herman Melville. "Silence is the general consecration of the universe." And Thomas Merton: "A man who loves God necessarily loves silence." And Jorge Luis Borges: "Absolute silence is the creative energy and intelligence of eternal being." And prickly, crusty, brave Job, who says to the Creator, "I put my finger to my lips.... I will not answer again." And again Melville: "Silence is the only Voice of our God."

To which I can only say silently, *Amen.*

Dear Lord, let me sometimes sense and practice
the extraordinary eloquence of silence.
—BRIAN DOYLE

February 29

So he went down and dipped himself seven times in the Jordan,
according to the word of the man of God; and his flesh was restored
like the flesh of a little child and he was clean.
—II Kings 5:14 (NASB)

W hat will you do if someone wants to wash your feet?" my wife Elba asked.

The conversation on the drive to church focused on the foot-washing service. I had never participated in one and I wasn't sure about doing it now. "I don't think I'd let them," I said. "If you choose not to be part of the ceremony, what message will you be sending?" In my heart I knew she was right because I am a minister.

At the service the pastor told us, "Jesus showed His servant spirit by washing the feet of the disciples. He was teaching them how they should serve others." Then Todd, six feet four inches tall and an executive with a major corporation, walked forward and slowly took off his shoes. He was followed by Betsy, a young mother in her thirties. I could sense the power of the ritual, but I kept hoping no one would ask me. Then I heard a familiar voice: "Pablo, I'd like to wash your feet." It was Terry, a new member of our congregation whose life had been totally transformed by Christ. How could I say no?

I walked to the front of the church, sat on a chair, took off my shoes and socks, and put my feet in the washbowl. Terry began to wash my feet and prayed, "Lord, thank You for Pastor Diaz. He has been a mentor to me. Bless his ministry and his family."

I was deeply humbled by the love Terry poured over me as he poured the water over my feet. And I was thankful that through this simple action, God was teaching me not to let my feelings get in the way of following Him.

Lord, help me to surrender to Your ways and
to step outside of my spiritual comfort zone.
—Pablo Diaz

March

March 1

Nevertheless God, that comforteth those that are cast down, comforted us.
—II Corinthians 7:6

*W*hen my husband Jerry was diagnosed with inoperable brain cancer back in October 1982, I couldn't imagine how I would continue to live. Fear and pain accompanied me everywhere, even in sleep. I wasn't angry with God; I would go on if only I knew how, but I didn't. It seemed I was totally helpless and no escape was possible. Family, friends, God's Word, prayer, phone calls, visits, casseroles, books of inspiration, hugs—nothing comforted me. I almost stopped eating, rarely slept, never laughed, couldn't read or concentrate. On one particular horrific night when Jerry was back in the hospital, the fear arrived promptly at three o'clock in the morning. I actually fled my bedroom to a guest room, I curled into a ball and cried out, "God, give me something—or I can't go on!"

God planted just one word in my pounding heart. *Nevertheless*. Eventually, I discovered it's used in the Bible more than two hundred times. I figured out that God isn't a God of *what if* but of *nevertheless*. Two months later Jerry died, but the power of "nevertheless living" got me through. I've come to agree with the astonishing statement of Gene Edwards in his little gem *The Inward Journey*: "Thank you, friend pain."

*Father, in the name of Jesus, I pray for life-changing comfort
for anyone who needs to hear from You right now.*
—Marion Bond West

MARCH 2

For God, who commanded the light to shine out
of darkness, hath shined in our hearts.
—II CORINTHIANS 4:6

Our church had just dedicated a new stained glass window in the sanctuary, high above the altar. In the center is the risen Jesus on a bright, cobalt blue background, His arms outstretched, a golden crown on His head. His robe shimmers with vibrant stripes of emerald, crimson and deep purple.

I was particularly anxious to see the window at night because several other churches in town have stunning windows that are lit after dark. So the first time I drove to church in the evening, I was disappointed to see nothing at all. The lights on the outside of the building didn't illuminate the window. But the following week, when lights were installed on the inside to shine outward, the stained glass revealed its beauty.

I think of the people I know who shine with the same kind of beauty, most alive with faith: the sisters at a nearby retreat center who maintain the prayer garden I've come to cherish, or the man at church who puts in so many hours organizing volunteers and donations for the downtown soup kitchen. Through their service, the light of Christ shines directly out from their hearts—you can't miss the glow.

At times I might have on all the outside lights, such as attending church and going to Bible study, but can anyone see Christ in me? It's not until I turn on the light of Christ's love inside my heart, through serving someone else, that the full beauty of that love can be seen.

Lord, bless the faithful whose first thought is to serve You
by serving others. Daily they inspire me to do the same.
—GINA BRIDGEMAN

MARCH 3

This one thing I do...
—PHILIPPIANS 3:13

*T*t was my usual end-of-day confession of failure. Letters I hadn't written, phone calls I'd intended to make, opportunities for kindness I hadn't seized upon. God must be as tired of hearing these bedtime laments, I thought, as I was of making them.

That's when some drawings I'd seen that morning popped into my mind: a two-page spread in a volume of cartoons in the dentist's waiting room. There were no captions, just thirty black-and-white drawings tracing a day in the life of a cymbal player. The musician wakes up, shaves, dresses, eats breakfast, studies his score. Finally he puts his cymbals in their case, travels to the concert hall and takes his place in the percussion section of the orchestra.

He waits quietly through most of the program. As his time to perform approaches, he seizes the cymbals and stands up, breathlessly watching the conductor's baton. The big moment comes! He clashes the cymbals together, one ringing, reverberating, perfectly timed note.

His allotted role accomplished, he leaves the stage, puts on hat and coat, travels home, enjoys dinner, yawns, puts on his pajamas, brushes his teeth, and goes to bed supremely content.

The cymbal player has done the one thing required of him. And was I, I wondered, remembering that picture-story, so capable and important—so central to God's plan—that He asked more of me? Maybe in the multiplicity of each day's events there was a single assignment for me. Maybe if I watched the Conductor more closely I would discover what it was.

Faithful Lord, what one thing have You for me to do this day?
—ELIZABETH SHERRILL

MARCH 4

The angel of the Lord appeared to him [Moses]
in a blazing fire from the midst of a bush.
—EXODUS 3:2 (NASB)

Each spring I always have a cord of oak firewood delivered to our house. It's stacked in our garage to cure and await the winter months and fireplace weather. There's nothing I love more than a chilly night, a blazing fire, a soft blanket and a good book.

Last night was such a night. Joyfully I carried the split oak logs to the fireplace, only to realize I had nothing with which to start the fire. Hearty oak does not burst into flame without the help of kindling, and I'd forgotten to fill the kindling box with pine scraps and wood shavings.

Over the years, I've discovered that developing my prayer life is much like building a fire in a fireplace. I need something to ignite the flame and get me started on my prayer journey. For me, devotional reading is kindling for my spirit.

On the table by my easy chair is the book I'm currently reading, along with my Bible and *Daily Guideposts*. The pages of these three books serve as my spiritual kindling every morning to spark a spirit of prayer. Reading them opens my mind to new thoughts and allows God's Spirit to speak to me.

All of us want to bask in the warmth of God's presence. But without spiritual kindling, it's difficult to build a fire within and keep it going. So don't neglect to fill your kindling box with good thoughts, interesting books and meaningful reflections. If you do, God will guide you by His light and fill you with His peace throughout the day.

Father, use my daily devotions to bring light and warmth into my life.
—SCOTT WALKER

MARCH 5

I received my doctor of ministry from Reformed Theological Seminary in Jackson, Mississippi. During the three years I studied at the seminary, I developed a good relationship with a classmate of mine who happened to be white. In fact, he gave me wise counsel on several occasions.

One day, on a "Grace Is Greater Than Race" tour, I traveled to the city where that old classmate is pastor of a church and met him for lunch. "Dolphus," he said, "I know you're trying to bring about unity within the body of Christ, but because of the attitudes of the people in the congregation I serve, I can't invite you to preach. I'm sorry."

"Well," I said, "keep working to educate them and one day they'll be open to my coming." My friend looked doubtful.

Three years later I walked into that very church and preached at an evening service. My message was received warmly. Now my friend wants to invite me back for a Sunday-morning service! The same people who were opposed to my preaching there are now leading the effort to get me back.

I need to be faithful in doing the work God gives me and remember that it's God Who moves mountains, not me.

> *Lord, thank You for Your faithfulness*
> *in moving the mountain of racial division.*
> —DOLPHUS WEARY

MARCH 6

He shall reward every man according to his works.
—MATTHEW 16:27

*B*asketball madness rocked the old Boston Garden in downtown Boston. It was the final game for the high-school championship of New England. A team from Connecticut and a team from Massachusetts were the finalists, and I was there rooting for the home team.

The score seesawed until the final seconds, when Massachusetts led by two points. Their eyes were on the championship, and I rejoiced. Then, suddenly, the Connecticut star worked his way under the basket where his easy layup would tie the score and send the game into overtime. At that moment the Massachusetts captain shoved him from behind and the Connecticut star missed the basket. Even the Massachusetts fans groaned. The Connecticut star was given two free throws. If he missed one, Massachusetts would win the championship. Hardly a clean-cut victory.

The Connecticut star made the first basket and the Garden fell silent. Then the young man crossed himself and bowed his head in prayer. What was he asking God for? Concentration? A forgiving spirit? Or victory? Whatever it was, it changed the mood of the game. That second shot swished through the net and the score was tied. The crowd roared its approval.

The Massachusetts captain apologized, and the Connecticut star gestured that it was all right. In overtime, the Connecticut star led his team to the championship. The shove from the Massachusetts captain hadn't decided the game; it was a push from above that sealed the hard-earned victory. Even I was pleased.

When I receive those unexpected jolts in life, dear Lord,
help me to know that I am being pushed closer to You.
—OSCAR GREENE

MARCH 7

I will proclaim the name of the Lord.
Oh, praise the greatness of our God!
—DEUTERONOMY 32:3 (NIV)

*P*lease, Lord!"
I often find myself praying this little prayer. When I'm scheduled for a checkup or biopsy, I pray, "Please, Lord!" when I think of the upcoming test. If I'm working on something important, I write "Please, Lord!" in the margin of the paper. I think of it as a way to keep my hopes constantly before God, a way of continually praying, "Please, Lord, let this happen for me." Until recently, I never thought of it as selfish.

Then I met Maryann. She's a ninety-four-year-old convalescent home resident who still speaks with the Irish brogue she brought to America as a sixteen-year-old girl. She has a fierce faith and is given to her own muttered prayers. When she's upset about anything, from rubbery meat loaf on her dinner tray to a distressing story on the news, she exclaims, "God bless us and save us!" When something goes particularly well, from perfectly cooked fish on her dinner tray to the election of her favorite candidate, she says, "Thanks be to the Man above!"

At the end of every visit, I tell Maryann when I'll be back, and she always says a fervent, "Please God!" At first, I thought she was making this small prayer in the same spirit I made mine. But Maryann's prayer is entirely different. My prayer amounts to "Please, Lord, please me." Her prayer is, "Lord, I hope this pleases You."

You can learn a lot from a ninety-four-year-old if you really listen.

Please, Lord, teach me to please You!
—MARCI ALBORGHETTI

MARCH 8

Can you guide the stars season by season
and direct the Big and Little Dipper?
—JOB 38:32 (GNT)

*T*t's four o'clock on Sunday morning, and I'm wakeful, feeling addled, anxious. *Lord, when I look back over my life, it seems so random, so accidental. I can't see the sense of it and the future is just as vague.* I wander out to the kitchen, click on the coffeemaker and step out into the early morning darkness. The air is wondrously crisp and clear. I stand there in my slippers, admiring an ebony sky strewn with diamonds and accented with a fingernail moon. Thin, Casper-the-Friendly-Ghost clouds drift slowly by, shuttering the stars off and on as they pass.

Lord, the universe seems so random, so accidental, as if You just took the stars in Your hand and hurled them into space. And yet there's order also. There are the Big Dipper and the Little Dipper, and up there is the stable North Star. High in the heavens, some geese pass silently over the moon. Lord, is it possible that my life is like the sky, with both order and disorder at the same time?

As I head back into the house, I think of a line by Alexander Pope I memorized in a college literature class. "All nature is but art, unknown to thee; all chance, direction which thou canst not see; all discord, harmony not understood." In a few hours I'll be sitting in church, praising God. But here in this cathedral of creation, I'm reminded that I need not understand exactly how God works. It's enough for me to walk by faith and to enjoy the beauty of His random order.

Lord, You are my North Star in a world of mystery and disarray.
—DANIEL SCHANTZ

MARCH 9

For anyone who enters God's rest also rests
from their works, just as God did from his.
—HEBREWS 4:10 (NIV)

*W*hat do you think God is saying to you in all this?" Pastor Tom asked
as he stood beside my hospital bed. Tom and I have asked each other
that same question numerous times while discussing spiritual matters.

I'd been in the hospital for two weeks already, and in two days I would
undergo more abdominal surgery. Coincidentally, just a couple of evenings
before, I had asked God a lot of questions: Why did I have to go through the
pain of diverticulitis, two surgeries and a lengthy recuperation? Couldn't He
heal me miraculously and instantly? God gave me an answer that surprised me.

So I told Tom, "God said, 'This is a time of rest for you.' It kind of shocked
me, because surgeries and sickness aren't what I think of as rest. But then God
said, 'Don't worry about anything. Trust Me. I'm taking care of everything.
Just rest.'"

That's what I did for the remainder of my thirty-three-day stay in the hospital.
Despite long nights of sleeplessness, I took God at His word. I rested, focusing
my mind on Him. I didn't think about work or finances or the bathroom faucet
at home that needed to be repaired. And during those long days and nights
an experience that could have been an ordeal became an occasion of intimate
communion with God.

Father, thank You for showing me that I can rest
in You no matter what difficulties I'm going through.
—HAROLD HOSTETLER

MARCH 10

In the day when I cried thou answeredst me.
—PSALM 138:3

DAY 1: BROKEN PROMISE, BROKEN HEART

*B*rock, we're just too different. I can't really love you. The engagement is over."

It was early in the morning, and my fiancée and I were sitting on the front porch of my house. For the past few days she had been withdrawn, not wanting to see me. Now I sat stunned as she got up, went to her car and drove away. Numb, I changed into my suit and headed to the office. That afternoon, my company was launching an offering and we had until 8:00 p.m. to get the details entered in our brokerage system. I managed to muster up enough adrenaline to get the job done. But when the rush was gone, I was desolated.

I arrived in the office early the next morning and soon realized I needed to get away. I was almost incoherent on the phone; my computer screen was a flashing irritant. The phone rang. "Brock, a Beth Baxter is here to see you." "Oh yeah, I'll be right down." Somehow I had forgotten to put the appointment on my calendar. Beth, a psychiatrist, is an old family friend. I lumbered down the stairs to greet her. "Hi, Beth! So glad you're here."

As Beth and I went over her investments, I was amazed at how hard it was to concentrate on them. She asked, "So how are you, Brock? You must be getting excited about the wedding!" I explained what had happened, and as we talked, I could feel the pain loosening its grip on me. As I walked her out, she gave me a hug. I had experienced my first full-blown meltdown, and here was the one person I knew best qualified to help.

Lord, when I didn't know where to turn, You sent me a miracle—
a small one perhaps, but a miracle nonetheless.
—BROCK KIDD

MARCH 11

To give unto them beauty for ashes....
—ISAIAH 61:3

DAY 2: AN OCEAN OF TEARS

*M*y engagement had ended suddenly, and I felt as though I was on the edge of a breakdown. I had to get out of town. My sister Keri had found a trip leaving for the Bahamas later that day. Before I knew it, I was on Grand Bahama Island, parked on a beach chair, looking out at the emerald green ocean. I stared for hours, not moving, as the waves rolled back and forth. And then came the crying.

After my second day, I started taking walks down the beach, thinking about why this had happened. My faith was one of the most important things that had come between my fiancée and me; she was unable to respect my belief in God. I thought I could save her from a life of emptiness and show her the hope and happiness faith can bring. That's why God was putting her with me, my family and our church. In my mind, the stage was being set for God to show up. But to her, He never did.

As I got a good distance down the beach, I began to talk to God. "How could You let this happen to us? This was all about You, after all! It was all there for her..." I was sobbing now, stumbling, the sun streaming red and pink lights throughout the stark blue sky. As the ocean continued its ebb and flow, the tide seemed to roar, *Why?* I was screaming now. "I'm dead inside, God! There's nothing left! If You're there, how can You get me through this pain? What can You possibly give me?"

Suddenly, everything stopped: the sound of the ocean, the wind, my anger. Into my mind, clear and instantly focused, came one word: *You.*

Lord, You have redeemed me and claimed me
and given me a strength that is not my own.

—BROCK KIDD

MARCH 12

As the hart panteth after the water brooks, so panteth my soul after thee, O God.
—PSALM 42:1

DAY 3: A SPACE FOR RENEWAL

As I was leaving the Bahamas, what I needed to do suddenly became very clear: I was to sell the engagement ring and go to Africa—alone. Normally, trips like this are planned at least a year ahead of time. The logistics for this one would take a miracle. But I believed if it was truly meant to be, it would somehow happen. I e-mailed my family from the airport and my father was the first to respond. "Great plan, Brock! I'll call Bill. He went several years ago and may have a contact."

By the time I got home to Nashville, Tennessee, my father had the number of a professional guide in Mozambique and my mother had bought me a new copy of Ernest Hemingway's *Green Hills of Africa*. A card from my sister was in the mailbox. On the front was a quote from Louis L'Amour: "There will come a time when you believe everything is finished. That will be the beginning." Then the phone rang. "Brock," said a heavily accented voice, "this is Simon from Mozambique. Your dad gave me the dates you can join us. I only have one three-week period open the rest of the year and that happens to be it. Because that's all that I have open, if you book now, I'll give you twenty-five percent off the whole trip."

"Absolutely, Brock," the chairman of my company said. "Take a month off if you need to." My sister had a list of quotes on flights to get me to Mozambique, where I was to take a three-hour flight deep into the African bush. Before I knew it, the die was cast. In the meantime, I was planning on spending a lot of time with my son Harrison and hoping that God would somehow show me how to heal all these wounds.

I know You are everywhere, Father, but sometimes
I need unfamiliar surroundings to hear You more clearly.
—BROCK KIDD

MARCH 13

Fear thou not, for I am with thee.
—ISAIAH 41:10

DAY 4: INTO THE WILD

*W*elcome to the bush, Brock," my guide Bryn said as I got off the plane in the interior of Mozambique. The setting was magnificent, as exotic and wild as anything I'd ever dreamed. Our days began before sunrise with a quick breakfast and then the tracking: almost ten miles a day, surrounded by elephants, impalas, kudus, zebras, warthogs and baboons. The adventure was there. But why was I there?

On the seventh day, we got up at 4:30 in the morning to find a group of dagga boys, mature bull buffalo that spend most of their time away from the herd. We followed them for hours and at one point got caught in a ditch surrounded with thicket and dozens of angry female buffalo. Suddenly, a large buffalo stuck her head into the bush where we were hiding and stomped her feet. Fortunately, she left the bush and didn't charge us. As the herd around us trampled off suddenly, we left our hideout. "Shoomba! " Bryn whispered, pointing to the reason the buffalo had left.

There, fifteen yards from us, was a large lion. As he bounded over the hill, we heard his incredibly powerful roar. "We'll stay clear of this area for the rest of the day," Bryn said. That was fine with me. Soon we were hot on the trail of a very large bull with big horns, the biggest we had seen. Bryn estimated he weighed more than eighteen hundred pounds. Although I was enjoying all of this excitement, I had a sick feeling of worry that I wouldn't be able to come through when I needed to. I began to shake. I started mentally repeating the Lord's Prayer, not just by rote, but fully conscious that I was saying it to God. After all that had happened, I was once again letting God into my heart.

Lord, it's when I'm thrown back on myself that I find my need for You.
—BROCK KIDD

MARCH 14

Now be strong...for I am with you, saith the Lord of hosts.
—HAGGAI 2:4

DAY 5: A HEART MADE WHOLE

*W*e spotted our great bull buffalo, along with two smaller bulls, in a thicket several hundred yards away in the Mozambique bush. It took my guide Bryn and me more than an hour, crouching and crawling, to get closer to the giant animals. *What if I begin to shake again?* I thought. As we slowly climbed the hill to where the bulls were gathered, I started to pray again, and suddenly I began to hear "Amazing Grace" in my head, as if it were being sung by my grandfather and the other people I've known who are now in heaven. Tears of joy were running down my face; I wiped them away as we got closer to where the big bulls were.

As we set up in front of the thicket, we realized that the bulls had spotted us. I kept praying, worried about the shaking. I could barely see the giant bull through the thicket, some fifty yards away. Then he turned and faced us. The bull was looking directly at me now, into my eyes, and he started to stomp. *Dear God, please be with me*, I prayed. Suddenly I felt a calm come over me. My body was tingling; the bull was staring into my eyes, and I was staring right back into his. Although I could feel my heart pounding, I wasn't shaking at all. I had never felt a sense of such peace. *This is why I've come*, I thought. Not for the buffalo or the adventure, but for God—to have Him in my heart again.

As I looked at the great old bull, I whispered under my breath, "My strength is in You, God." All I heard was an answering whisper in my heart: *I am always here.*

> *Lord, help me to remember that underneath all my fears,*
> *You are there to be my strength.*
> —BROCK KIDD

March 15

"Whoever believes in me, as the Scripture has said,
streams of living water will flow from within him."
—John 7:38 (NIV)

Day 6: A Father's Message

It was a glorious sunrise in the bush. The sky was a burning orange, and now the noises around me were comforting. I felt I had started a new life. I began to record the sunrise, talking out loud to Harrison, speaking a message I felt suddenly called to send. "Harrison, when you grow up and become a man, there will be times when you will be sad and maybe angry, and maybe your heart will feel like it's broken and you won't think you'll ever be happy again. Growing up, I was very blessed to have Mimi and Big Dad for my parents. One of the greatest gifts they gave me was a strong heart. You have that same strong heart. Just ask Mimi or Big Dad, Uncle Ben or Aunt Keri, and they will tell you.

"Harrison, now I know why I came to Africa. It was to share my story—our story—with you and the lesson it taught me. Every one of God's children has been given a cup. Even in our saddest and hardest times, God is always there with a pitcher overflowing with the water of life, but it's up to us to pick ourselves up, go out into the world and hold our cup up to God. He will fill it to overflowing with His power and love, and we will be happy once again.

"I am so glad to have you for my son. I love you, buddy." I turned off the camera. It was time to go home.

Lord, in Your mercy, even my tears can become the water of life.
—Brock Kidd

Oh that men would praise the Lord for his goodness.
—PSALM 107:15

DAY 7: THE NEW LIFE

*A*s my plane touched down in Nashville, Tennessee, I experienced a passing wave of sadness. I thought of my ex-fiancée and all those who build walls that keep out God. And then something happened: A wave of anticipation swept over me, and I knew that the minute my feet touched ground, a new beginning was ripe for the picking. New priorities were already shaping up, and in the next weeks I acted on them. When my son Harrison was with me, night walks replaced video games and I began to talk to him more about God and the goodness of our lives.

The responsibility of serving my clients became a privilege. I resigned from the boards of two organizations so I could give more time to a third that serves needy children in our community. My church was preparing for an uncertain new season with the retirement of my father, who had served as minister for thirty-eight years. As an elder, I was asked to chair a new committee focused on reenergizing the church and spreading the good news. An assignment I would have laughed at six months ago suddenly became my calling.

A part of me will always linger in the African bush, where I came eye to eye with all the horror the world holds in the form of the terrifying charge of a Cape buffalo. And I'll always hold fast to the knowledge that even though disappointments, dangers and fears will come, God is always with me. But just as important as my time there was that day sitting across the table from my client Judy: "Brock, you have to tell this story," she said to me.

*I hope I will spend my life remembering—and living—both. Father,
even the scars I carry in life are reasons to sing Your praises.*
—BROCK KIDD

MARCH 17

And of his fulness have all we received, and grace for grace.
—JOHN 1:16

*M*y big sister is a major card-sender—birthdays, anniversaries, Valentine's, St. Patrick's Day, you name it and Mary Lou graces my mailbox with a card. She never forgets. Me, I'm a slacker. I'll buy the occasional greeting card but never seem to actually get around to sending it. The convenience and instant gratification of e-cards has made it only slightly more likely that I'll send one.

But I love Mary Lou's cards. My birthday just wouldn't be complete without her greeting, or Valentine's Day without the burst of a heart-red envelope in my mailbox. I don't even need to decipher her left-handed scrawl to know it's from her. And she's the only one who actually mails me a St. Patrick's Day card (in a green envelope).

Mary Lou has been a world-class big sister to me all my life, ever since she got to name me after her favorite uncle (Hi, Uncle Ed!) because she was so upset about our mother having to go to the hospital and have me. I'm the baby of the family, and you know what that means. I got away with a lot of stuff the other kids never could. A little spoiled, you might say—just a little.

And maybe all these years later Mary Lou is still spoiling me a bit. Not that I deserve it. I'm too old. Yet Mary Lou's cards keep coming. They remind me of grace: We don't necessarily deserve it; it just comes. Maybe it's God's way of spoiling His children just a bit. Next time the occasion arises, I'm sending Mary Lou a card. I wonder if she'll recognize my handwriting.

I'm blessed, Lord, in so many ways I don't deserve. Thank You
for the miracle of Your grace and for world-class big sisters.

—EDWARD GRINNAN

MARCH 18

The God of all comfort, who comforts us in all our troubles....
—II CORINTHIANS 1:3–4 (NIV)

*W*hen my husband Whitney and I moved south one gray, wet January, I was terribly homesick for the house in New York where we'd lived for eighteen years. Our new cedar house atop a small mountain in Kingston Springs, Tennessee, was beautiful. But so different from New York, I thought sadly as I began unpacking.

Everything I pulled out held a memory of "back home." Here was a lamp from the table in the living room next to the window overlooking our rambling stone wall. Here were knickknacks that had sat on the big windowsill where I watched the horses in the field. Here was the teakettle that had poured so many steaming cups for friends.

By the time dusk was falling through the bare winter woods around our new house, I was a maudlin mess. I just wanted to go home. But then, in the distance, my ears picked up a sound I'd heard many times in my childhood home in Pennsylvania: the wail of a train whistle. Through the rain-beaded windows, the long-forgotten sound came closer and closer, and then faded away, leaving a warm comfort, just as it had when I was a child falling asleep to its mournful wail. Every night I could count on it like clockwork. As I could count on God.

Now, fifty years and six hundred miles away in Kingston Springs, the sound of home had followed, a timely reminder that, like clockwork, I could still count on God.

Father God, thank You for the housewarming Your presence brings.
—SHARI SMYTH

MARCH 19

*For as the heavens are higher than the earth, so are my ways higher
than your ways, and my thoughts than your thoughts.*

—ISAIAH 55:9

*S*olomon, my five-year-old, gets upset by things that don't follow the rules of cause-and-effect. Whenever he comes across something that doesn't seem quite right, he furrows his brow and demands an answer. So when Faith, a classmate of his, was diagnosed with leukemia, Solomon tried to make sense of it all. "Why did this happen?" "Why is Faith too tired to play?" "Why did she lose her curls?" "Will she die?" "Will I die?" "Will you die?" "When will we die?" "Does dying hurt?" At that moment I longed for the innocent "What's that?" of Solomon's toddler years. How could I explain that I had no idea why Faith was sick, that sometimes bad things happen for reasons we can't explain? Instead, I found myself hugging Solomon tightly and being thankful he was in my arms and healthy.

"Why are you crying, Mommy?" Solomon asked.

"I don't know," I said. "I don't know why Faith got leukemia. I don't think anyone knows."

Solomon's face perked up. "Mommy, I know who knows."

"Who?" I asked.

"God. God knows everything. He's got a plan."

"You're right," I said.

"But, Mommy, how can we figure it out? How can we know the plan?"

"I don't think we can. But we can pray for Faith and her family."

"Oh, okay," he said. "I have another question."

"Okay."

"How come the teacher never picks me to be line leader?"

I'm happy to say that Faith is doing well. Her leukemia is in remission. Her curls have grown back, her energy and smiles have returned. Aptly named, Faith has filled us all with hope and gratitude.

Dear Lord, when there are no answers, let me always trust Your plan.

—SABRA CIANCANELLI

March 20

O taste and see that the Lord is good.
—Psalm 34:8

I'd looked forward to everything about the Rhine cruise except the guided tours scheduled for various stops. Ever since boyhood, I'd secretly resisted being force-fed historical facts, dates or the biographical details of long-dead potentates. The first tour was the city of Antwerp. As I followed the other passengers down the gangplank, I saw to my horror five huge buses lined up on the dockside quay. Tib and I had been assigned to bus five. Beside it stood a guide holding a long stick topped by a dinner-sized paper plate with the number 5 on it, looking for all the world like a giant lollipop.

Everyone trooped off the bus in the center of town where, with a whispered farewell to Tib, and the pang of guilt I always felt at my lack of historical curiosity, I slipped away from the lollipop parade to enjoy the city on my own. I walked through the diamond center on Appelmansstraat and along the rows of houseboats, chatting with cordial English-speaking Belgians. For lunch, I dined at canal-side stalls, sampling raw herring and the Low Countries specialty e*rwtensoep*, a pea soup so thick my spoon stood up by itself.

Comparing notes with Tib back on the ship, I thought how differently we'd delighted in the day. Tib learns about a place primarily through its history and its art; I through encounters with the people who presently live there. "Why ever should you feel guilty?" she asked when I confessed feeling I was missing something others found important. "Aren't yours and mine just different ways of exploring God's world?"

Help me, Father, to treasure the many ways
You've given us to experience Your limitless creation!
—John Sherrill

MARCH 21

Feed me with food convenient for me.
—PROVERBS 30:8

*Y*ou've gained three pounds," Dr. Serafin said without even a hint of a smile.

"Oh, no problem," I answered, perched on the examining table for my annual physical. "I'll lose it in a flash."

My first plan was simple: no snacks. That lasted until I went to a party with particularly tasty hors d'oeuvres.

Okay, a new scale. I'll weigh myself every day until I lose the weight. The new scale said I'd gained two more pounds. I increased my morning exercise and started carrying weights when I walked. I am woman. I can do this. Six months later, I was still five pounds overweight.

One day, over coffee, a friend of mine told me about her struggles with alcohol. "So many of us have the notion that the solution to our problems is within ourselves," she said. "Thanks to Alcoholics Anonymous, I've learned that the only way I can solve my problems is to turn them over to God."

My problem was certainly a tiny one compared to my friend's, but the principle was the same. "God," I prayed, "could You show me how to lose those pounds and fill the space they leave with something better?"

Once I asked, things started happening. We traveled to Africa, where I discovered that most of the people in the world get by on one meal a day. After we returned, I read three articles that emphasized that our bodies need half as much food in the second half of our lives. I developed the habit of never taking more than I needed. God had given me the motivation to start looking at food differently.

I thought losing weight was all about me. But as soon as I bothered to ask, God started showing me it was about something bigger. And as for Dr. Serafin, I can't wait for my next appointment. I think he's going to be surprised!

Father, I hunger for the satisfaction of following Your ways.
—PAM KIDD

*"You're blessed when you care. At the moment
of being 'carefull,' you find yourselves cared for."*
—Matthew 5:7 (MSG)

*R*ecently I woke up missing my children and grandchildren. They know I don't need anything, and they don't often send letters or call. I was indulging in a grand pity party, so I prayed, confessing my whiny self-absorption. Then I read the Beatitudes to see what Jesus said would make His followers feel blessed. My eye stopped at "You're blessed when you care."

I decided to care for everyone I met that day. *Maybe everyone like me needs to be heard*, I thought. *So to care for the people I meet today the way God does, I can let them tell me about their lives.* It was a remarkable day. At each of my appointments, I asked the receptionists and nurses for their names. At the restaurant, I asked the waiter for his name and introduced myself and my wife to him. I didn't preach or force conversation on people, and not everyone responded.

But the simple act of really listening to the people I encountered had a striking effect: God had filled my day with warm and caring people.

*Lord, when I make my days full of simple caring,
I really do feel cared for. Thank You for the blessing.*
—Keith Miller

MARCH 23

Rejoice always, pray without ceasing.
—I THESSALONIANS 5:16–17 (NRSV)

*D*o you ever have trouble figuring out what the Bible means for your everyday life? When the participants in a Bible study I was leading pressed me one day on the above passage, I had to swallow hard and say, "Pray without ceasing? I really don't know how to do that." How do you pray all the time? Not just when someone is sick or you have something to say to God, but all the time? I knew my prayer life wasn't like that. I felt that I had failed as their teacher. Worse, I wondered if I was also failing as a man of faith.

That night while watching the news, I was mesmerized by the story of a photographer from the *Los Angeles Times* who took stunning pictures of some firefighters deploying their silver emergency shelters when a devastating Southern California wildfire overran their position. When asked what was going through her mind when she was taking the photographs, she said simply, "I would stop shooting and start praying."

Pray all the time? Figuring out what the Bible means sometimes is as simple as doing what the Bible says, as best you can, as often as you can, in as many places as you can.

Teach me something new about Your Word today,
God, so I may live it out tomorrow in praise of You.
—JEFF JAPINGA

Now to the King eternal, immortal, invisible,
the only God, be honor and glory forever and ever.
—I Timothy 1:17 (NASB)

I love books and coffee. After a long day at work, I sometimes drop by a favorite bookstore and spend thirty minutes with a hot espresso, browsing through the stacks of books. These moments clear my mind and restore my spirit. They also put a dent in my wallet!

Not long ago I was leafing through a book on English history and discovered a story about King Canute, the battle-hardened Viking who ruled England from 1016 to 1035 and built a North Sea empire that stretched from Greenland to the Baltic, and from England to Russia.

One day Canute ordered his nobles to gather on the seashore. He had his throne carried to the beach and placed where the tide was advancing across the sand. Sitting on the throne, Canute commanded the waves of the ocean to advance no further. Sternly, he glared at the surf as it continued to rise, covering his feet with salt water. Finally, thoroughly drenched, Canute ordered his throne returned to his palace and stomped away in sodden disgust.

Several days later a wise Canute declared, "Let all the world know that the power of kings is empty and worthless. There is no king worthy of the name save God, by whose will heaven, earth and sea obey eternal laws." Canute never wore his crown again.

As I sat in the bookstore and drank my coffee, I could see myself in that imperious king. I've had moments when I commanded the waves of my life to advance no further. Every time I've gotten my feet wet, God's waves remind me that there is no king in all this universe save God.

Lord, help me to take the crown from my hard head
and give it back to You. Amen.
—Scott Walker

MARCH 25

*W*hen the cardiologist scheduled me for a stress test because of a suspected blockage in one coronary artery, I was more surprised than frightened. I'd been working out on my treadmill for years, and although my family history included heart disease, I always thought I'd been careful enough to avoid it.

After we moved, however, I had spent six hours one day hauling boxes out of the garage, unpacking them and then shelving an entire library of books. I might have, in the doctor's words, "knocked something loose."

The test would consist of two series of pictures of my heart, each taking about twenty minutes. I would have to lie very still, with my hands behind my head, or they'd have to start the test over again.

I hadn't counted on my bursitis. After five minutes into the first series, my left shoulder started to hurt, and soon the pain was so bad I was afraid my body would begin to shake, ruining the pictures.

I was determined not to have to take the test over, and I tried to find all kinds of things to take my mind off of my painful shoulder. Nothing seemed to have an effect until I started reciting the Twenty-third Psalm: "The Lord is my shepherd; I shall not want." I could still feel the pain, but it seemed further away, and I was no longer apprehensive that the test would be ruined.

Before they took the second set of pictures, I told the nurse about my problems in the first test, and they were able to pad my shoulder so I didn't have any pain. So I switched from the Twenty-third Psalm to Psalm 150:6: "Let every thing that hath breath praise the Lord."

Thank You, Lord, for Your wisdom in giving us a psalm for every occasion.
—RHODA BLECKER

All the days ordained for me were written
in your book before one of them came to be.
—Psalm 139:16 (niv)

*V*isiting a museum, I paused in front of a picture by the surrealist René Magritte. In the painting, an artist sits before an easel, staring at an egg placed on a table. On the canvas, though, he's not painting an egg but a feathered, full-grown bird. Puzzling, when there were more than enough puzzles in my life just then! My husband and I were trying to sell our home of fifty years in the worst housing market in decades. Moving near family in another state meant leaving not only friends, but longtime doctors and dentists, service people, our church. How could we ever find replacements for these things? Which belongings could we take to a small apartment? How would we manage if the house didn't sell?

I turned away from Magritte's perplexing painting and then looked again. The artist in the picture, clearly, was painting not what he saw but what he knew. The beak, the claws, the feathered wings on his canvas—all this, in time, would develop from an egg. The artist saw the end from the beginning. *I'm seeing only the egg,* I thought, *things as they are at present. I can't see the life-in-the-making that will someday take shape. But an Artist is at work in my life and every life, One Who sees the completed picture and knows the people, the places, the specifics of a future still invisible to me.*

Help me put anxiety aside, Father, and watch
Your brush at work on the finished portrait.
—Elizabeth Sherrill

MARCH 27

I call to remembrance my song in the night:
I commune with mine own heart.

—PSALM 77:6

*T*was awake again at 3:00 a.m. *Quick, Marion, before those troubling thoughts attack your mind. Sing!*

Singing the old hymns I learned as a child keeps away the "what ifs" that like to attack in the middle of the night. I don't sing out loud, just silently in my spirit. After a while I can usually get back to sleep.

I sang my last song several times as I hovered on the brink of sleep:

Jesus is the sweetest name I know

And He's just the same as His lovely name.

That's the reason why I love Him so.

Oh, Jesus is the sweetest name I know.

Right then I was ambushed by an unexpected attack: *Jesus doesn't care about you or your stupid songs!*

Oh, Lord, don't let that thought stay with me and make me doubt. Somehow, show me that You care.

"The piano tuner will be here by nine," my husband Gene reminded me the next morning. Neither Gene nor I play the piano, but he cherishes our baby grand. It's about ninety years old and has been in his family forever.

When Bobby Howington finished his work, he gave us our annual mini-concert. Gene and I sat side by side on the sofa listening intently as music from the perfectly tuned piano filled our living room and our souls. Bobby's skilled fingers lovingly played,

Jesus is the sweetest name I know

And He's just the same as His lovely name.

That's the reason why I love Him so.

Oh, Jesus is the sweetest name I know.

Your faithfulness amazes me, Father, time and time again.

—MARION BOND WEST

For they shall all know me, from the least of them to the greatest, says the Lord;
for I will forgive their iniquity, and remember their sin no more.
—JEREMIAH 31:34 (NRSV)

I'd been staring at my computer screen for the better part of the morning, with precious few words of the report that was due by the end of the day to show for it. "I can't seem to focus," I said to my colleague Keith as we headed to the cafeteria for a quick lunch. "Every time I try to draw some conclusions and recommendations, I keep thinking about the report I messed up three weeks ago. And my mind just seems to freeze."

"My basketball coach taught me something I've never forgotten," Keith responded. Keith had played college ball about twenty years before. "He always said, 'You'll win some games, you'll lose others. But never lose the same game twice.'"

"When you get back to your desk," Keith suggested on the way back from the cafeteria, "print a copy of that old report, say out loud what you learned from it and toss that copy in the trash. And this time, mean it. Then see if you can move on with your current work."

I did finish my report that afternoon. It wasn't half bad.

Help me to believe, oh, God, that Your grace is greater than my guilt,
calling me each and every day to rise above those times when I fail You.
—JEFF JAPINGA

MARCH 29

"Unless a grain of wheat falls into the earth and dies,
it remains by itself alone; but if it dies, it bears much fruit."
—John 12:24 (NASB)

*T*his year our dearest African friend, Samuel Nimubona of Burundi, was assassinated on a quiet Saturday evening in the capital city of Bujumbura. He was thirty-three years old, had a wife and two beautiful daughters, loved Jesus with all his heart, and worked tirelessly for peace and reconciliation between the Hutu and Tutsi ethnic groups in his troubled nation.

The news of his death crushed my wife Joy and me, and I got angry at God. On the Sunday morning after I got the news, I paced up and down and finally shook my fist at the sky and yelled, "If this is Your plan, God, I want out!" I began to weep and couldn't stop. God seemed silent, and that was just fine with me. I didn't want to talk to Him anyway.

That night an e-mail came from Samuel's closest friend, who had been the first person on the scene and had driven Samuel to the hospital. He told of how the news spread through the country on Sunday, and thousands gathered to mourn our friend. Then he wrote these words:

> But after all this sad story, let me comfort you, dear brother. Samuel is a hero. He is a hero to Jesus, and to the Burundi people. For the first time in our country, we have seen a miracle when all ethnic groups and all religions mourned somebody together. Samuel is harvesting what he has sowed. Friends, it is a very sad time for all of us, but I can assure you that Samuel has not died. His work will remain with us forever.

My own tears came again. God had to give up His own Son at thirty-three to save the world. Maybe Samuel had to give his life to save Burundi.

Dear Father, I cannot see Your hand in this, but I trust You to cause Samuel's life to bear much fruit. Please let my life count for something as his did.
—Eric Fellman

"Martha, Martha," the Lord answered, "you are worried and upset about many things, but only one thing is needed. Mary has chosen what is better."

—LUKE 10:41–42 (NIV)

*M*y wife Kathy and I had been up late chatting with Maria and John, friends who were with us for the weekend, so we were still in bed when the phone rang. It was our son Ryan, calling to see if he, his friend Jennifer and her children could come for a visit at ten.

Kathy and I shifted into high gear. After breakfast with Maria and John, we loaded the dishwasher. There was plenty of time for showers and a trip to the recycling center.

"Kathy, could you take a load of laundry down when you're finished with your shower?" I called as I headed downstairs to load the garbage and recycling bins into our car.

Kathy's arms were full of laundry when everyone arrived fifteen minutes later, so she gave Ryan and Jennifer and Mandy and Jim a one-handed hug and a kiss.

"Mom, can we talk to you in the kitchen for a minute?" Ryan asked.

"You bet, Ryan, but let me get this load of laundry started first."

It was while she was in the basement, pouring detergent into the washer, that it struck her. *I think Ryan asked Jenn to marry him!*

Kathy went charging back upstairs. Ryan and Jennifer were standing alone in the kitchen when she turned the corner. "Now, what was it you wanted to talk about?" she asked. There was no answer. "Is there a ring I should see?"

When I walked into the family room, a spot on the sofa was saved for me. I hugged and kissed everyone. Then, while talking over my shoulder, I went into the kitchen and began unloading the dishwasher.

"Ted, come in and sit down," Kathy said. "We have a Mary moment for you, and it shouldn't wait any longer."

Lord, please help me recognize when I need to stop being Martha and enjoy the Mary moments in my life.

—TED NACE

MARCH 31

The memory of the righteous is a blessing.
—PROVERBS 10:7 (NRSV)

The sun was warm, but the wind had a sharp edge to it as I lifted the sap bucket off the maple tree. The bucket was full, and I focused my attention on the task of removing it from the small hook that held it securely to the tree.

When the ground thawed, the sap was drawn upward toward the branches to give the tree new life. This was the liquid we would boil down to make maple syrup.

I lowered my eyes to the gathering pail on the ground and carefully poured the gallons of clear liquid into it. As the last drop fell, my eyes moved from the bucket to the granite marker that sat beneath the maple tree. It had been resting there for more than eleven years. On the stone were engraved the names of four family members who had passed away. Just looking at their names brought a rush of fond memories.

I paused for a moment and retreated from the labor at hand to remember my dad, my aunt, my cousin and my mom, and the impact each had on my life. The memory of their love flowed into my soul just as the sap flowed from the maple tree into the bucket. God felt very close on that warm spring day as I gathered maple sap by the old rock wall.

Thank You, Lord, for allowing me to remember all those
who were Your hands and heart here on earth, those
who shaped my life and helped to make me who I am today.
—PATRICIA PUSEY

April

APRIL 1

"Let your light shine before others."
—MATTHEW 5:16 (NIV)

*I*t was a sunny spring day in New York City's Central Park. Daffodils bloomed by the path; somewhere, people were singing. And I trudged beneath the budding trees feeling every one of my seventy-five years. My feet hurt, my vision was blurred, my back ached, I was short of breath. Was I ready for a rocking chair?

I could see the singers now, a large crowd, maybe two hundred people, on the path ahead. As I came closer, I made out the words of the perky tune: "This little light of mine, I'm gonna let it shine...." I walked faster, eager to pass them. My light didn't feel very shiny just then.

Only as I drew near could I see that half the crowd was in wheelchairs. In their teens and twenties, they all had cerebral palsy. Heads drifted to the side, arms were strapped to chair arms, eyes wandered. Did they even hear, I wondered, as their attendants sang? "This little light...."

I was surrounded by them now, the path blocked by wheelchairs, many tilted back bed-like. "Let it shine." What light could shine from the seemingly cruel limitations around me?

And then I saw it. The young woman's fingers were curled against her palm. But with that fist she was rapping the padded arm of her chair. Up, down, up—as far as her restraints would allow—in perfect time with the music.

And I saw not a little light, but a very big one. Bright enough to shine through the self-absorption of one passerby and light up even that future rocking chair in a world where the smallest reflector can still shed His glory around us.

Shine Your light, Father, on my slower pace today.
—ELIZABETH SHERRILL

And the earth brought forth grass, and herb yielding seed
after his kind, and the tree yielding fruit, whose seed was in itself,
after his kind: and God saw that it was good.

—GENESIS 1:12

This week my wife Shirley and I arrived back in Pennsylvania. I tell people in Florida that we go north early to see the daffodils—and see them I do, out our kitchen window. Their bright yellow heads dance in the cool wind, just as William Wordsworth described them in his oft-quoted poem:

A host, of golden daffodils;
Beside the lake, beneath the trees,
Fluttering and dancing in the breeze.

Also in spring bloom is a saffron field of forsythia we brought with us when we moved here from Princeton, New Jersey. Our former neighbor Mrs. Vaughn, then in her eighties, loved forsythia. (She called it "for-sigh-thia.") Up and ready to open their eyes, too, is another transplant, our Virginia bluebells. What makes them special is that they were a gift from another neighbor, Mrs. Braden, who majored in botany and could call everything in her yard by its Latin name. The plants she gave us have multiplied, and we have passed some of them along.

A rain-dampened Shirley, who's been weeding around some beautiful magenta tulips, just came inside, singing, "Though April showers may come your way, they bring the flowers that bloom in May." I answer with a riff from that old hymn "Showers of Blessings." I'm still thinking of Mrs. Braden and the blessing she was. I remember her for her kindness and generosity. Those aren't bad traits to be remembered by at this time of year when nature everywhere speaks of God's bountiful handiwork.

Dear Lord, in all things bright and beautiful I see Your great love and creativity.

—FRED BAUER

April 3

My soul is exceeding sorrowful, even unto death.
—MATTHEW 26:38

O n the wall of my office, facing the photo of Dr. Van Dusen, is a watercolor of a village in the high, dry Altiplano of Bolivia. In the foreground, a group of Aymara Indians guide their llamas toward town. The focus of the painting is a church with whitewashed walls and a massive bell tower looming above mud-and-wattle huts.

The watercolor takes me back to the year Tib and I spent as teachers in Bolivia, and especially to a car trip we made during Holy Week to explore the high desert country.

Though we were fourteen thousand feet above sea level, the peaks of the Andes rose high above us. Villages crouched in their immense shadows, always with a church like the one in the watercolor. The church interiors were simple, bare and beautiful—except for the crucifix. Here was a writhing, agonized Jesus: blood streaming from real nails in hands and feet and from a savage circle of three-inch thorns.

Back in La Paz, I asked a longtime missionary about this emphasis on painful death. "Where's the victory of the cross?" I asked.

"The Indians identify with pain," Ed Barber explained. "They're perpetually poor, often cold and sick. Not so long ago, the only life they knew was toil in the silver mines 365 days a year."

Missionaries, Ed went on, were attempting to make the risen Christ real to the Aymara. "But they have a lot to teach us too: The joy of Easter has no meaning for any of us apart from suffering. Better than most of us, Indians have incorporated pain into their understanding of God."

So today I tape a strand of Easter grass to the frame of the watercolor, reminding me that when suffering strikes family, church, neighborhood, country, I can thank God that He has woven this into the very fabric of His story.

Risen Lord, help me to stay with You through the painful days of this week.
—JOHN SHERRILL

APRIL 4

The simplicity that is in Christ.
—II CORINTHIANS 11:3

*D*uring my early morning walks I inevitably became bored as I huffed and puffed. A jogging friend explained that she fought the boredom by praying for her neighbors as she passed their homes.

Approaching Bobby and E.J.'s house the next morning, I asked God to do something simple for my friends of more than forty years. E.J. had been diagnosed with Alzheimer's and ALS (Lou Gehrig's disease). Bobby, his wife of almost fifty-seven years, cared for him at home with astounding love and patience. "Lord, give them laughter," I prayed. "Let E.J. remember something funny today."

Every morning as I passed their house, I prayed for Bobby and E.J. Then one day Bobby confided to me, "I just want him to go to heaven from our home, not some facility." It didn't look likely. Just to get E.J. to eat, Bobby had to feed him, one spoonful at a time. I wasn't sure how long she could handle it alone.

One day E.J. waved to me from their open front door, smiling. "Thank You, Lord," I prayed. "He's still at home. Content and kind—just much leaner." Early Easter morning, walking by their lovely brick home, I left a small basket filled with jelly beans. E.J. and I both adored them. The sun was barely up one sultry summer morning when I passed Bobby and E.J.'s house, unable to think of what to pray for. Finally I said, "Lord, do something brand-new for E.J. today."

After I got home, I checked my phone messages. One had been left early that morning. "Marion, Bobby wanted you to know that E.J. left this life from his beloved recliner in the bedroom around 6:30. She's okay, and she knows he is too."

Father, You stand ready to answer even the simplest,
most hurried prayers in Your magnificent way!
—MARION BOND WEST

APRIL 5

"And I will ask the Father, and He will give you another Helper, that He may be with you forever.... I will not leave you orphans; I will come to you."
—JOHN 14:16, 18 (NKJV)

Looking into the worried eyes of His disciples, Jesus knew they realized He would soon be killed. They would be left alone without their leader.

It was at that moment that Jesus talked with them about the coming of the Holy Spirit. They would not be left alone like orphans. The very presence of God—Father, Son and Holy Spirit—would be forever with them.

When I was fourteen years old, my father suddenly died of a heart attack. After his death, we moved from the Philippines back to my mother's hometown, Fort Valley, Georgia. I remember the fear of those first weeks of grief and separation and readjustment to a new world and a new life. I was afraid my mother would also die and my sister and I would be left alone in a world we did not know and could not trust. It was a terrible anxiety for a teenager to live with. I didn't want to be an orphan thrust into the care of people I didn't know.

So it was with Jesus' disciples. And so it is when I fear that God isn't with me, doesn't hear me, is far away from me. In these moments I need to hear the reassuring promise of Jesus: "I will not leave you orphans; I will come to you, ...the Father will give you another Helper, that He may be with you forever."

Dear Lord, reassure me that You are with me. May I witness the presence of the Spirit moving in my life today.
—SCOTT WALKER

APRIL 6

Jesus said to him, "Judas, is it with a kiss
that you are betraying the Son of Man?"
—LUKE 22:48 (NRSV)

The machine for the audio tour at the Metropolitan Museum of Art looked a little like an iPod, but the guide assured me that all I had to do was punch in the right numbers and I could hear about hundreds of works of art in the collection.

I tried it, delighted by the information the machine gave. For instance, who knew that the little man staring out of a huge Tiepolo is the artist Giovanni Battista Tiepolo himself? Or that in a large painting of the chemist Antoine-Laurent Lavoisier, his wife is depicted with a portfolio of drawings because she was an artist too?

Then I came to a medieval sculpture with a familiar scene, Christ's betrayal. It was easy enough to identify the characters: Peter raising his sword, Judas with his back to the viewer, Christ gazing on with compassion. I wondered what the audio tour would have to say about it. I punched in a number.

"This poignant scene," the voice on the tape said, "was part of a choir screen in a cathedral. No one could really see the back of it, but it's worth looking at today." I walked around to the back of the sculpture. "Here you can see Judas's face. Now compare him to Christ. You'll notice something startling: The sculptor has given them the same features." Was this the artist's joke? Or was he making a statement that could only be read when the sculpture was put on the floor of a modern museum?

I thought of the subject again—Christ's betrayal. But wasn't it Judas' betrayal too? In betraying his Lord, he betrayed himself and all that was Christlike about him.

I returned to my tape with a lot on my mind.

Forgive me, Lord, when I forget You.
—RICK HAMLIN

APRIL 7

*Then they went home and prepared spices and ointments
to embalm him; but by the time they were finished it was the Sabbath,
so they rested all that day as required by the Jewish law.*
—LUKE 23:56 (TLB)

For Jesus' followers and friends, Saturday was a day of rest. It was their Sabbath. They had long hours to sit and think, remember, cry and maybe, from time to time, hope. "He did say something about 'rising on the third day,' didn't He?"

This Saturday I concentrate on cleaning the house and planning tomorrow's Easter dinner. It's what I call "the day in between." It's a "normal" day, like thousands of others.

But deep inside the tomb, deep inside the Father's heart, resurrection life is stirring. Is this the day Jesus "descended into hell" to lead forth those who would come with Him? Is He there now as I dump clothes into the washer? Are the angels on edge with anticipation? I wonder as I spread out a clean tablecloth and set a glass vase of my daffodils in the center. At what moment will the power of God's love overrule death and leave those grave cloths empty in Joseph's tomb? Has it happened already? I remove the brownies from the oven.

I can't follow Jesus on this day; no one but He and the Father know exactly what happened when.

*Lord God, Lord Jesus, thank You that the ultimate joy of tomorrow
still lies ahead for all of us, no matter how horrible or humdrum today is.*
—ROBERTA ROGERS

APRIL 8

Then the same day at evening, being the first day of the week, when the doors were shut where the disciples were assembled...Jesus came and stood in the midst, and said to them, "Peace be with you." When He had said this, He showed them His hands and His side. Then the disciples were glad when they saw the Lord.

—JOHN 20:19–20 (NKJV)

*A*ccording to John's gospel, at sunrise following the Sabbath, the women coming to anoint Jesus' body discovered the empty tomb. Peter and the beloved disciple ran to investigate. They found the grave clothes on the rock ledge of the tomb wall; only the face covering had been laid aside by itself. Perplexed, the disciples returned to their place of hiding.

When night came, the door to their secluded room was closed and bolted. Suddenly Jesus stood in their midst. The wounds of His Crucifixion could be clearly seen. He spoke to them and then disappeared.

The next day, Luke tells us, He appeared to two of the disciples walking to the city of Emmaus. Though they talked for hours as they hiked together, the disciples did not recognize Jesus. It was only when they stopped at an inn for dinner that they identified Him by the unique way He blessed and broke the bread. Again, He disappeared.

Holy Week begins with the raising of Lazarus and ends with the Resurrection of Jesus. Lazarus's body was raised just as it was before his death; Jesus' body was completely transformed. Jesus was physically present and yet not bound by time or space.

The Resurrection of Jesus is shrouded in a mystery I can't possibly understand or imagine. But when I live in Easter faith, I learn there's a truth beyond my understanding, there are realities beyond my imagination, and God is the Lord of life and death and all creation.

Father, thank You for the wonder, the mystery
and the miracle of Jesus' Resurrection.

—SCOTT WALKER

APRIL 9

We know that all things work together for good to them that love God,
to them who are the called according to his purpose.
—ROMANS 8:28

*E*very time I buy a novel or check one out of the library, I think of my grandmother Smith, who lived with us a while when I was in my early teens.

Grandmother was a tall woman who wore long dresses and piled her waist-length hair into a bun on top of her head. She loved to read, and I kept her supplied with books from the library. In my mind's eye, I can see her in her rocking chair, glasses (which she bought at the dime store) perched on her nose, completely absorbed in a book.

Grandmother Smith had one very annoying habit: Whenever I brought her a new novel, she would turn to the last chapter and read it first. Although I didn't say anything, my annoyance must have shown, because one day she said to me, "Kenneth, I know it bothers you for me to read the last chapter first. But at my age, I don't want to invest a lot of time and energy in reading a book if I don't like the way it ends."

Over the years, I've had to make many decisions without knowing exactly how things would work out. And I've often wished that, like Grandmother Smith, I could skip ahead and know the outcome in advance. I can't, of course. But I can find guidance. Some of it comes as I think through the choices I face or discuss them with friends whose judgment I respect. And I can pray for help in interpreting what I already know. After all, the One Who wrote the Book knows the end of the story.

Father, let me face life's decisions with confidence in Your providential care.
—KENNETH CHAFIN

Not giving up meeting together, as some are
in the habit of doing, but encouraging one another.
—HEBREWS 10:25 (NIV)

*A*fter moving a few months ago, I started attending a new church nearby. I went every Sunday, singing the songs and listening to the sermon. I even took notes. The only problem was that was all I did. I didn't join a Bible study, volunteer to hand out bulletins or play for the softball team. I usually arrived a few minutes late and left immediately after the service concluded, so I didn't get to know any of my fellow churchgoers. Then one Sunday I ran into Rachael, a friend from college. She had been attending the church too. But unlike me, Rachael had gotten involved. She was attending a Bible study and had helped with registration for the upcoming retreat. She was part of the community.

Driving home from church that day, I finally understood that showing up on Sunday morning isn't enough. Having a relationship with God requires having relationships with His people, because it's through them that I will give and receive His love. This past week I arrived early and met a few folks before the service started. Who knows? Maybe I'll even start handing out bulletins.

Lord, Your Word compares the church to a body.
Please show me the part I was meant to play in it.
—JOSHUA SUNDQUIST

But by His doing you are in Christ Jesus, who became to us wisdom from God.
—I CORINTHIANS 1:30 (NASB)

*S*ome of my dearest friends are people I've never met. Many are poets, gone long before I was born but intensely alive when I read or hear their words. Though we lived centuries apart, John Keats and I met when I was in college. In Keats I discovered a young man deeply enchanted with the beauty of life and swept away by love for a young woman he could never marry. In his twenties Keats realized that he would die from tuberculosis before he was thirty. On the night I read his anguished poem "When I Have Fears That I May Cease to Be," I keenly realized that every day of my young life was a precious gift, a priceless opportunity to create, to love, to work and to be.

Now in my fifties, I am awed by the poetic craft of Alfred, Lord Tennyson. To read "Ulysses" for the first or thousandth time is to know that though half of my life is over, it is not too late "to seek another world...that some work of noble note, may yet be done." But above all, the poetry of the Bible is a sumptuous feast for the wise and the simple. The beautiful metaphors of the psalmist accompany us through every moment of our day and night. And to read the Gospels and hear the parabolic poetry of Jesus is to glimpse the ultimate truth of God. Take time to read, reflect and ponder the poetic wisdom of the ages.

And above all, listen to the words of Jesus. His voice reveals God's truth.

Father, may the wisdom of the past introduce me to present truth.
And in all things may I hear the voice of Jesus. Amen.
—SCOTT WALKER

He hath made every thing beautiful in his time.
—ECCLESIASTES 3:11

So here we are again with one of those hard-to-understand lines. Koheleth, author of Ecclesiastes, has just written of fourteen pairs of opposites. Each pair includes a positive and a negative. The negatives include such words as *die, kill, weep, mourn, rend, hate* and *war*. Yet he follows those contradictory pairs with the statement that "he hath made every thing beautiful." But the sentence ends with "in his time." So we're back to where we started—with time, *His* time. *What*, I wonder, *is His time?* What could it be other than all time? And what could all time be but eternity, a vast and ever-expanding now? Somewhere in God's eternity are the answers to all of my questions. Today I ask the silence, "How does God transform hate, killing and weeping into beauty?"

Think about your father who treated wounded soldiers on a Navy troopship in World War II.

Consider how gentle and caring he was when he came home. Could it be that war had mellowed him?

Sometimes hatred is deeply buried childhood pain masquerading as bravado, misdirected and acted out.

Asking and receiving forgiveness is the cure. It has the power to transform hatred into love. And tears. Is there anyone who has never wept?

Tears are the great releaser, cleanser of pain, healer of overburdened lives. This is the beauty of weeping.

Holy Father, I confess I don't really know how You transform
the harmful into the beautiful. I only know You do it in Your own time.
—MARILYN MORGAN KING

APRIL 13

Ye shall seek me, and find me, when ye shall search for me with all your heart.
—JEREMIAH 29:13

On the Friday after Easter, my colleague Ptolemy and I made a trip to the Abbey of Gethsemani outside Louisville, Kentucky. The place has been a spiritual landmark for me because of the writings of its most famous resident, Thomas Merton. A gifted poet and author, he entered the monastery in his twenties to devote himself to a life of prayer, teaching and study. Here he wrote his autobiography, *The Seven Storey Mountain*, and it inspired me in my own spiritual search. But somehow a visit to the place where he lived was less than inspiring. Yes, we could see the sanctuary where he worshipped and the garden where he walked. In the bookstore we even spoke to one of the brothers who knew him. But I didn't feel as if I was meeting Merton.

"Go for a walk in the hills," a brother urged us, giving us a map. Ptolemy and I set off along the trail, trudging across fresh-mown pasture, winding through wooded hills, pausing at a sculpture garden, climbing a mountain where there was supposed to be a view of the abbey (hard to see through the trees). For a moment we got lost, and I worried that I'd brought Ptolemy on a wild-goose chase. He was good-natured, but I was fretting. It was getting late, and we needed to get back to Louisville. Then we came out of the woods onto a dirt lane leading to a meadow with a rusty old tractor, a red barn and a rough-hewn cross.

That's when I met Merton...in that humble scene before me. I was reminded of how faith can transform the things of everyday life and how when you follow an unknown path—searching, trusting—God will lead you somewhere.

God, I know that in my seeking, however lost I feel, You are there.
—RICK HAMLIN

If I must boast, I will boast of the things that show my weakness.
—II CORINTHIANS 11:30 (NRSV)

*N*oelle, my eight-year-old daughter, is in ballet class. She is learning *relevés*, *pliés* and *ronds de jambe*. The little girls cross arms and join hands and then amble left to right and right to left. Tiptoeing, aware of their posture and position, with their heads held high, they create as much beauty as their little bodies will allow. Truthfully, it's mostly a chaotic swirl of bodies in motion, but it sure is cute.

One girl in the class doesn't blend in, even though she's dressed in a leotard that perfectly matches the others. Lindsey is using a walker. Her hands clutch the handles tightly. Her legs don't allow her to do even the simplest dance step. She is assisted by a young woman who moves her from place to place, and oftentimes that is simply out of the way of the others.

After class, Noelle sat on the floor with the other girls, chatting, taking off their ballet shoes, putting on sweaters, stuffing dance clothes into their bags. Meanwhile, Lindsey was being tended to by her caregiver.

Today Lindsey might not have performed a soaring *jeté*. But in a sense, I think she did. She took an art form defined by the long lines of an extended leg, the poetry of a turned wrist, and a lighter-than-a-feather gallop across the stage, and said that definition didn't apply to her. And so, with a piano clanging in the room, her leotard on, mirrors in all directions, girls flowing all around her, Lindsey stood in one place, not moving an inch, and in a way known only to her, danced.

Lord, no matter what my limitations, give me the courage to try.
—DAVE FRANCO

APRIL 15

And the Lord God said, "It isn't good for man to be alone."
—GENESIS 2:18 (TLB)

*M*y daughter Maria and I decided to walk in the Komen Race for the Cure with our church's team. All over the United States these races raise money for breast cancer research, screening and education. When we picked up my new friend Karen, I was surprised by what she was wearing: a pink shirt, signifying she is a breast cancer survivor.

"Oh, I didn't know," I stammered.

"That's okay," Karen said. "I'm three years cancer free and feeling great!"

Karen seemed excited to get to the race, and when we arrived I understood why. The crowd was filled with pink shirts. The survivors received special gift bags and pink hats studded with rhinestones and then snacked on fresh fruit at linen-covered tables in the Pink Hat Café. Live music, laughter and loud voices created a party atmosphere. Later we cheered as Karen crossed the finish line in the Survivors' Race, arm in arm with other women in pink shirts.

Fighting any difficulty alone can't be what God intended for us. There's power when we unite; for one thing, thirty-seven thousand people raised two million dollars for the cause that day. But beyond that, these survivors showed everyone the power of God's Spirit in His human creation. Through even the worst circumstances, He helps us hold each other up, strengthen one another and celebrate one more day of living for the gift that it is.

Thank You, Lord, for Your Spirit that brings us together
and strengthens us for the tough battles we face.
—GINA BRIDGEMAN

APRIL 16

Blessed be the God and Father of our Lord Jesus Christ!
By his great mercy he has given us a new birth into a living hope
through the resurrection of Jesus Christ from the dead.
—I PETER 1:3 (NRSV)

The Sunday after Easter, I stood in our church basement looking at the lilies that had adorned the sanctuary. Like the blossoms turning brown, the joy of Christ's Resurrection I'd experienced last Sunday was fading. After the spiritually uplifting services of Holy Week, the past week of the daily grind had left me feeling listless. Pointing to the wilting lilies, I lamented to another parishioner, "What a shame to throw them away."

"We don't throw them out," she responded. "I'm going to plant them around the church grounds where they can bloom again each summer."

"That's a great idea!" I exclaimed. The bulbs would be nourished underground for months and then would send up new shoots and flower again.

I began thinking about how I could do the same thing. How could I plant the Resurrection joy of Easter in my heart and keep it flourishing? Maybe I needed more quiet times for prayer and Scripture reading. Or perhaps I could be like St. Seraphim of Sarov, who greeted everyone at all seasons with "Christ is risen!" and called each "my joy."

There was no need to feel listless. Easter wasn't so far away at all. It was ready to bloom at all times. All I needed was the nourishment from God's Word, some regular doses of prayer and the willingness to see people as "my joy."

Oh, Lord, open the eyes of my heart to see Your gifts. Please remind me
of the triumph of Your Resurrection in my daily struggles.
—MARY BROWN

APRIL 17

When Jesus saw that he answered wisely, he said to him,
"You are not far from the kingdom of God."
—MARK 12:34 (NRSV)

group of Pharisees came to Jesus with a series of trick questions, and Jesus amazed them with His answers. But one question seemed to come from the heart of a seeker. Seeing how wise Jesus was, a Pharisee asked Him, "Teacher, which is the greatest commandment in the Law?" (Matthew 22:36, updated NIV).

Jesus answered, "Love the Lord your God with all your heart and with all your soul and with all your mind.... Love your neighbor as yourself" (Matthew 22:37, 39, updated NIV). We will never know for sure, but I believe this man was among those mentioned in Acts 6:7 who "believed and obeyed" Jesus' teaching after the Resurrection.

When traveling in India recently, I met a man from a remote region closed to influence from the outside world. He had been a passionate follower of Jesus since his teens. I asked him how that could have happened. "My father was a fisherman," he told me, "and often we would go out on the water and come back with empty nets. Then he would tell me, 'We will look elsewhere. The fish are there. We just need to find them.' When I told my father I wanted to find God, instead of telling me what tradition to follow, he gave me the same instruction: 'Keep seeking.' One day an older friend who had gone to the city gave me a copy of the gospel of John, and when I read Jesus' statement, 'I am the way, the truth, and the life' (John 14:6), I had the answer I needed. I have been following Him ever since."

Lord, let me find You in the confusion of my life today.
—ERIC FELLMAN

The Lord God has given Me the tongue of disciples,
that I may know how to sustain the weary one with a word.
—ISAIAH 50:4 (NASB)

One of the associate pastors of our church asked me to give my testimony in front of the congregation. Anything but that! *Please, Lord, no!* I thought. Public speaking has always been the number-one fear in my life. But I didn't want to turn down my pastor, so I said I would. A week of dread and sleepless nights followed.

The next Sunday I was playing the piano in the praise band and looking at the stage in front of me, knowing that the following Sunday, I'd have to be there, microphone in hand, speaking to all those people. God would have to do a mini-miracle to get me calm enough to be of any use to Him.

When our praise songs were over, I had to get off the stage and find a seat in the congregation. Stage right seemed like a good choice, so I took a few steps in that direction until my shoe got caught in a cable. I didn't fall, but it took a series of modern-dance-like movements to keep me standing. My face turned beet red, and my ears began to sizzle with embarrassment.

The next Sunday I walked up onstage to give my testimony with a lot more confidence than I'd ever had before. Compared to last week's mishap, speaking seemed like a breeze. And after church a man came up to me to tell me that what I'd said had touched him deeply.

If I hadn't tripped the week before, I don't think I'd have been as effective a speaker that Sunday. I guess God will do a mini-miracle to get His message out, even if it's sometimes a little hard on the messenger.

Lord, help me always to speak Your Word boldly.
—DAVE FRANCO

APRIL 19

But each of us was given grace according to the measure
of Christ's gift...for building up the body of Christ.
—EPHESIANS 4:7, 12 (NRSV)

A friend was telling me about two boys in his son's high school class a few years back who shared the exact same name but seemingly little else. One was an all-state swimmer on his way to being class valedictorian and about to choose one of the six elite universities that had offered him scholarships. The other often skipped class, refused to play sports (although he was built like a linebacker, my friend said) and likely wasn't even thinking about college. Two very different kids headed in two very different directions.

"That just doesn't seem fair to me," I said.

My friend smiled. It turns out that both ended up going to college and both are doing very well. Do you know why? Because the talented kid decided to invest some of his talents in another kid with the same name—and it all added up to two successful young men. "You're right, of course," he concluded. "Life isn't fair. But God is. That's why God gave me what I have, not just for my own use but to benefit the lives of the world around me."

That day a friend shared his wisdom with me. Today I'm passing it along to you. After all, it's only fair.

Show me, generous God, where I can use what
You've given me to benefit someone else.
—JEFF JAPINGA

April 20

As it is written, "No eye has seen...no human mind has conceived
the things God has prepared for those who love him."
—I Corinthians 2:9 (niv)

Reading the verse above, I began to wonder, if heaven will have sights even more wonderful than what I recall from my growing-up years?

Will heaven have libraries where children tiptoe into their hushed interiors to check out storybooks as exciting as Billy Whiskers, The Bobbsey Twins, Nancy Drew, David and Goliath, Joseph and His Bad Brothers?

Will neighbors gather to hand-crank homemade ice cream? Kids sucking on scattered ice chips—compliments of an ice-house man who slings fifty-pound blocks with black tongs onto a car's bumper for the ride home? Will red-checkered tablecloths cover plywood tables shaded by the trees lining the crystal streams?

Will there be stellar circuses with outlandish clowns and trapeze stunts and brassy bands and hawkers shouting "Free peanuts! Free popcorn!"?

Will we be in the heavenly host congregating on Saturday nights for sacred concerts in a celestial band shell, parking on golden streets to people-watch, joining others for sodas beneath oscillating fans until the hands of a courthouse clock signal curfew?

Will there be treadle sewing machines transforming cloth into gossamer wardrobes for us? Rocking chairs to nod in? Yellow roses and verbenas and hollyhocks thriving under inundations of environment-safe soapsuds tossed from dishpans off kitchen stoops?

Things I'm sure won't be in heaven: potato bugs and tomato worms to pick off plants, washboards to scrub laundry, potbellied coal stoves with teakettles whistling full-speed ahead, outdoor bathrooms with crescent windows, wool long johns that itch, glued-on shoe soles. It wouldn't be heaven, you see, with these things.

But as for what it's like...I think I've caught a glimpse of those sights.

What an infinite future You must have for us, Father,
far beyond what we can possibly imagine!
—Isabel Wolseley

Lord, I know that people's lives are not their own;
it is not for them to direct their steps.
—JEREMIAH 10:23 (NIV)

*T*was in the office, working through my agenda, when an e-mail arrived: "Greetings! This is Chi from AA flight to LGA. I can't believe it's already been over a week since we met. My time in NY was quite nice and meaningful; especially from the beginning as how God seemed to place us next to each other to connect in many ways."

Our paths had crossed in an airport when her flight was delayed and I was on standby, trying to get home to my family. During the flight, we enjoyed small talk until she asked me about my work at Guideposts. That opened the door for her to share her faith and the recent loss of her father, who had suddenly passed away, leaving Chi, her mother and her sister. Chi's words were filled with pain, loss and grief. *What if this were my daughter?* I thought to myself. *What would I want someone to say?*

I sensed this was not a time for me to talk but to listen. Chi spoke proudly. "My father came from Korea and worked hard to give my sister and me a better future in the United States. He valued education, family and faith." The more she shared about her dad, the stronger Chi became. When the airplane landed at LaGuardia Airport, I promised to pray for Chi and her family and to send her some Guideposts publications. When we said good-bye at the baggage claim, I didn't expect to hear from her again. But when I read her e-mail, I knew it was no coincidence that God had put us next to each other on that plane.

Lord, thank You for rearranging our plans so we can cross paths
with those You want us to touch with Your love.
—PABLO DIAZ

May he give you the desire of your heart and make all your plans succeed.
—PSALM 20:4 (NIV)

Last winter I found myself at a shopping mall in the foothills of the Rocky Mountains, searching for clothes to fit my shoestring budget. As I carried a pair of socks (on sale, two dollars) to the checkout counter, an advertisement for a contest caught my eye.

"Tell us your dream!" it said. *"We'll pay for it!"*

At that time several months remained in the ski racing season, and I was nearly broke. But I did have a dream of going to the Paralympics—that's why I was racing. So I grabbed a brochure for the contest, paid for my socks and headed out to my car for the long trip back up to the mountains where I train. When I got home, I wrote an essay for the contest, committing my dream to paper—and prayer.

Time went by, and when I hadn't heard anything, I assumed I hadn't won the contest. But I did make the Paralympics team, and I managed to travel to Torino, Italy, to compete there. Three days before I was going to fly back to the States, I got a call from the clothing company. I had won the contest, but more importantly, I'd already gotten the chance to follow my dream.

Lord, You are the dream giver. Thank You
for putting these desires in my heart.
—JOSHUA SUNDQUIST

You know when I sit down and when I rise up;
You understand my thought from afar.
—PSALM 139:2 (NASB)

I'm a doubting Thomas. I recognize and admire faith in others, but to follow God myself, I want one more sign, one more confirmation. It's been the same with my career. *Are You sure, God?* I've found myself asking. *Do You really mean for me to do this work?*

This spring I attended a women's conference with five hundred participants. At the end of the conference many door prizes were given away—lovely artwork, gift certificates from fancy salons and ornate floral arrangements. *I never win anything,* I thought as the numbers of the winning tickets were called out. *And those flowers are too frilly for me anyway.*

Then the last gift was rolled out: a brand-new computer chair. I'd been borrowing my twelve-year-old's chair to work in. I dug in my purse to find my crumpled-up ticket: *433.*

Father, I'm not asking for the chair as a sign. It's wrong. But I sure would love to work in that chair.

"Ladies, the winning number is four-seventeen. Are you still here, four-seventeen? Okay, we'll draw again." She jiggled the box. "Number four-twenty-two!"

Never mind, God.

A woman screamed and ran down to the front of the hall. "That's me, that's me!"

See, God. How silly of me to ask.

"Oh, I'm terribly sorry, but you're number four-twelve." Blushing, the woman left the stage.

"Folks, how about number four-thirty-three?"

"Woo-hoo!" I screamed cheerleader style, ran onto the stage and twirled in my new chair. My friends wheeled me out to the car.

Okay, Lord, I'll keep working. You knew I wanted the chair even before I asked.
—JULIE GARMON

Wondrously show Your lovingkindness, O Savior
of those who take refuge at Your right hand.
—PSALM 17:7 (NASB)

The dog run where I take Millie for her exercise and canine social life is also an interesting place to observe people. The other day I overheard a conversation between two women sitting next to me on a bench.

Older Woman: What day is it?

Younger Woman: Fifteen.

OW: Congratulations.

YW: Thanks. I never thought I'd make it, especially last night. I really wanted to.

OW: But you didn't.

YW: No. But I'm ashamed of myself for wanting to. I just kept praying and the urge passed. I went to a meeting first thing this morning and talked about it to the group.

OW: What will you do the next time the urge hits you?

YW: Pray. Pick up the phone. Find a meeting.

OW: You're going to be all right then. Don't be ashamed. The one thing you can always do is pray. God understands.

YW: I never believed in God, let alone prayer, before. Now it's saving my life, I guess.

OW: I'm praying for you too, dear. Lots of people are.

The older woman rose and retrieved her dog, and the younger woman pulled out a book. I watched Millie chase another golden retriever in a big circle until they skidded to a stop. Then I stole a peek at what the woman was reading—the *Big Book*, the Alcoholics Anonymous spiritual blueprint for recovery from alcoholism, a day at a time. She turned the page, and I closed my eyes. She had one more person praying for her.

You are there for us, God, as our highest power in our hardest times.
—EDWARD GRINNAN

Seek ye the Lord while he may be found, call ye upon him while he is near.
—Isaiah 55:6

*I*n a conversation I had recently with one of my children, I mentioned entertainer Arthur Godfrey, whose heyday was on television and radio in the 1950s.

"Who was Arthur Godfrey?" Laraine wanted to know. I swallowed hard at the thought that somebody so prominent a few—well, more than a few—years ago was unknown to a woman in her forties. But, of course, each generation has its people, places and things, who eventually pass out of sight and out of mind.

I still remember my magazine interview with Mr. Godfrey in his New York City studio. I was looking for a spiritual hook on which to hang my story, but I'd been told he wasn't interested in religion. He seemed to have nothing to say when I tried to guide our conversation toward morality, ethics or values. Everything we discussed seemed superficial, and I was about to give up hope of finding anything worth writing about. Then I remembered he had had a bout with lung cancer, and I asked him about his trial. Suddenly, he grew serious.

"I thought I was a goner," he confided. "But the Man Upstairs must have had more for me to do."

"Do you believe God had a part in your healing?"

"Well, before I got cancer, I wasn't sure He paid much attention to people like me. But thousands of listeners wrote to say they were praying for me, and... and I believe that prayer is what saved me."

After that, we talked for a long time about faith and belief, and I found my story. What was it theologian Paul Tillich said, that all people have an "ultimate concern" about where they came from, why they are here and where they are going? Arthur Godfrey, who was reputed to be uninterested in spiritual things, proved the point for me.

Lord, give us patience with those who seek,
Teach us when to be silent and when to speak.
—Fred Bauer

APRIL 26

The Lord is good, a refuge in times of trouble. He cares for those who trust in him.
—NAHUM 1:7 (NIV)

*I*t was a sorrowful day for my friend, who was moving out of her home following a divorce. "I'm trying to be cheerful, but I can't do it," she told me. "How can I face this cross?"

That evening I took my son to a youth meeting at our church. As the meeting began, the youth pastor announced, "We're under a severe weather watch. If the tornado siren goes off, we go to the bottom of the storage stairwell."

About twenty minutes later, the siren went off. As we stood up to head down the stairs, someone suggested we bring the pizzas and soft drinks. Once we were downstairs, we squeezed in amid the cardboard boxes of lightbulbs and bathroom tissue, opened the pizza boxes, and started talking. After a while we weren't even aware of the siren.

Once the rough weather had safely passed, I realized that although it was the first time we had been in church when the siren went off, we weren't afraid because someone had a plan. A survey of the church building had been done, and the safest places had been identified beforehand. When we needed to know, the plan was communicated to us. All we had to do was grab the pizza and follow the plan.

Finally I had an answer for my divorced friend: It's not cheerfulness we need when we're faced with difficult things, but trust. In my moments of greatest need, I trust that God has a plan that will lead me to a place of safety. And that's why I can take heart on the very worst of days.

Father, on the most difficult of days I put my hand in Yours, trusting that even in this, You know where we're going.

—KAREN BARBER

APRIL 27

And the children of Israel said to Samuel, Cease not
to cry unto the Lord our God for us.
—I SAMUEL 7:8

*M*ost mornings find me at the gym in a high-intensity aerobic cycling class—a sweaty, heart-pounding hour of running uphill on a stationary bike. The grunting and groaning of the participants is drowned out by the pounding soundtrack. Today, the one repeated line of a song caught my ear: "Say a prayer for me." I had to smile through my pain. This was Monday morning, and as we have for decades, Guideposts starts the week at 9:45 with Prayer Fellowship, where we get together as a staff and pray with you. As my friend Van Varner used to say, "If you want to know what's important in people's lives, find out what they pray for."

In my years at Guideposts, I have seen the breadth of spiritual longing in the requests you send in. Last week we prayed for everything from a combat unit in Afghanistan to a sick goldfish in Oklahoma, and we prayed equally for both. We pray for everything from world peace to peace of mind. Most prayer requests are for family, health, finances, forgiveness or simply God's protection in a changing world. In these Monday morning sessions, I have come to understand that prayer not only joins us with God; it also connects us to each other.

Thank You, Lord, for prayer, by which we stay
connected to one another through You.
—EDWARD GRINNAN

APRIL 28

And the children of Israel did eat manna forty years.
—EXODUS 16:35

I use a lectionary for my daily Bible reading, and it's remarkable how often these preset passages seem chosen especially for my situation at that moment.

The Exodus account of manna falling from heaven, though, fell on what seemed a wretchedly inappropriate time for me. The Israelites are trudging across a bleak and barren landscape longing for earlier, happier times—I could identify with that! Both my husband and I had had surgery recently on joints crippled by arthritis—old people's problems. Our house needed repairs too, but hospital bills were more than anticipated. Work assignments were overdue, and I didn't know where the time and the energy and the money were going to come from.

What does God do for the Israelites? Rains provisions for them right out of the sky. Food they don't have to work for, bread lying on the ground for the taking—exactly what they need for each day.

Where was the manna for me? I demanded of the Exodus verses. Where was my supply tumbling out of the heavens?

What was this miraculous manna anyway? Trying to make twenty-first-century sense out of the passage, I got out my Bible dictionary to see what the thing was.

But manna, it turned out, is not a thing. It's a question. Manna means "What is this?" The Israelites had no idea what those small round white things on the ground were. They certainly didn't recognize them, at first, as the answer to their need.

What unrecognized supply was lying at my feet too? I wondered. How often I have regarded the new and unknown with suspicion. A new form of worship, a new technology, a new boss at work—only to have "What is this?" turn out to be God's perfect provision.

Faithful Lord, what unexpected shape will Your supply for me take today?
—ELIZABETH SHERRILL

April 29

He said to them, "Go into all the world
and preach the gospel to all creation."
—Mark 16:15 (NIV)

*O*ur pastor described the guest speaker visiting our church as "a true
visionary." And he was right. Vernon Brewer of World Help is taking the
Gospel to the forgotten people of the world. He explained to us the principle
that guides such a daunting task: "Every day I try to live my life in such a way
that I accomplish at least one thing that will outlive me and last for eternity."

That sure put a new spin on my Sunday afternoon to-do list. Should I attend
the local tour of homes or call that friend who just lost her husband? *If you
accomplish only one eternity-minded deed every day, Roberta,* God seemed to be
telling me, *you'll change your life and the course of eternity. You don't have to do it all
in one day. Just one thing each day.*

When I was growing up, we had a little plaque hanging in the entry of our
house that read "Only one life, 'twill soon be past. Only what's done for Christ
will last." Over the years I'd forgotten the powerful simplicity of that maxim,
but thanks to a true visionary, I'm remembering it afresh.

Help me to keep eternity's values in view, Lord.
—Roberta Messner

*"I am concerned for you and will look on you with favor;
you will be plowed and sown.... I...will make you prosper
more than before. Then you will know that I am the Lord."*
—Ezekiel 36:9, 11 (niv)

ecently I met an out-of-town acquaintance I'd not seen in years. "Hi, Mary Lou," I greeted her. "Are you still writing newspaper columns?"

"No, the new editor fired me eleven months ago. Even though I take some comfort in knowing my work was good, I'm still grieving and feeling humiliated."

"What are you doing now?" I asked.

"Nothing much. I have no self-confidence left. Even God has let me down."

"Of course He hasn't!" I answered. "You know something? I was also fired by an editor. That editor's parting words, 'You're a pretty good writer. Go write for somebody else!' seemed tattooed on my brain. I couldn't erase my grief, either. Then a friend came up with a thought. She quoted Ezekiel 36:9, 11 and added, 'God's concerned about you. So do as the man said: Submit your work elsewhere and see what happens!'" I took her advice—and God at His Word—and sent my stories to another publication. That happened thirty-five years ago, and I've been writing for Guideposts ever since.

*Dear Lord, help me always to remember that You're watching
over me and that You will not allow anything to touch me
that is not in Your will and for my good.*
—Isabel Wolseley

May

MAY 1

My sorrow is beyond healing, My heart is faint within me!...
Is there no balm in Gilead? Is there no physician there?
—JEREMIAH 8:18, 22 (NASB)

*D*riving to work yesterday, I stopped at a red light. As I absently looked at my hand on the steering wheel, I noticed the long scar on my wrist. Suddenly I drifted back in memory thirty-six years to the summer following my high-school graduation. I was living in my hometown of Fort Valley, Georgia, and working on the assembly line at the Blue Bird school bus factory. Eighteen years old, I was making school buses so I could save money for college.

Bus-body assembly lines are dangerous places. Amidst powerful machinery, hydraulic presses, hot metal and a vast assortment of high-powered tools, it's easy to be injured. One day, as I cut through a steel beam with a blow torch, my wrist grazed the sharp, molten edge of the beam. Suddenly I was cut to the bone with a wound that would scar my wrist for life.

For a while the scar was prominent and jagged. Sometimes it would swell, becoming inflamed and painful. But I noticed yesterday that now the jagged scar is smooth, faded, almost unnoticeable. Time has worked its healing wonder.

Sometimes events in our lives wound us so deeply that an emotional scar is left for a lifetime. The death of my father when I was fourteen years old cut much more deeply than that steel beam. Yet, over time, I have learned that God has a way of making emotional scars grow smaller too. A grief we feared would consume us; a disappointment so intense it maimed us; a shameful mistake that seared our self-image—all of these can be healed by time and the loving grace of God.

Father, I am thankful that in You I have found a balm
in Gilead that can make the wounded whole. Amen.
—SCOTT WALKER

MAY 2

And he sent them out to proclaim the kingdom of God and to heal the sick.
—LUKE 9:2 (NIV)

This year I started having trouble with one of my knees. I was trying too hard to keep up with the boys when we were out skiing, and my knee started to give a little. Soon I was in a lot of pain.

The doctor ordered an MRI and then showed me the pictures of how my knee was put together: two bones joined by ligaments and protected by cartilage. My case was simple: The doughnut of cartilage called the meniscus was partially torn, and the loose flap was the cause of my pain. Like a piece of loose carpet under a doorway, it would catch every so often when the knee moved, and the result was agony. The treatment, said my doctor, was to drill three small holes in the knee, insert two tiny viewing scopes and an arthroscopic tool through the holes, and shave off the torn piece. "Then God takes over, and you'll be as good as new," he promised.

After six weeks, he proved to be exactly right. I was amazed at how pain-free and "like new" the knee felt. I left the doctor's office after the follow-up visit full of awe at what he'd accomplished with his amazing tools and skills.

Sometimes people ask, "Why doesn't Jesus heal today as He did in the New Testament?" I guess I found out He does, every day, in countless ways. He just sometimes uses doctors to do the preliminary work.

Dear Lord, thank You for the healing You do through Your power
at work in the hands of our doctors and in the miracle of our bodies.
—ERIC FELLMAN

MAY 3

I come seeking fruit on this fig tree, and find none: cut it down.
—LUKE 13:7

New Hampshire is too cold and gray for me to raise figs, yet I'm disturbed by the image of the poor plant in the parable being threatened with destruction because it doesn't bear fruit. It's worn out and needs help.

The wise gardener in this Scripture pleads for time, a year "to dig about it and dung it." Digging about, or cultivating, will break up compacted soil and let both water and nutrients reach the plant's roots. Though the plants need water only two or three times a season, the soil needs to be loose to let it through. Thus nourished, the plant has a fighting chance of producing fruit. Once the soil is loosened, the fig tree can be propagated from a branch bent into the soil. More plants mean more fruit.

And why is this parable about figs rather than dates, which are so common in the Holy Land? Perhaps because dates contain only one large seed and the fig contains hundreds. Each tiny fig seed produces yet more fruit, a hefty return from simply breaking up the hard soil and letting in life-giving water.

So I ponder the fig. How many times do I harden myself by complacency or pride or anger and not produce fruit? How can I replenish myself? Like the fig, sometimes I need help from others—and a little time.

Lord of creation, thank You for the quiet wisdom of flowering things.
—GAIL THORELL SCHILLING

MAY 4

*Forgetting what lies behind and reaching forward to what lies ahead, I press on
toward the goal for the prize of the upward call of God in Christ Jesus.*
—PHILIPPIANS 3:13–14 (NASB)

*S*ometimes I think my golden retriever Beau was born with a tennis ball
wedged in his mouth. His goal in life seems to be to chase the balls I throw
for him.

But there's one problem: Whenever Beau retrieves a ball, he refuses to return
it to me. He races back to me, proud of his successful recovery but determined
not to surrender his prize. He's eager for me to throw the ball again, but he
doesn't understand that if he doesn't give me the ball, I can't throw it.

Sometimes I'm a lot like Beau in my relationship with God. I want Him to
zing that next challenge out in front of me, but I don't want to let go of the
security of my last accomplishment. I want to hold on to the past and race
toward the future at the same time. But to remain vital and alive, I need the
exhilaration of another race, another challenge, another opportunity to do
what I do best. And that means I must release the victories of yesterday and
trust God to throw the ball for me one more time.

*Father, help me to forget what lies behind
and reach forward to what lies ahead. Amen.*
—SCOTT WALKER

Lead a life worthy of God, who calls you into his own kingdom and glory.
—I THESSALONIANS 2:12 (NRSV)

*W*hen I volunteered to work several hours a week as a caregiver for an elderly woman in our community, I felt quite smug about my decision. I envisioned the loving friendship that would develop between the woman and me. She would be gentle, she would be kind. And grateful, of course.

Instead, she proved to be an angry, bitter person who did nothing but complain about everyone she'd ever known. Soon she included me in those complaints. All my attempts to make her comfortable and content met with verbal abuse.

One day as I was standing in my kitchen, putting together a box of food and supplies to take to the woman, I exploded in rebellion. "God, I don't like being around this woman. I don't think I'm worthy to serve You in this area with an attitude this bad. Maybe I shouldn't try to help her. Maybe I should just quit."

God's answer sounded as clearly inside my head as if I'd heard the words spoken out loud. *Don't worry about your attitude. She needs you, and that's all that matters. Get to work.*

A weight lifted from my shoulders. God already knew my limitations, of course, but He could use me anyway, worthy or not! Eventually my attitude toward the woman changed, and I was able to view her with a little of the love and forbearance I'm sure God had felt for her—and for me—all along.

Father, help me reach out today to someone who is difficult to be with,
even as You reach out to me when I'm not at my best.

—MADGE HARRAH

MAY 6

All who have this hope in him purify themselves, just as he is pure.
—I JOHN 3:3 (NIV)

*D*uring my last year at college, I spent days in front of my computer, working on my senior thesis. Outlines turned into drafts, drafts transformed into revisions, revisions into new revisions and, before I knew it, November had turned into April. Somehow in the midst of all that work I found myself slipping away from having time with God. Sure, I still went to Bible study, but I kept thinking of all the other things I needed to do before I could get back in God's good graces: catch up on my Bible reading, update my prayer list, clean my room so I'd be more focused in prayer.

I spoke with a friend from home. "I have to go," my friend said only a few minutes into the conversation. "The housekeeper is coming tomorrow, and I have to get this place straightened up." I hung up, laughing to myself. Who would clean house before allowing a housekeeper inside?

As crazy as that sounds, that is just what I was doing with God. He wants to talk, even if I haven't called in a while or if the pages of my Bible have become a little dusty. All I have to do is take the first step. He'll cover the rest.

Lord, turn my feet toward Your path and help me remember that I don't need a perfect heart to talk to You, only a willing one.
—ASHLEY JOHNSON

MAY 7

I'd agreed to write a book that I had no idea how to write. When the editors made the final critique, my heart sank. Many chapters had to be omitted, but the story had to stay connected and flow smoothly.

Wearily, I lined up all fifty chapters on the floor like a long train, snaking from the front door through the living room and into the kitchen. I flopped down near the front door by chapter one, my head in my hands. "Lord Jesus, You've been my helper so far, but if You don't come through now, I just can't finish this." I added a desperate, ridiculous-sounding request. "Lord, would You lend me about thirty IQ points for, say, four hours?"

Slowly I lifted my head. I felt a new energy, and clear thoughts marched into my mind. Ideas and solutions filed into neat rows. I scooted around on the floor, mumbling, rearranging, pulling out chapters, scribbling in pencil for hours. Finally, I crawled back to the front door and sat there with my heart overflowing with gratitude, my back and head resting against the wall. Even with my eyes closed, I sensed an intense golden light, sweet and encouraging, surrounding me and some of the chapters.

Some people might say it was just the setting sun hitting a sliver of beveled glass in our front door. But to me, it was a sign from the One Who had rescued me—the job was done.

Lord Jesus, You are the same today, yesterday and forever.
—MARION BOND WEST

MAY 8

Worship the Lord in the beauty of holiness.
—I CHRONICLES 16:29

I stepped out of our hotel early that morning, hoping for better air than we'd breathed since touching down at Bangkok's Suvarnabhumi Airport the evening before. But again the city's stench assaulted me. A swarm of three-wheeled Tuk Tuk taxis roared by, leaving blue smoke clouds behind them; a beggar's face was masked against the foul smog; a dog with runny eyes sniffed at an orange peel in the gutter.

My walk took me to the refuse-clogged Chao Phraya River. And it was there that I saw her, a tiny woman with pitted skin and shaking hands. She wore a threadbare ankle-length green dress and was as bony as the dogs scrounging for food in every alleyway. Around her neck was a rope of tiny purple orchids so fresh and perfect they must have been in the orchid market ten minutes earlier. As I watched, she took the lovely flowers from her neck, placed them on a small quayside altar, arranged them with great care, stepped back to judge the effect, made a few small adjustments and left. This lady's religion was not my own, but her gift was also a gift to me. She was bringing an offering of beauty, creating an oasis of order and harmony in one corner of a chaotic city.

From that moment on I began to see Bangkok differently. I noticed a woman scrubbing the sidewalk in front of the closet-sized store where she sold spools of thread; a man cleaning his ancient but gleaming car with a feather duster; a teenager helping a blind man onto the bouncing ferryboat that crosses the river. All works of beauty are manifestations of God, and by the time I left Bangkok, I was seeing Him everywhere. It's a beautiful, beautiful city!

Help me bring some of Your beauty, Lord, to my corner of the world today.
—JOHN SHERRILL

MAY 9

At Gibeon the Lord appeared to Solomon during the night in a dream, and God said, "Ask for whatever you want me to give you."
—I KINGS 3:5 (NIV)

Recently, I was in the middle of a particularly busy stretch at work—too many tasks, too few hours in the day. As the week dragged on and I got further and further behind on my to-do list, I grew increasingly short with my colleagues. "Nothing," I answered the first time someone asked what was wrong...and the second time and the third.

The fourth time, I said something. "I think it's obvious I could use some help here, but I don't beg."

My colleague smiled. "Someone once told me that a Christian is a beggar telling another beggar where to find bread. We owe our lives to the generosity of someone else. Now how can I help you?"

There are certain things I know to be true about myself: I'm studious and cautious; conservative; I don't embrace change very easily. And I'm shy; I don't say a lot and certainly don't demand a lot from others.

I never thought I would change—until that horribly busy week at work. That's when I learned I could be a little less self-reliant and a little more God-reliant, and even ask for help.

Like Solomon, God, I rely on You for all that I am. May I never be too busy or too proud to ask for Your help.
—JEFF JAPINGA

MAY 10

Whether we live therefore, or die, we are the Lord's.
—ROMANS 14:8

I am walking in the woods, spring violets peeking through the dead leaves, when suddenly I recall a childhood memory. I am ten years old. Mother, an apron tied over her work dress, is talking to me. "I think we could grow some violets here," she says, pointing to a shady spot. I stare at the bare patch of ground near the corner of our farmhouse. "We could dig them in the woods." Already she is moving toward the tractor shed for the shovel.

Soon Mother and I are headed through the gate toward the back pasture and the woods that border it. I am not sure how much help my small hands will be, but I like being with Mother, being a part of whatever she suggests we do together. We easily find a patch of violets, and Mother begins to dig. Carefully I wrap the plants in the newspaper we've brought and nest them into a small basket. "I think that will be enough, don't you?" I nod.

The month of May is a difficult one for me. Next Sunday is Mother's Day; a week later, it's Mother's birthday; and the end of the month brings Memorial Day. Those first few Mays after Mother's death, I could scarcely comprehend how one small set of squares on the calendar could hold so much sadness. My grief has mellowed over the years. The hurt is more like a tender spot than a gaping wound. Life has gone on. The violets Mother and I dug and replanted that spring took hold and bloomed every year until we sold that farm and moved to another. I like to think they might be blooming still.

You are Lord of life and death. I place myself—and my loved ones—in Your eternal care.

—MARY LOU CARNEY

MAY 11

The joy of the Lord is your strength.
—NEHEMIAH 8:10

*T*he weekly prayer meeting in our living room began with singing, and there was never any question about one person's choice. "Rejoice in the Lord!" Jean Nardozzi would say. Whatever the crisis or need before the group, Jean wanted this song. We sang it in unison; we sang it in rounds. Because it was so short, we sang it over and over.

I got tired, finally, of endlessly repeating "Rejoice." In Lent, I suggested we sing the lovely solemn hymns appropriate to the season. We did, that year, though in Jean's eyes I could see "Rejoice" longing to burst out.

It wasn't that Jean had fewer problems than the rest of us. Her beloved husband Bob had diabetes, their three grown sons the usual struggles. She taught both a morning and an afternoon kindergarten class at an overcrowded, understaffed school, despite serious health problems of her own. Yet every week she chose this hymn.

And then her husband died. It was a sorrowful group indeed that gathered in our living room for the first time without Bob. We went around the circle offering what we could—a poem, a prayer, a special memory. When it came Jean's turn, she suggested a song. And, of course, it was "Rejoice in the Lord."

There's a word in the verse I'd overlooked as we sang "Rejoice." The word I've invoked in times of sorrow ever since: *always.*

Whatever today brings, Father, teach me to rejoice in You.
—ELIZABETH SHERRILL

Stand up and bless the Lord your God for ever and ever: and blessed be thy glorious name, which is exalted above all blessing and praise.
—NEHEMIAH 9:5

*O*ur minister brought a large vase filled with cut roses of various colors and set it on the altar. He asked the members of the congregation to gather in a semicircle at the front of the church and face the altar. Because we're a small church, there were maybe thirty people in that circle. The minister then asked each of us to come, one at a time, and select a rose from the vase, face the congregation and name someone who had been a blessing in our life.

Some people named a parent or a friend or a teacher or a co-worker. When my husband Larry went forward, he selected a yellow rose and said, with a catch in his voice, "Thank You, God, for the women in my life."

He walked over and handed the rose to me, but I knew that special tribute included not only me but also his mother and our daughter. Years later, I still have the pressed petals from that rose.

Today I'm thinking again of those who have blessed my life. The list is long, including Larry, our children, our grandchildren, our parents, our friends. Topping the list, of course, is God, ever present, ever loving.

Lord, today I will thank someone who has touched and blessed my life.
—MADGE HARRAH

The Lord does not let the righteous go hungry.
—PROVERBS 10:3 (NIV)

I was invited to speak at the community-wide homecoming at a rural church one Sunday morning. This is a big event for many churches in Mississippi, when every family attends services at the church, followed by a celebration in their homes. My wife Rosie and our grandson Little Reggie went with me for the occasion.

Afterward we were invited to the home of a family with ten children—seven girls and three boys—some of them older than Rosie and I, others younger. Their mother moved around in a motorized wheelchair. They had prepared a reunion feast, and we had the opportunity to share pig's feet and ham hocks with them. We talked about the difficult times, about not having much but the joy of having each other. It was a great time of fellowship and food.

As we drove away, Rosie and I blessed this matriarch, nearly ninety years old, surrounded by all her children and grandchildren. We were overwhelmingly blessed as we saw a grateful family gathered at the home of their mother. Over the years they'd gone through ups and downs, but truly the Lord had not let the righteous go hungry. And on this day there was plenty of physical food—and no hunger for love either.

Lord, help me to know that You are shaping me to be
a part of Your greater family, now and in glory.
—DOLPHUS WEARY

MAY 14

Thinking he was the gardener, she said....
—JOHN 20:15 (NIV)

*S*everal months after my sister Susan's house burned down, we took a short trip to the coast of South Carolina to escape some of the stress. On Saturday afternoon we visited a small town where we were drawn to a little cypress-wood church overlooking a tidal marsh. We roamed the grounds, hoping to find a sign telling when Sunday services were held. But all we saw was a casually dressed man with graying hair pulling weeds in a flower bed. "He's probably with a lawn company and doesn't know anything about services," I told Susan doubtfully.

Nevertheless, we approached the man, and he told us there'd be a service featuring a praise band on Sunday morning.

On Sunday, as we settled into a pew, Susan nodded toward the minister sitting up front in spotless white robes. "That's the man who was pulling weeds yesterday afternoon," she whispered.

The bulletin listed a Saturday-evening service, and I realized that the minister must have been on his way to prepare for it when he had taken a moment to tidy up the flower bed.

I smiled, wondering if perhaps the Holy Spirit had caused the minister's eyes to notice those weeds so he would linger a moment in the churchyard—precisely where we could find him to learn about the service.

The rafters of the church rang as Susan added beautiful harmonies to the praise songs. The service filled both of us with renewed joy. And I left with a new sense of how the humble acts we sometimes unconsciously pause to do can turn into divine appointments we could never orchestrate ourselves.

Father, help me to see the small signs of humble service that invite,
"Wait here for your next heavenly appointment."
—KAREN BARBER

He will beautify the humble with salvation.
—PSALM 149:4 (NKJV)

Lord, I know I complain a lot, but today I just want to thank You. Not just for the things that are right, but also for the things that are wrong.

Thank You for my limited energy. When I see the mistakes my high-energy friends make—overextension, ill temper, neglect of family—I'm glad You measure out my strength with an eyedropper. I have enough and not too much.

Thank You for my anxieties, which stalk me like mosquitoes. Like the check-engine light on my dashboard, they warn me that something needs attention. When I listen to them, it leads me to prepare, and preparation brings success.

Thank You for my poor memory. My wife has a great memory, but I see how she struggles to forget hurts and failures, how the past crowds into the present and ruins her day. I'm glad things fade quickly for me.

Thank You for my quietness. I envy people who can carry the conversational ball, but that's not me. Hey, all these talkers need someone to listen to them, and that's where I come in. I like to listen, to ask questions, to be supportive.

Thank You for the freedom to make my own mistakes. When I look back on my life, I'm appalled at my stupidity and I'm ashamed of some of my choices. Yet, without the freedom to make those choices, I would never have become who I am today.

Thank You for the aches and pains of aging. Like an early-warning system, they serve to remind me not to overextend myself. They urge me to stop and rest or to ask for help when I need it—lessons I wish I had learned long ago.

It's good to know, God, that even my afflictions can reflect Your glory.
—DANIEL SCHANTZ

MAY 16

Teach us to number our days, that we may apply our hearts unto wisdom.
—PSALM 90:12

*A*nother year, another birthday. I could hear excited laughter from the kitchen as my wife Carol and the boys put the finishing touches on their preparations. Soon the ritual would begin. Andy, our six-year-old, would escort me to the living room couch, snap out the lights and leave me alone in the dark for a minute or two. Then I'd hear the familiar tune of "Happy Birthday" and my family would march through the doorway, bearing a huge chocolate cake blazing with candles.

Too many candles, I thought gloomily. I couldn't believe another year had gone by.

"Dad, come here!" the kids shouted from the kitchen.

"Quickly!" added Carol.

I rushed in, expecting there had been an accident. Instead, everyone was smiling and pointing at the metal exhaust hood that sloped at a steep angle above the range. A single red birthday candle sat balanced on the metal in utter defiance of gravity. It was clear that the slightest breath would knock it over.

"I was getting the candles from the cabinet when one slipped out of the box," said Carol. "It landed on its end and just stayed there."

"It's a miracle!" said Andy.

No doubt about it; the odds of the little candle falling several feet and staying upright on such a steep slope must have been a million to one. I grabbed our camera and took a roll of photos. Then Andy blew on the candle, and it toppled over.

Carol stuck the candle in the middle of the cake, all alone. As I blew it out, I thought about other, deeper miracles, about life and love and the warmth of a family, and I thanked God for the many years that had brought these many gifts my way.

> *Gracious God, teach me to give thanks for the blessings*
> *of past years and to await humbly those still to come.*
> —PHILIP ZALESKI

MAY 17

For if I go not away, the Comforter will not come unto you;
but if I depart, I will send him unto you.
—JOHN 16:7

*M*y seven-year-old granddaughter Hannah gave me a big squeeze as I was about to end my visit. "It's hard to say good-bye," she said. My throat tightened. My home in the Midwest was a long way from hers on Alaska's Kenai Peninsula. "I know about good-byes," Hannah continued. "I had a friend named Flora when we lived in Kaktovik (an Arctic island Eskimo village). I didn't want her to leave, but she had to go away to college. After Flora left, I found out we were moving too. So then it was a fair good-bye because we both had to go."

A fair good-bye—I had never linked those words before. So many farewells seem wrenchingly unjust. Whether it's death or divorce or a move or a visit that ends, farewells create a gap that someone didn't want, and the heart cries, "Unfair!"

Jesus knew that pain of farewell, and so at His Ascension, He promised His followers, "I go to prepare a place for you.... I will come again, and receive you unto myself; that where I am, there ye may be also" (John 14:2–3). He emphasized, "I will not leave you comfortless" (John 14:18), speaking of the Comforter—the Holy Spirit—Who He said will "abide with you for ever" (John 14:16). No matter where the partings are in my life, Jesus shares those empty spaces with me. His comfort is totally there...and totally fair.

Jesus, faithful Friend, through all my good-byes
You are the One Who never leaves.
—CAROL KNAPP

MAY 18

"I, the Lord...will take hold of your hand."

—ISAIAH 42:6 (NIV)

The district of Columbia subway system boasts some of the longest escalators in the world. Being afraid of heights, I try to stay away from certain stations. The fear is especially fierce when I'm riding up. On some level the scenario reminds me of the spirit's journey at death: Even though I'm traveling toward the light, I'm venturing precariously farther and farther from the solid ground of the bottom stair.

Last month, when my older sister Alice came to visit, we rode the subway and got off at a stop unfamiliar to me. I saw the escalator and gasped. "Oh, it's too high. I can't."

"Come on," she coaxed. "You're not alone. You can do this."

"Stand in front of me," I said, "so I can see you, and just hold my hand." Which she did, all the way to the top.

This morning a friend asked me, "If you could choose one person to be at your side when you die, who would it be?"

"Alice," I answered quickly—she who knew me from birth, who held my hand in childhood photos, who walked into the hospital with me the morning our dad passed away. "I'd want her to hold one hand." And Jesus the other.

Lord, whether I'm facing life or death, whenever I'm afraid, take my hand.

—EVELYN BENCE

MAY 19

"Be reconciled to your brother or sister."
—MATTHEW 5:24 (NRSV)

It's a favorite hymn at our home church in Mt. Kisco, New York. But whenever the organ plays the opening bars of "Fairest Lord Jesus," I am back for a moment in West Germany.

It was 1968 and most Germans were still denying that the Holocaust had ever happened. In only one town had there been a sustained effort to face the truth. In Darmstadt, a group of Lutheran women recorded the stories of concentration camp survivors, ministered to their needs and prayed for God's forgiveness on their nation.

That year I was with the first group of Americans to go on retreat at their center in Darmstadt. We, too, had sins that needed forgiveness. For me, a blanket hatred of Germans, fanned as a teenager during World War II.

A group of Germans were also holding a retreat at the center. We'd pass them on the path between the refectory and the chapel, eyeing each other warily across a tragic history. Did they hate us too? I wondered. Americans who'd firebombed their cities?

Only as they were leaving did we learn that each of the Germans had been given the name of one of us to pray for all week. How to thank them? In the chapel that morning we'd sung "Fairest Lord Jesus." "It's an old German hymn," our translator had pointed out.

Why not sing this song for the German group?

And so we trooped into the refectory as they ate their farewell meal, each of us choosing a chair to stand behind as we sang. Afterward they rose and embraced us, many of them in tears. The woman to whom I'd sung fumbled in a handbag and drew out a scrap of paper with a typed name on it.

"Bitte (please)...who?"

And, of course, the name written on the paper was my own. When God draws people together, He is doing what He likes best.

Give me words today, Father, that will "make the woeful heart to sing."
—ELIZABETH SHERRILL

MAY 20

Then Jesus told his disciples a parable to show them
that they should always pray and not give up.
—LUKE 18:1 (NIV)

I have a good friend who sometimes can barely get herself to leave her house or even answer the phone. Once, during a particularly bad bout, she let over six hundred unopened e-mails pile up in her in-box. Eventually, a mutual friend went over and helped her go through them. Later our friend told me, "Her hand trembled on the mouse the whole time. Jenny was just terrified of doing anything."

Jenny has a kind of paralysis caused by anxiety. What brings on that anxiety no one can say. She is very smart, usually quite independent, runs her own business and has a solid faith. Why, then, does she allow herself to be made prisoner by her own irrational fears?

I've tried to reason with her. That doesn't work, of course, because Jenny's problems are rooted deep in her psyche. So I resort to prayer, asking God to make Jenny better. Yet every time Jenny has another setback, I find myself more and more dismayed. *Why aren't my prayers helping? Doesn't she want to get better?*

The other day our friend mentioned that Jenny had been making progress, so I e-mailed her just to see. "I'm getting better," she typed right back. How? "I've stopped asking God to fix me. Instead, I ask for help with the small things. 'God, help me get out of bed. God, help me brush my teeth and get dressed. God, help me walk out the door.' I stay focused on the next thing. Little victories."

Sometimes it's the people we pray for who teach us how to pray. Now I pray for the small things too—not just for Jenny, but also for myself. When we break down our problems for God, He helps us see them in perspective, which is itself often the most powerful answer to prayer.

Help me, Lord, to see that prayer is a process guided by You, not me,
and meant to bring You into every moment of my life.
—EDWARD GRINNAN

*After this manner therefore pray ye: Our Father
which art in heaven, Hallowed be thy name.*
—MATTHEW 6:9

*M*y grandfather was a quiet, skinny man who smiled a lot. He liked to sit on the front steps of our house with us grandkids and, as he said, watch the parade of the world wander by. He taught us much, sitting on the steps. One day he taught me a prayer that he said would be food for the long voyage ahead. Being Irish, he taught me the prayer in Irish Gaelic.

"Ar nathair," he said, "which is Our Father, *ata ar neamh,* Who is in heaven, though, of course, He is in us and everywhere and that's a stone fact. *Go naomhaitear d'ainm,* hallowed be Thy name, *go dtaga do riocht,* Thy kingdom come, which it is already, as we see by just paying attention to the miracle of what is. *Go ndeantar do thoil,* Thy will be done, *ar an talamh mar a dheantar ar neamh,* on earth as it is in heaven. *Tabhair duinn inniu,* give to us, *ar n'aran laethuil,* our daily bread, and *agus maith duinn ar bhfiacha,* forgive us our debts, *mar a mhaithimidne dar bhfeichiuna fein,* as we forgive our own debtors, which it would be hilarious if anyone ever owed us money, the very idea, eh? Well, boy, the prayer as usually said then goes on to say *agus na lig sinn i gcathu,* and lead us not into temptation, but Himself would never lead His children astray—we are all too good at going astray on our own. *Ach saor sin o olc,* deliver us from evil, and we finish with *aimein,* which let us say together as men do."

So *aimein!* we said together, sitting and smiling and watching the parade of the world wander by. And forty years later I'm still watching, with my grandfather's prayer humming in my heart.

*Dear Lord, thank You, from the bottom of my heart, for grandfathers
and prayers and parades and hummings in hearts.* Aimein!
—BRIAN DOYLE

MAY 22

Don't let anyone look down on you because you are young, but set an example for the believers in speech, in conduct, in love, in faith and in purity.
—I Timothy 4:12 (NIV)

Kristina, the youth director at our church, asked me if I could teach her high school Bible study. I agreed, but I wanted to meet her students and observe her class first.

She introduced me to the three students who were attending that week's study. Kristina asked about their week, prayed and then jumped onto a chair. "I want two of you to grab my hands and see if you can pull me off this chair." All three of the students were boys, two of them large enough to lift Kristina and the chair easily if they chose. Only one shyly stood up to take Kristina's right hand, so I volunteered to take her left hand. With very little effort, we pulled her forward and she had to jump from her chair to keep from falling.

Kristina climbed back onto the chair and said, "Now I'm going to lift Tim up to my level." She couldn't, of course. "It's a lot easier to pull someone down to your level than it is to lift someone up," she added. Kristina had four students that evening. I know the spirit of her oldest student was lifted high.

Dear God, thank You for the gift of faith that is measured by depth, not by years.
—Tim Williams

I delight to do thy will, O my God.
—PSALM 40:8

While traveling in Africa, the frequent delays there taught me to relax in God's timing. But any trip has delays and they're teaching me something else: God may allow delays because there's something He wants us to do with the "wasted" time.

I hate the long wait to get through airport security. My friend Sandra says she handles waiting by finding something to do, like praying for those waiting with her. I've been trying this too. I inch forward, shove my suitcase ahead of me and ask God to bless that kid with the heavy backpack. I find I can maintain this altruistic attitude about fifteen minutes before those I'm interceding for become again simply the people ahead of me in line.

But for those fifteen minutes, waiting has another dimension, and I've begun to look for ways to make all airport delays useful. Once when a flight was delayed, I entertained a wiggly two-year-old while his tired mother went for a cup of coffee. Another time I scribbled down loudspeaker messages for a deaf lady. Recently I listened for half an hour to a man who was on his way to his wife's side in a hospital; he thanked me for my excellent advice, when I hadn't spoken more than five words.

Whenever I remember to listen for God's assignment, I come away from the experience certain that in His economy there are no unusable minutes. The plus in delays—anywhere, at home or away—is that they wrench us from our schedule, that road we were barreling down with tunnel vision. When our agenda is put on hold, we just may get a glimpse of His.

Lord of the journey, help me to know that there are no delays
in Your schedule, only plans You didn't tell me about in advance.
—ELIZABETH SHERRILL

MAY 24

My cup runneth over.
—PSALM 23:5

*A*few years ago the quilters of Gee's Bend, Alabama, hit the headlines. For generations, the women of the community had been making quilts from the scraps of their husbands' work clothes: corduroy, denim, twill. Their children grew up sleeping under piles of patchwork every winter, because most of the houses in the town—populated almost entirely by still-poor descendants of slaves—had no heat. Then an art dealer came to town and told the ladies their quilts were really something else: They were art.

Within months Gee's Bend quilts were selling for hundreds, even thousands, of dollars. An exhibition toured museums. The designs—beautiful geometric patterns that resembled modernist paintings—were slapped onto coasters and ties and rugs and note cards. Awash in newfound celebrity and unprecedented wealth, some of the quilters bought furniture, cars, a new stove for the first time in thirty years. Then the distrust began to build. There were lawsuits. There were allegations that the dealer wasn't passing profits on to the women. There were claims of financial mismanagement.

One day I went to talk with one of the oldest quilters. We sat on her rickety front porch, on one of those suffocatingly hot southern afternoons. I went into nosy-journalist mode, all my questions revolving around one theme: She clearly hadn't gotten rich, but didn't she want to be? Wasn't she upset? Gazing out at the dusty road, she told me about the old days, about the civil rights movement, about how poor the town had always been, about God's faithfulness throughout. Then she stopped talking. All I could hear was birdsong. Finally she turned to me. She had an answer to my questions, a favorite Psalm she wanted to share: "The Lord is my shepherd." She paused and then continued, stopping after each word for emphasis: "I. Shall. Not. Want."

Never let me forget, Lord, that my truest riches lie in knowing You.
—JEFF CHU

MAY 25

And seeing the multitudes, he went up into a mountain: and when he was set,
his disciples came unto him: And he opened his mouth, and taught them.
—MATTHEW 5:1–2

Recently, my wife Shirley and I and nine other members of our family visited China. Whenever I go to another country, I'm always intrigued to learn more about its religious beliefs and practices. Since the seventh century, China has been strongly influenced by the teachings of the Buddha. Not surprisingly, many shrines and temples feature statues of the Buddha, but what did surprise me were the various expressions on the faces of the statues, happy and sad and prayerful and angry.

One temple visit reminded me of a huge Buddha I saw many years ago in Japan, the famed Kamakura Buddha, south of Tokyo. That statue was fashioned from bronze in 1252 and was once housed in a temple that was destroyed by a tsunami more than five hundred years ago. Now the enormous image is in the open. The memorable thing about that Buddha is that visitors can go inside the statue and get a bird's-eye view of the world. I remember thinking at the time, what an experience it would be if we could see things from God's perspective.

Then it came to me: That is exactly the reason God sent Jesus—to share with humankind His love, His very nature, His wishes, hopes and dreams for His creation. Nothing, it seems to me, captures a God's-eye view of life better than the Beatitudes, which advise all who would follow Him to be humble, seek righteousness, be merciful and makers of peace.

Help us God, to see the needs of others first,
Your will to seek with deep hunger and thirst.
—FRED BAUER

MAY 26

"I will not leave you orphaned."
—JOHN 14:18 (MSG)

*M*y brother Earle was killed in a plane crash when I was a boy. After my dad died, I said to my aunt, "All my life I've had this delusion that my father loved Earle more than me." Without missing a beat, she said, "That wasn't a delusion. He really did like him a lot more. We all felt so sad for you."

I was stunned. Then I remembered Dad going off to Earle's baseball games. Earle, five years older than I, already played very well. I was too little to go, but I practiced all the time, hoping Dad would want to be with me. One Saturday, with two mitts and a baseball, I finally got up the courage to ask, "Daddy, will you please go out and play catch with me?" Frowning, he nodded and took the mitt I offered him. In the next five minutes I discovered a horrible thing: Dad couldn't catch a ball! He'd run track at Oklahoma University, so I assumed he was an all-around athlete. Dad was very embarrassed; I was heartbroken. I saw that Dad's interest was in Earle, not in baseball.

My dad was a fine man and taught me a lot about integrity and determination in coming back from his own failures. My need to get Dad's attention motivated me to become a tenacious competitor in sports and in life. And it left me in a place where I was able to hear God whisper, *"Keith, you have a Father now Who will never be too busy to hang out with you, teach you, encourage you when you win, console you when you lose—and love you forever. And you'll never have to be alone again."*

> *Lord, I'm very grateful for the way my loss*
> *and pain led me to a miraculous life in You.*
>
> —KEITH MILLER

To set the mind on the flesh is death, but to set the mind on the Spirit is life and peace.

—ROMANS 8:6 (NRSV)

*Y*ears ago our family celebrated Pentecost Sunday in a Russian Orthodox church in Wiesbaden, Germany. The service concluded with lengthy "kneeling prayers" for renewal in the Holy Spirit. As we knelt, I tried to pray— but mostly I struggled to hold my squirming ten-month-old son Mark and inwardly complained about my sore back. I also looked forward to the delicious brunch we would eat afterward with some new friends from America. Finally the service ended, and we drove to the restaurant.

After the meal we lingered in the hot, humid banquet room. I began to be irritated by my children's interruptions and annoyed with the other family's grandpa's long-winded tales. Soon our foreheads glistened with sweat, and we fanned ourselves with menus. I looked longingly out the window at the blue sky, the sunshine shimmering on the lawn and the leaves quivering in the breeze. Then our friend Ted said, "Maybe I can get this window open." He tried a crank, but the window didn't budge. "*Hmm*, it seems to be locked." He felt along the window, released a lever and then pushed the window open. A cool draft wafted over us. "How wonderful that feels!" "What a relief!" we exclaimed. I finally relaxed and enjoyed the sweet fellowship, speaking English and sharing what we missed about home. Grandpa's stories now seemed charming!

Sometimes my life feels like that stifling banquet room. I see glimpses of blue sky and green trees glistening in God's kingdom—a glorious Spirit-filled life—yet I seem trapped by problems, challenging relationships or my not-so-glorious life. Pentecost is a special opportunity to open my heart to let in God's light and fresh breeze of love.

Come, Holy Spirit. Fill my life anew that I may enter into deeper union with You and others.

—MARY BROWN

MAY 28

If your enemies are hungry, give them bread to eat;
and if they are thirsty, give them water to drink.
—PROVERBS 25:21 (NRSV)

We probably all know someone who has been affected by violence or war. You may have lost a son or daughter, a niece or nephew or grandchild in Iraq or Afghanistan. Or you may have been there in support of a friend who lost someone. If my friend Bill hadn't experienced this sort of loss himself, I don't think a Bible verse could have possibly made him as angry as this one from Proverbs did.

Bill lost his son in the fighting in Afghanistan almost four years ago. Not a week goes by when he doesn't break down in tears—the sort of thing Bill had never done before tragedy entered his life. Bill and I were in Bible study together, and our leader was reviewing all of the passages in Scripture that talk about loving and praying for our enemies. In addition to the verse above, we also heard, "But I say to you, Love your enemies and pray for those who persecute you" (Matthew 5:44, NRSV). Even though those words come from the Sermon on the Mount preached by Jesus Himself, they infuriated Bill for a long time.

I'll tell you what: God works miracles. After weeks of seeking God's help, Bill is praying once again, and he tells me that praying for the men who killed his son has begun to heal his own wounds.

Dear Jesus, when sorrow makes me feel like lashing out,
grant me the gift of forgiveness.
—JON SWEENEY

MAY 29

All were amazed and perplexed, saying to one another, "What does this mean?"
—ACTS 2:12 (NRSV)

*T*was on a roll...or so I thought.

Leading a workshop for about fifteen people, I watched heads nodding in assent to what I was saying. That told me I was connecting with these folks in the ways I hope for when I teach.

Except for one person, an older woman, third row, left side of the room. No matter what I said, she didn't nod; she didn't show glimmers of recognition or understanding. She didn't look like she was enjoying the experience at all.

Which is why I was surprised when she approached me after the session, extended her hand and expressed her thanks. "I didn't think you were enjoying this," I responded. "All the others, they were nodding"—I moved my head up and down—"but you...."

She smiled. "I used to listen simply for things I agreed with. But I find I learn much more from what surprises me. So I listen hard for what I didn't know before."

That surprised me. And I've never forgotten it. In fact, it's become a part of my own life and learning, especially in areas like my devotions or adult education at church. I don't just listen anymore for someone to confirm what I already believe. I listen for a challenge, to become what I haven't yet understood.

Open my eyes today, God, to a person or idea I have never considered—but one You have placed before me.

—JEFF JAPINGA

MAY 30

Flowers appear on the earth.
—SONG OF SOLOMON 2:12 (NIV)

lowers don't just appear on the desert earth where I live. If the earth receives enough winter snow, and if March stays cool and overcast, and if we get some rain in April, flowers will appear. But even when all the "ifs" aren't in place, stubborn flowers like the sego lily and the many hues of desert paintbrush still grace the baked earth for a few colorful weeks.

Not even sagebrush can grow on the south-facing hillsides that steam and dry in the winter sun while shaded valleys still hide under several feet of snow. These eroded slopes remain barren for eleven months, from June to May, and then, no matter how dry and hot the weather, a lone white primrose appears. The next day it looks as though a crazed florist has flung baskets of white, yellow and pink primroses across the rocky earth.

I always call the first primrose I see the "Dargie primrose." Dargie lived in one of the poorest homes in the neighborhood of poor homes where I grew up. Both her father and mother were alcoholics. One of the surest signs of spring I remember is Dargie emerging from her house on a Saturday morning with a plateful of cookies, coaxing even the roughest young bullies on the block into her backyard to listen to some Bible stories. I shyly watched boys who had beaten me up the previous week listen to a young woman explain that God loved each one of them. I watched the belief in their hardened eyes, a belief born from the kindness of the messenger. I don't know how many unloved young boys bloomed under her care or for how long they continued to bloom. I do know that for at least a single spring morning, beauty reigned in a barren place.

Dear God, help me to be a "Dargie primrose" today.
—TIM WILLIAMS

MAY 31

Wait on the Lord: be of good courage, and he shall strengthen thine heart.
—PSALM 27:14

*M*y husband has been dead four years. "It will get easier," I was assured. It didn't. It got harder! When the church phoned, requesting pictures for a new directory, I couldn't stand the thought of mine being put in it without him at my side. "It's okay," the secretary said, "I understand. We'll just list your name."

Later that day I went to take a load of trash to the bins at the edge of the road—formerly my husband's job. Trash had been pulled out of the plastic bags and was scattered down the street. *Bother, that drat raccoon has been at it again!*

As I retrieved a couple of cans that had rolled over to my neighbor's chain-link fence, I was greeted by a sunflower. It had struggled up through a tangle of brush inside the fence and pushed its bud through one of the links. It bloomed alone, a flower enormously large and bright...like a smile from God to brighten up my day. "Thank You, Lord," I whispered.

I took courage from that flower; I, too, could bloom alone. I would phone the church and arrange to have my picture put in the directory.

> *Lord of eternal light and love, when my heart is lonely,*
> *I praise You for the encouragement of sweet surprises.*
> —FAY ANGUS

June

JUNE 1

Set your hope on the grace to be brought to you
when Jesus Christ is revealed at his coming.
—I Peter 1:13 (NIV)

*H*e lived across the street from us as I was growing up, a blind, bedridden old man. I'd see him on rare occasions, being wheeled from the house to the car, to my young mind a picture of hopelessness.

How wrong I was! When I learned to type, Mr. Seldon hired me one afternoon a week after school to answer the letters that came from all over the country to this one-time organist and music teacher. His replies were long, personal and detailed—largely encouragement to former students.

I also helped him organize his huge collection of 78-rpm records. There was usually music playing when I arrived, often "Amazing Grace."

"I want to be just like John Newton," he said once.

I was startled; he'd just finished telling me about Newton's life as a drunkard and a ship's captain in the slave trade. "I mean," he added, "like Newton after he lost his sight." Newton, he went on, had had a tremendous conversion and had become a minister and hymn writer. Then the man who wrote, "I once was blind, but now I see," became blind.

Newton's spiritual sight, however, grew keener than ever as he went on preaching and writing hymns. When he reached his eighties, friends urged him to retire. "Do you know what he said?" Mr. Seldon asked. "He admitted that his eyesight was gone and his memory failing, but he said, 'I remember two things: I am a great sinner. And Jesus is a great Savior.'

"Bad eyesight isn't such a disadvantage," Mr. Seldon said. "It helps us overlook the unimportant things and set our sights on the ones that matter."

Show me the things this day, Father, that matter to You.
—Elizabeth Sherrill

June 2

Are not two sparrows sold for a penny? Yet not one of them
will fall to the ground apart from your Father.
—MATTHEW 10:29 (NRSV)

*B*irds have fascinated me all my life. I've hunted them with my binoculars all over the globe, but my best bird-watching takes place in the backyard around the birdbath and feeder. There are always new birds coming to my table, some for the season, others just passing through, like the flock of warblers that showed up today. They were myrtles, or yellow rumps, so named because of the lemony swatch on their backsides.

A couple of them had the misfortune of flying into the kitchen window. When I heard the thud, I hurried outside and found two birds, both females, under the bushes, one out cold, the other stunned and drowsy.

Sometimes I've had luck reviving an injured bird by warming it in my hands, so I tried holding bird number one. I knew she was alive; I could feel her heart racing beneath the black and white feathers that had kept her from freezing during her high-altitude flight from South America. But when she didn't respond after five minutes, I turned to bird number two. She was now conscious and when I raised her on one finger, she left in a hurry without so much as a chirped thank-you.

The first bird would now sit on my hand, but nod and tip over, so I put her in a box to rest. Fifteen minutes later she was improved. Eyeing me suspiciously as if to say, "You're not my mother," she spread her wings and flittered off in the same direction as bird number two.

I'm always pleased to read the Bible passage that says not even a sparrow falls without God's knowledge. It reassures me that He knows of my movements too, of my goings out and comings in, of my ups and downs, of my gains and pains. In other words, He cares. That's good news for all of us.

When I forget, Lord, to give life its reverential due,
Remind me that all things were created by You.
—FRED BAUER

June 3

Why are ye fearful, O ye of little faith?
—Matthew 8:26

We are on a bus driving through an off-road thicket, deep in a moonless landscape. There is no electricity for miles, and I can see nothing as I stare out the window into the darkness. The bus rumbles to a halt, and my husband David and I and our fellow passengers stumble toward a pontoon boat. Within minutes we're anchored in the middle of a forbidding bay. "This is the strangest tourist attraction I've ever seen," I whisper nervously to David.

Earlier, after we'd arrived on the Isle of Vieques for a special holiday, our taxi driver had said, "Put the Bioluminescent Bay at the top of your agenda." So here we are, listening to the pilot of the boat say, "To experience the miracle of the bay, you must jump into the water." No one moves. This is ridiculous. The water is as black as the night. We all wait. Suddenly, David stands up and jumps into the unknown. In the pool of darkness, his body takes on a bright glow. His every movement radiates a flowing blue-green light. Mesmerized, I jump in, and others follow.

I wave my arms and make angel wings, and then twirl and swirl in a trail of fairy dust. By now, everyone is laughing and splashing as our every move turns the night magical. The moment seems part fantasy, part science fiction as the energy of our bodies sets trillions of microorganisms aglow.

Later, back on the boat heading for shore, I think of the fear that wrapped around us. There in a dark bay, magic was waiting—waiting for someone who believed enough to take a chance and jump in.

Father, take away my toe-first inclinations and fill me with a leaping faith.
—Pam Kidd

JUNE 4

When they walk through the Valley of Weeping it will become a place
of springs where pools of blessing and refreshment collect after rains!
—PSALM 84:6 (TLB)

*H*e was the famous "singing cowboy," hero to a generation of small boys, our son Scott among them. At the end of each TV episode, toy guitar in hand, Scott would sing along, "Happy trails to you, until we meet again."

I had gone to interview Roy Rogers, not about his screen life but his personal faith. We sat in the family room of his unpretentious California ranch house while I listed just a few of the charities he and his wife Dale Evans supported: orphanages, shelters for abused women, programs for troubled teens, aid for the handicapped and chronically ill—"Dale and I just try to give back a little of what God's given us," he said, cutting short the recitation.

Someone else, I suggested, might focus instead on what God had taken away. Roy's first wife, I knew, had died of an embolism soon after the birth of their son Roy Jr. The Down syndrome baby born to him and Dale died before the little girl's second birthday. Their twelve-year-old adopted daughter Debbie was killed in a church bus accident. That same year their adopted son Sandy died during peacetime army service. Hadn't there been times, I asked, when his faith was shaken?

"Never!" he said. "God's become more real to us with every sorrow."

If there were no valleys along the trail, he explained, there would be no mountains either. "The valleys are where I learn how small I am, the mountaintops where I see how great He is."

Happy trails indeed, I thought, when both pain and joy lead to God.

Faithful Lord, be with me wherever today's trail leads.
—ELIZABETH SHERRILL

JUNE 5

*Then some people came, bringing to him
a paralyzed man, carried by four of them.*
—MARK 2:3 (NRSV)

*I*t's a scary thing to have your son phone, offhandedly chat a while, and then finally give the real reason for his call. "Mom, I have some health problems that will involve some serious surgery. But don't worry."

Of course I worried. *What if something happens to John?* Now, my children may be married and away from home, but they're still my kids. And in situations like this, I turn to God even more than usual.

That's when I recalled the story in Mark of the sick man carried to Jesus by four friends. *Why four?* I wondered. The Gospel doesn't say, but it seems logical that if the man was too sick to make it on his own, he'd need a stretcher and four carriers, one for each corner.

If it worked in biblical times, it should work now too, I reasoned. So with motherly concern, I looked for four friends of my own—friends who truly believe in prayer—who would agree to carry John on a "prayer stretcher." I think it helps to pray specifically—not just a vague, "Lord, take care of John." So I said, "Mary, will you take the left front corner, please? Sue, right front. Bonnie, left rear. Kathie, right rear." My position? I reasoned that every team needs cheerleaders. I'd be one, encouraging each prayer and giving them updates on John's condition.

For two months, the four stretcher-bearers continued their faithful vigil. When surgery day came, John's wife Marie said, "Neither of us is afraid. We both sense John is being carried on a bed of prayer."

And how does the story in Mark end? When Jesus saw the faith of the four friends, He said to the paralytic, "Get up, take your mat and go home" (Mark 2:11, updated NIV).

And within a short time, that's just what John did.

*Father, You've told us that anything is possible if we have faith.
Please show me how to have that faith—the faith that moves mountains!*
—ISABEL WOLSELEY

JUNE 6

In every thing give thanks, for this is the will of God.
—I Thessalonians 5:18

"In everything give thanks" was the lectionary reading that morning. *Could I do this?* I wondered. *Thank God for everything for an entire day?* I decided to try...and promptly forgot the lofty experiment in the thousand things to do for an upcoming trip.

It was one o'clock before I remembered the morning's resolve. Well, I'd make a fresh start in the car on the way to the post office. Surely on this glorious fall afternoon, there'd be no end of things to thank God for. In this elevated mood, I pulled out onto the street...where the first thing I saw was a dead squirrel.

What kind of miserable irony was this! Was there any possible thing to thank God for in this all-too-common small tragedy?

I tried being thankful that the poor little animal must have died instantly. But the joy was gone from the day. The pumpkins on the doorsteps, the red of the maple trees—every sight was overlaid with the image of the dead squirrel. And because I could not forget it, God used it to speak to me.

I did not will the death of My creature, He said, *but you can learn from it.*

The squirrel, God told me, had been very busy. Climbing trees, dashing across streets, digging holes, tucking away acorns, so intent on preparing for the future that it was blind to the present. Animals, of course, can't alter behavior programmed over millions of years. *But you have a choice,* God said. *All morning you've reminded Me of a squirrel, so busy getting ready for tomorrow you forgot that the present moment is the only time you can be with Me.*

Busy? Of course I was busy. Remember God in the midst of my busyness? Of course I could. "In everything give thanks"—isn't this God's way of saying, *Whatever is happening right now, that is where I am.*

Bestower of blessing, thank You for this moment.
—Elizabeth Sherrill

JUNE 7

Underneath are the everlasting arms.
—DEUTERONOMY 33:27

*I*t stands with other mementos on a table in the family room, the framed tribute our daughter Liz gave to her dad on his eightieth birthday—six brief paragraphs recalling ways John had been there for her from earliest childhood through school, marriage, work and raising children of her own.

In addition to the typed message, Liz had pasted two small black-and-white photos of herself and John, taken when she was two. They show a favorite game—one that brought me out into the yard with a camera one summer afternoon.

In the picture at the top of the page, John grips Liz's legs and lifts the tiny girl high in the air. The game is to see if Liz will be brave enough not to hang on to him but to hold herself erect and balanced, hands behind her back. She does it! In her face is the triumph of overcoming fear and hesitation.

In the lower left corner of the framed page is the scene seconds later as Liz collapses, squealing with laughter, into her father's embrace. I looked at those photos this morning, seeing in them the kind of faith I want to have in my heavenly Father. Isn't this what trust in Him does? Lets us stand straight and strong, knowing Whose arms support us...lets us fall gratefully into those arms when our own strength fails.

Faithful Lord, let me feel Your everlasting arms beneath me today.
—ELIZABETH SHERRILL

JUNE 8

Then He arose and rebuked the wind, and said to the sea, "Peace, be still!"
—MARK 4:39 (NKJV)

*W*hen I was a boy, I preferred Sunday evening services because they were more informal. The song leader would often ask for favorites, and my hand would be the first one in the air. "Sing number one-oh-two, 'Master, the Tempest Is Raging'" (Mary A. Baker, 1874). The dramatic song sent chills through me. It was about the disciples in the boat during a storm on Lake Galilee. When we got to the chorus, I would sing out like a drowning man:

> Whether the wrath of the storm-tossed sea,
> Or demons, or men, or whatever it be,
> No water can swallow the ship where lies
> The Master of ocean, and earth, and skies;
> They all shall sweetly obey Thy will,
> Peace, be still! Peace, be still!

I still think of that song when life gets stormy, when the winds of change rock my boat, when waves of anxiety wash over me, when I feel like I'm drowning in work, when the thunder and lightning of conflict frighten me. At such times I remind myself that nothing can sink my ship because Jesus is in the boat with me. He made the sea and the sky, and He can say, "Peace, be still!" and things will settle down. They always do.

> *Father, the sea is big and my boat is small, but I feel safe*
> *because You are here in the boat with me.*
> —DANIEL SCHANTZ

JUNE 9

Each man has his own gift from God.
—I CORINTHIANS 7:7 (NASB)

When I was in high school, I longed to be a majorette like my friends. But the rules stipulated that majorettes must play a band instrument. The long-suffering band director finally suggested, "Try the triangle, Marion. Anyone can play it." Not me.

So I went out for basketball. Of the thirty who wanted to play, only two of us didn't make it. I tried cheerleading next—until I discovered that I couldn't smile and cheer at the same time.

An observant English teacher asked, "What's wrong, Marion?" "I can't be a majorette, a basketball player or a cheerleader. I'm a...nothing." The teacher sat down in the empty seat in front of me. "You've gotten A's on all your essays, despite your spelling. Maybe your gift is simply different. What do you really enjoy?"

I was always delighted when an essay was assigned, beamed when everyone else moaned. I'd waited on the cold granite steps for the library to open each summer morning. Books had become the brothers and sisters I didn't have, keeping me company while my mother worked. Sometimes I would lie in bed, thinking about words I enjoyed—such as *tapestry, September, pristine* and *pensive*—and authors I adored—Pearl S. Buck, W. Somerset Maugham, Edgar Allan Poe, Sinclair Lewis, Emily Dickinson. Tiny Tim, Heidi, Nancy Drew, Tom Sawyer and Lassie were cherished friends. The batons, musical instruments, basketballs and pom-poms are long gone. My own gift from God remains alive.

Oh, Father, here's a long overdue, deep-down thank You
for knowing, even way back then, the gift for me!
—MARION BOND WEST

JUNE 10

If I take the wings of the morning, and dwell in the uttermost parts of the sea;
Even there shall thy hand lead me, and thy right hand shall hold me.
—PSALM 139:9–10

*T*was beachcombing with my husband along the Pacific Ocean south of Seattle. We were dismayed to discover a stranded harbor seal pup that had apparently washed in on the tide. We didn't know what to do except feel sorry for it.

The next day, from the deck of my sister-in-law's home on Gray's Harbor, we noticed a cluster of people carrying a baby seal to a small secluded beach. They released it on the mud flats, where it flopped awkwardly toward the water. Its mewling carried to us on the wind.

My husband left to find out what was going on. The people returning the seal pup to the sea were community animal control volunteers. The mother seal had gone to deep water to feed, depositing her baby on a sandbar. The waves swept it in to shore, leaving it too weak and tired to follow the tide back out. That's when we had stumbled upon it.

Now the rested pup was being returned to the water near its birthing place, plaintively calling for its mother. She could distinguish her pup's cry underwater and would swim to find it. As we watched the little seal disappear in the waves, our dismay of a day earlier became anticipation at the reunion soon to take place.

There are times when, whether carried away on a tide of my own making or pounded by breakers not of my choosing, I feel separated from God. Then, like that seal pup, I'm out of my element, exhausted and floundering. But wherever I am, God hears my cry. He knows I am His and He will find me.

Loving Lord, help me to remember that You are always near me.
—CAROL KNAPP

Because I live, ye shall live also.
—JOHN 14:19

*T*was in anguish as I wandered down the mall from the pharmacy to the bookstore. In the face of my mother's death, the biblical truths I'd claimed for most of my life suddenly seemed shallow, and I found myself asking questions that had never before entered my mind: *Is heaven a real place? Is Mother really with Jesus?*

I became even more upset as I remembered the final conversation I'd had with Mother as she slipped into a coma. "Do you know who I am?" I asked her. To my horror, she had no idea. *Dear God, she's forgetting everything!*

A tap on my shoulder interrupted my reverie. It was Frank from work. He stood quietly by my side as I gathered a stack of books on coping with grief and then put them back on the shelf. I'd missed several weeks of work to care for Mother, and I didn't have the luxury of extra money for books.

"Think some bibliotherapy might help?" Frank asked softly, reaching into his wallet. "I have this coupon for a discount shopping spree. I've been saving it for something special."

I did some quick calculations and discovered that the money a friend had tucked inside a sympathy card would cover the books.

In the quiet of my home, those books returned me to the foundations of faith that grief had caused me to forget and doubt. And they helped me to recall the second part of that conversation in Mother's hospital room.

After Mother had failed to recognize me, another question spilled out from a place of desperation deep within me: "Do you know who Jesus is?" I asked her.

My two sisters and I hovered over her bed, but Mother's faraway look didn't take us in. "He's our Savior," she answered as if it were the surest thing in all the world.

Dear Lord, the promise of Your salvation is the surest thing in the world. And life ever after with You? I can't wait.
—ROBERTA MESSNER

JUNE 12

Nathanael saith unto him, Whence knowest thou me?
Jesus answered...when thou wast under the fig tree, I saw thee.
—JOHN 1:48

*M*y cousin lives up a narrow canyon road on the outskirts of Los Angeles. My favorite spot when I visit her is a rock ledge beneath a spreading live oak overlooking a large grassy field. When I hold very still, the space around me reveals all sorts of activity. The creatures feel safe to show themselves.

One day I sat in the sun and silently began to greet all that I saw. *I see you, coyote, prowling in the grass. I see you, gecko, climbing on the rock. I see you, dragonfly, flitting by. I see you, squirrels, peering at me. I see you, hummingbird, darting among the blossoms. I see you, scampering rabbits. I see you, butterfly, floating on the breeze.*

I spoke aloud and my soliloquy became a dialogue. "Jesus, what do You see?" His answer, calm and sure, filled my heart. *I see you, Carol, sitting under the oak tree, sunning your legs.*

I felt a sudden breathlessness, an acute awareness that Jesus really does see me. He knows every detail—my thoughts and dreams, my battles, my motivations and limitations, the pangs of body and soul, the secret joys and triumphs of my heart. I sensed His deep compassion and caring for me. And like the creatures around me, I knew it was safe to show myself.

Jesus, I love Your eyes that see exactly who I am—and who You intend me to be.
—CAROL KNAPP

JUNE 13

Believe in the light.
—JOHN 12:36

Ray Charles was one of the most influential soul singers of all time. His music, often upbeat, sometimes plaintive, could set my feet to tapping and rock my soul with emotion. Shortly after his death I saw the movie *Ray*. It showed how he began to go blind when he was seven years old and how his mother, a poor sharecropper in Florida, did all she could to help him overcome his disability. One scene in particular stood out in my mind.

Imagine this boy, now totally blind, walking into his cabin and falling to the floor. The audience sees him there, screaming out for his mother. She stands nearby, perfectly still; she knows instinctively that her son must overcome the darkness on his own.

Thinking he is alone, the boy slowly picks himself up off the floor. He moves toward the fireplace and feels the heat. From the open window he hears a horse and buggy passing by. He realizes he is going to be okay. His mother, hovering all the while, weeps and finally embraces her boy.

That scene reminded me of a night when I felt completely alone. I had thought that if I tried hard, God would make everything okay for me, but it hadn't worked out that way. I sat in my backyard in anguish, feeling totally abandoned. But now this memory took on a new dimension. I realized God had been hovering near, feeling my pain, ready to embrace me with a hug. All I had to do was pay attention. All I needed to do was listen. And with Him by my side, I could pick myself up and feel my way to the light.

Father, in the dark times, keep me believing in the light.
—BROCK KIDD

171

Nation shall not lift up a sword against nation, neither shall they learn war any more. But they shall sit every man under his vine and under his fig tree; and none shall make them afraid: for the mouth of the Lord of hosts hath spoken it.

—MICAH 4:3–4

A young friend of mine is just back from Iraq. He was twenty-three years old when he left, and now he is a thousand times older than I. We sit in the sun and he talks a while.

"I don't regret my service," he says. "I did a good thing, protecting my friends, trying to help the people there find a peaceful life where they can just work and pray and argue like normal people.

"I prayed, sure. You bet I prayed. I prayed all the time. And I tried to do everything with my fullest attention—that's a kind of prayer too. When I cleaned my weapon, I was intent on cleaning my weapon. When I helped build a shed for a family, I built the best shed there ever was.

"Someday I'll go back. I have to go back. Those poor people, they were just like us. The kids trying to get out of doing their homework, and somebody forgot to let the dog out, and whose turn is it to do the dishes? The prayer of every day. I bet I prayed that prayer more than any other when I was there: 'God, grant us the miracle of a normal day.' I mean, really, what more powerful prayer could you ever pray?"

Dear Lord, on my knees I beg You this: Grant us the miracle of a normal day. I know full well that every day is a miracle, but You know what I mean. And can You shove the world toward being a place where no child has to go to war?

—BRIAN DOYLE

JUNE 15

Jesus spoke to them and said, "Take heart, it is I; do not be afraid."
—MATTHEW 14:27 (NRSV)

I was cleaning up the debris from Hurricane Gustav. Although I'd breathed a sigh of relief, it wasn't over yet. Hurricane Hannah had turned toward the East Coast, but Ike was on its way into the Gulf and Josephine wasn't far behind. *Lord*, I prayed silently as I picked up broken branches, *watch over us. I'm afraid.*

As my brief prayer ended, I heard voices coming from the tennis courts across from my backyard pond. Two women were playing. As they hit the ball back and forth, one called out, "God always sees us through." "Yes," her partner called back, "we just have to let go of our fear and latch on to our faith." *What a perfect message for me today*, I thought.

The next morning in church, I listened to the story of Jesus calming His disciples on the stormy Sea of Galilee. "Do not be afraid," Jesus had said. That afternoon I walked outside and gazed across the pond. My fear was gone.

Father, thank You for the words that comfort me
through the storms in my life.
—MELODY BONNETTE

JUNE 16

Give to them as the Lord your God has blessed you.
—DEUTERONOMY 15:14 (NIV)

Only Brock," my sister Keri teased, "would travel all the way to Zimbabwe and end up in the investment business!" I had just picked up my family at the airport on their return from that country, and Keri was bursting with stories to share. I had made the long journey to Zimbabwe the year before, visiting the farm for AIDS orphans that our family, church friends and many *Guideposts* readers support. While touring a clinic that serves as an awareness center for people infected with HIV, I met a young entrepreneur who refused to let AIDS affect his spirit. His name was Tapiwa, and he had helped write a book that served as an educational tool for many sick folks. He helped to fund the printing of this book by making and selling maputi, a popcorn-like snack popular in Zimbabwe. He had dreams of expanding his business so he could help his family.

"Back in America," I told him, "I work for an investment company and I'd very much like to invest in your business." I pressed some money into the disbelieving boy's hand and looked into his eyes. "I'll be back someday to see how we're doing." That was that, or so I thought. On her visit to the AIDS clinic, Keri learned that Tapiwa was eager for me to return. It seems he has a lot to share with his American partner. He's turned those first dollars into a small factory where he prepares and packages his corn. He has two employees and several roadside stands. He's keeping his family afloat.

Keri laid out the entire story with great pride. "Brock," she said, "this is the best investment you've ever made!" My sister had never been righter.

Dear Lord, thank You for the daily opportunity
You give me to invest in others.
—BROCK KIDD

JUNE 17

Thou art my father, my God, and the rock of my salvation.
—PSALM 89:26

I saw my father angry at my mother only once.

Dad was a private detective with an office in New York City, twenty-five miles from our home in the suburbs. To a child, it seemed fun and glamorous, knowing behind-the-scenes stories about kidnappings or murders. What I didn't know about was Dad's perpetual fear that someone he had helped send to prison might seek revenge on our family.

On the day I remember so well, Mother answered a phone call. "He's not here," I heard her say.

"That's funny," she said as she replaced the receiver. "The man just hung up."

A family rule was that unidentified calls be reported to the office. Mother called Dad and then turned to me. "Lock the front door! I'll get the back one. Then help me lower the shades."

Thirty minutes later I heard a car slow and stop, and then footsteps on the walk. Peeking from an upstairs window, I saw one of Dad's operatives station himself at the front door. Minutes later Dad himself arrived. The locked doors, the drawn shades, the sentinel at the door, none of it made such an impression on me as Daddy's voice raised to Mother: "Never, never, never say, 'He's not here'!"

She never did again, I'm sure.

But don't I say that too, anytime a problem overwhelms me? Don't I hear God telling me now, "Never, never, never say, 'My heavenly Father is not here'"?

Faithful Lord, teach me to say when trouble calls, "My Father is right here."
—ELIZABETH SHERRILL

JUNE 18

Jesus said: "I'm telling you once and for all, that unless you return
to square one and start over like children, you're not even going
to get a look at the kingdom, let alone get in."
—MATTHEW 18:2–3 (MSG)

I sat up in bed, unable to get back to sleep. "God," I prayed, "I love You. But to be honest, my prayer life is just not working. Please give me a hand." I opened the Bible at Matthew 18 and tried to read, but my spirit wasn't in gear. Then I had a strong nudge: *Focus on what you're reading. It's for you!* Jesus was saying to His disciples, "I'm telling you once and for all, that unless you return to square one and start over like children you're not even going to get a look at the kingdom, let alone get in." *Keith*, God seemed to be saying, *you can't see reality from My perspective—or what to do—unless you become like a little child again.*

Immediately I remembered the Lord's Prayer, the only prayer Jesus gave as a model. Although our translations begin it with "Our Father," in Aramaic, Jesus' native language, it began "Abba" ("Daddy"). I bowed my head. "Daddy, I'm a lost little boy trying to control everything instead of listening as Your little child." Instantly tears came, and I grasped the problem with my prayer life. When praying to "Our Father," I prayed adult to adult, as if God were a peer with expertise in an area I hadn't mastered (and Whom I could fire if I didn't like His advice). But when I prayed to "Daddy," I prayed as a listening child. Simply saying "Daddy" brought me what all my studying and meditation had not: a new set of ears.

Daddy in heaven, thank You for teaching me to come
to You childlike, eyes wide open and ears listening. Amen.
—KEITH MILLER

JUNE 19

"But you will chase your enemies and they will fall before you."
—LEVITICUS 26:7 (NASB)

When one of my thirtysomething-year-old children asked me to pray about a particularly painful trial, I immediately did so. But when I didn't see much result, I wondered if my prayers were making a difference. Was God really hearing me? Discouraged, I was about to give up the battle as I headed to the mailbox one hot morning in June. I'd written what I hoped was a letter of encouragement, but I wasn't certain I should mail it.

As I stood hesitating at the mailbox, I heard a loud commotion overhead. I looked up, shading my eyes with my hand and squinting into the bright sun. An unbelievably tiny bird was screaming loudly as she chased a huge hawk. Again and again they circled in the sky above a small wooded area. Were the little bird's babies there? Relentlessly, the small bird pursued the enormous hawk, darting in front of him as if daring him to catch her. At last the hawk began to grow weary. Fascinated, I watched as the exhausted hawk flew slowly out of sight and the victorious little bird returned to her babies. I continued to stare up at the cloudless sky long after the battle was over and the birds were gone, and listened with my heart.

I thought I heard clearly: *You can't imagine how effective your prayers are. The enemy is growing weary.* "Yes!" I said out loud joyfully, and I dropped my letter into the mailbox. Even as I walked back to the house, I prayed for my child with new energy.

Father God, teach me to be a patient, persistent prayer warrior.
—MARION BOND WEST

JUNE 20

My heart rejoiced in all my labour.
—ECCLESIASTES 2:10

Today is my day off. But this will be no holiday. Guests are coming to our house tonight for dinner, and I have a to-do list a mile long.

As I mop the kitchen floor, I suddenly hear the echo of my mother's voice: "Keeping a house clean is like shoveling a sidewalk in a blizzard!" For the past few hours I have "shoveled" valiantly to change chaos into order under our roof.

Moving from mopping to dusting, I gaze across the living room at the antique furniture my wife Beth and I have collected over the years. As I wipe dust from an old English chest, I smell the citrus scent of the furniture polish, and peace pervades me. Slowly, the patina of the dark mahogany becomes richer, glowing softly in the lamplight. For a moment, cleaning is not work; it's a pleasure, a comfort to my soul. Somehow the dusting of furniture and the polishing of wood have become a form of prayer. As I work, God works beside me, cleaning me up, dusting away the worries, polishing the dreams that have grown dull.

As the sun dips behind the tree line and Beth arrives home from her office, I'm smiling, humming, feeling more energetic. The house may not be spotless, but polishing furniture with God has been the solace I needed. A day of work has become a day of rest.

Lord, today as I try to shovel snow in a blizzard, help my heart grow quiet, my thoughts become focused and my soul find healing in You.
—SCOTT WALKER

JUNE 21

I delight greatly in the Lord.... For he has clothed me with garments of salvation.
—Isaiah 61:10 (NIV)

I've never gotten a letter from an item of clothing—until now.

As I start to snip the large tag on the new skirt I just purchased, I notice this message on the back:

Hello! I am your special garment from Bali. I am unique and often handwoven, hand-beaded, hand-printed and hand-painted. My defects are part of my beauty! Please treat me with special care. Thank you.

I look closely at the skirt: It has huge pink flowers and wonderful lime-green leaves. Beads and sequins are worked randomly into the pattern. A silk pocket on the front rests inches from the hemline. Yes, it is unique. And, perhaps, a tad flawed. But it is lovely nonetheless. I glance at myself in a nearby mirror. Like the skirt, I'm less than perfect. I wish my hair were curly. I wish I were taller. I wish my waist...well, I wish I *had* a waist!

My defects are part of my beauty. If I can believe that of a garment, why not of myself?

As I cut the tag with the scissors and it falls into my hand, I see what's on the other side—the name brand on the skirt: FAITH.

Maybe this piece of clothing is perfect after all!

You made me in Your image, God. What a humbling
and empowering thing! Help me to understand that in loving myself—
imperfections and all—I'm also loving You.
—Mary Lou Carney

He maketh me to lie down in green pastures:
he leadeth me beside the still waters. He restoreth my soul.

—PSALM 23:2–3

*Y*ou've never been to a place like Costa Rica," a friend who had once lived there told me when he heard Shirley and I were going to travel there with our family. (We had ten in our entourage—kids, mates and grandkids.) And he was right. The people were unbelievably open and friendly, the weather when we were there in June idyllic, and the country breathtakingly beautiful— from its verdant mountains and lush valleys to its yawning shores and beryl-blue sea.

Our first destination was Arenal, a still-active volcano northwest of the capital, San Jose. We rented a van that accommodated all of us and our luggage, and slowly made our way on less-than-smooth, mountainous roads. But it was the beautiful countryside, not the bumpy thoroughfare, that captured our attention the first morning. Around every bend was a new piece of eye candy: towering rainforests, fast-flowing streams, majestic waterfalls and panoramic valleys that seemed to meander forever.

It was in one of those mountain folds that we took a midmorning rest. Cattle grazed contentedly in a high meadow above a pond that shimmered in the morning sun, and the quiet was palpable. For the first time in the hurry-scurry of packing, getting to the airport and flying to our destination, a peacefulness swept over me, that sense of well-being we all experience when we pause to really appreciate the wonders of God's handiwork, take time to see the awesomeness of His creations.

Thank You, Lord, for a world of beauty. Inspire
its preservation as our sacred duty.

—FRED BAUER

JUNE 23

The LORD is trustworthy in all he promises and faithful in all he does.
—PSALM 145:13 (NIV)

*G*et out and step away from the vehicle!"

The border guard's words were harsh. My friend and I moved uneasily to a spot about fifteen feet from our van. We had been stopped as we were leaving Yugoslavia to enter Romania back when Communism ruled eastern Europe. Inside was a load of Bibles for the Romanian underground church.

In those days I was traveling for Brother Andrew, a man known as "God's Smuggler." On this trip, as on every such mission, we had sought God's guidance and were led to this passage: "The Lord watches over you—the Lord is your shade at your right hand" (Psalm 121:5, updated NIV).

At the border, when we opened our doors, a handle came loose and clattered to the concrete. Immediately the guards became suspicious. They swarmed over the van, removing door panels, pulling out seats, examining everything from the engine compartment to the undercarriage, which they probed with a mirror on a long pole. They even rapped along the sides of the van, checking whether anything might be stuffed inside.

But they didn't find a single Bible. You see, before the trip, my friend and I had prayed the "smuggler's prayer" Brother Andrew had taught us: "Lord, when You were on earth, You made blind eyes to see, but we are taking Bibles to Your children. Please make seeing eyes blind so the guards won't see what You don't want them to see." Minutes after the guards' fruitless search, we drove off toward our rendezvous with the underground Christians, rejoicing that our cargo of seven hundred Bibles was intact.

Father, continue to remind us that Your promises never fail
so we'll trust in You, no matter what challenges we face each day.
—HAROLD HOSTETLER

JUNE 24

Hear my voice when I call, Lord.
—PSALM 27:7 (NIV)

*S*unday morning found me in the Seattle, Washington, airport, waiting to catch a plane back to Chicago. I moved through the crowded boarding area, too restless just to sit and wait. Other travelers checked their watches, read their books or worked on their laptops. But mostly, they talked on their cell phones.

I caught snatches of conversations as husbands phoned wives, sons checked in with their mothers, sisters caught up on all the news. It seemed as though everyone was talking to his or her family!

Everyone except me. I looked at my new cell phone, cute and snug in the side of my purse. Problem was, I'd forgotten to charge it the night before, and my battery was too low to make any calls. How could I have been so forgetful?

I was working myself into a bad mood when I happened to glance out the window. The sky seemed to go on forever, a pale blue broken by patches of angel-hair clouds. On the horizon, stately pine trees poked their heads toward the arching expanse. A wide-winged bird came briefly into view before veering off and soaring out of sight. And like that bird, my spirit began to rise too. *I don't need a cell phone to communicate*, I thought. So there in the midst of the hubbub of Gate C7, I closed my eyes and began a silent conversation. *Hello, Father. I just thought I'd check in with You....*

A few minutes later, as I boarded the plane, I watched the other passengers stow their cell phones. Smiling, I patted the side of my purse, grateful for the low battery that led to my leisurely preflight conversation with my heavenly Father.

> *How good it is, God, to know that I can always*
> *"phone home" and find You waiting for my call!*
> —MARY LOU CARNEY

June 25

Whose hands have gathered up the wind?
—PROVERBS 30:4 (NIV)

I watched the strong winds move across the water on my backyard pond. A storm was approaching and the wind gusts were close to twenty miles an hour.

"It's so easy to see the wind on the water now," I mused. Not so when I was a teenager vacationing in Florida. I spent the summer sunning, waterskiing and learning how to sail from a tanned blond instructor named Robby. I remember sitting in his small two-person Sunfish when he said, "You've got to maneuver the boat into the wind. Look for the breeze on the water and tack toward it." He pointed ahead to a darkening rippled area. "The wind on the water looks a bit like fish feeding below the surface."

I squinted into the sun, looking out across the water for some sign that the wind was approaching. I shook my head, frustrated. "I don't see it."

A few minutes later the wind filled our sails. Robby trimmed them and turned toward me. "We can't see the wind, but we can see its effect on the water," he said. "It's a little like noticing God in our life. We can't really see Him, but we can see His effect."

Looking out into my backyard now, I watched my grown children and young grandchildren attempt to fly a kite in the breeze. I watched the wind race across the pond, reach the kite and lift it high. My grandbabies, their soft, wispy hair blowing in all directions, ran after the kite. My children and their spouses cheered, and Misty, my oldest daughter, video camera in hand, documented it all. I joined along in the cheers, not just for the kite high in the air, but for the ability to see the effect of God's gracious love on my family and me.

Powerful Creator, may I always see Your presence in my life.
—MELODY BONNETTE

JUNE 26

And the children of Israel said to Samuel,
Cease not to cry unto the Lord our God for us.
—I SAMUEL 7:8

*W*hen I saw the name in the "From" line in my e-mailbox, I couldn't wait to open the message. Freddie and I had met in seminary and developed a friendship. After we graduated, we worked closely together at a church in Boston. People called us Batman and Robin—we were the dynamic duo of ministry. Just two months earlier, we'd reconnected while I was in Boston on business. "You look great," I told him. He was doing well and felt he was at the top of his game.

I opened Freddie's e-mail and started to read, but I couldn't get past the first line: "The doctors discovered that I have cancer, and I've had surgery."

It was too late to call, so I prayed for him. The next day I called him at home. I could barely hear him as he began sharing his ordeal. "It was touch and go, because the cancer was near the brain," he explained. "It takes faith to get through cancer. And I have a great family and caring friends." His voice got stronger as he talked about his support system.

"Freddie, I have a strong prayer network of friends," I said. "I'll ask them to pray for you."

"Thank you, Pablo. I really need their prayers."

I hung up the phone and called Efrain and Gisela in Connecticut, Maria and Pedro in Florida, Angela at the Peale Center, and Felix in Cleveland. I sent a prayer request to Guideposts Prayer Fellowship and put a few more on the Internet.

Freddie is right. It takes faith and friends to get through cancer...and a whole lot of prayer.

Lord, bless all the members of our family.
And please keep Freddie in Your special care.
—PABLO DIAZ

JUNE 27

When the day of Pentecost had come, they were all together in one place.
—ACTS 2:1 (NRSV)

O n Pentecost Sunday, we read the account in Acts of the once confused and frightened followers of Jesus empowered by the Holy Spirit to preach, heal and carry the glad news of His salvation to the ends of the earth. But Pentecost is not just a Sunday. Pentecost ends the fifty-day Easter season, making way for the six-month season after Pentecost, the longest in the year and, for me, the most challenging, because after Pentecost the story is open-ended. After Pentecost the story is still being written. For the twenty-six weeks after Pentecost, the Word asks what I am doing with the Spirit's gift.

I'm uncomfortable with the second half of the year. Me, carry the sacred story forward? Me, become Jesus' hands and feet and voice? How can I? How would I know His will? How would I find the strength? By coming together, the Word tells me on Pentecost, with other believers. Pentecost is the birthday of the church, that great body assembled "from every nation, from all tribes and peoples and languages" (Revelation 7:9, NRSV). On Pentecost I renew my commitment to church attendance and to joining with fellow believers wherever I can. It is when we gather all together in one place that the Spirit gives us wisdom and power. It's from that place that He sends us out, as He sent the disciples on Pentecost, to carry His blessings to the world.

Holy Spirit, draw us together, that when we go each to our own assignment, we may go in the strength that comes only from You.
—ELIZABETH SHERRILL

JUNE 28

The Lord...be not far from every one of us.
—ACTS 17:27

*W*hen my brother Bob and I were small boys growing up in Ohio, our father used to take us sometimes to an amusement park where one of the attractions was a maze, a labyrinth of artfully planned mirrors in which it was possible to get completely lost. Wherever you looked, whichever passage you chose, you ended by running into a reflection of yourself.

Being a minister, my father couldn't resist pointing out a moral. "This maze," he would say, "is just like life. No matter where you go, you can't escape from yourself. So you had better try to be a worthwhile person, because you'll never get away from that person no matter what you do!"

That was a valid lesson, and I remember it still. But what I remember best is the very first time we entered the maze and I somehow got separated from Bob and my father. Becoming more and more panicky, I finally cried for help. What a relief it was to hear my father's strong, reassuring tones: "This way, Norman. I'm right over here. Just follow my voice. I'm right over here!"

And so he was. What a blessing it was to find him. And what a blessing it is to know that whenever we're feeling lost or panicky as we move through life, a Person of infinite strength and love is calling out to us, "Just follow My voice and you'll find the Way. I'm right over here!"

Dear Savior, teach us to reach for Your hand,
knowing that it will always be there.
—NORMAN VINCENT PEALE

JUNE 29

So let us not grow weary in doing what is right,
for we will reap at harvest time, if we do not give up.
—GALATIANS 6:9 (NRSV)

*T*he note was on my desk the last day of school. It read: "Thanks for putting up with me. I guess maybe some of what you said is right. At least I'm willing to let God back into my life—for a while, anyway. Your student, Dina."

Not much of a confession of faith, but to me it was a rainbow in a cloud-darkened sky. I teach religion at a girls' school, and our students can't graduate without passing two semesters with me—and God.

Dina sat through the first few days of class with a belligerent smirk. After a class discussion on the nature of God's love, she angrily announced, "This is all a bunch of junk. I used to believe that, but when I needed God, He wasn't there for me. I learned you can't expect anything from anyone—especially God." She folded her arms across her chest and gave me a "Now what are you going to do?" look.

Refusing to take the bait, I said, "Lots of people feel that way when they've been hurt. But the truth about God doesn't depend on how we feel, but on who He is. Keep your mind open. Keep listening. Class dismissed."

It was a long semester. Dina kept challenging, testing, questioning. Some days I was sure her defiance was beginning to crack; at other times she seemed more resistant than ever. By semester's end, I was certain I'd done nothing to draw her closer to God; I only hoped I hadn't driven her farther away.

And then I found the note. It reminded me again that it's God Who brings the harvest; all I have to do is be faithful to my part of the process. I tucked Dina's note in my pocket and said a quick prayer. My teaching time with her was over, but I knew His was just beginning.

Lord, help me to remember to be a faithful worker
in the field where You place me.
—PAMELA KENNEDY

JUNE 30

Then shall all the trees of the wood rejoice.
—PSALM 96:12

I've always loved trees. As a child, I had a favorite neighborhood tree in which I'd sit to read my book. I can't remember what my college professors looked like, but I can describe the autumnal pinkish-orange of a glowing young maple on campus. As a young mother, I admired an elegant fir holding court in a bare field. My children and I called her the "Queen Tree." Today I can show you where a gnarled old soldier of an apple tree used to grow near our Minnesota home before a country road was widened.

Trees have always been friends, but on one particular day they offered me a special comfort. It was time to leave my home in the Alaskan woods. For ten years, as the children grew to young adulthood, I had waved them off on their adventures from this sturdy sheltering house.

Now my husband had gone ahead to a new job in another state. I was the last one to leave our home. As I locked its doors and paused in the rutted drive for a final look, I thought forlornly, *Who's going to wave good-bye to me?* I felt suddenly overwhelmed by the new path my life was taking.

Just then my eyes were drawn to the tall, supple birch trees encircling me. They were bending and swaying in the wind, dozens of them, waving their leafy boughs in a group farewell. My trees, in God's perfect timing, were the ones to wave good-bye.

> *Loving God, Maker of all things, make me aware*
> *of Your presence through the things You have made.*
> —CAROL KNAPP

July

*Make every effort to add to your faith goodness; and to goodness, knowledge; and
to knowledge, self-control; and to self-control, perseverance; and to perseverance,
godliness; and to godliness, mutual affection; and to mutual affection, love.*
—II PETER 1:5–7 (NIV)

*W*hen I raise my blind in the morning, I see velvet-red roses at my
window, given to me by my mother. Sometimes the large blossoms
are slightly bowed with raindrops glistening on the leaves, beautiful works of
art. But it was not always so.

The plant was struggling to survive when I moved it from my old home
where, truth to tell, I had neglected it. After transplanting it and myself, I read
up on roses and watered the plant faithfully. I fed it and sometimes buried cut
banana peelings in the soil (gives needed phosphorus, one book said). I checked
the leaves for aphids and black spots, and used the appropriate sprays. With all
this attention, the plant came alive.

I'm not so unlike my roses. When Jesus came to live in my heart, I received
His divine nature. But I must cultivate the love and faithfulness that were
planted then, or I won't grow to my full potential. What God has worked in, I
am to work out with diligence.

*Dear Father, help me make every effort to nurture
the fruit of the Spirit in my life.*
—HELEN GRACE LESCHEID

*Therefore, if anyone is in Christ, the new creation
has come: The old has gone, the new is here!*
—II CORINTHIANS 5:17 (NIV)

Rwanda is one of the jewels of Africa, a Maryland-sized place with verdant peaks, crystalline lakes and one of the world's last populations of rare mountain gorillas. It's also desperately poor; most of Rwanda's people survive on incomes of less than a dollar a day. Recently I traveled to Rwanda for my job with a business magazine.

One afternoon I went out to the countryside, to a small town where seventy-six women, all survivors of the nation's 1994 genocide, have formed a cooperative to knit scarves. For some of these women, their handiwork—which, by the time it reaches markets in the United States, can go for eighty dollars apiece—is producing the first earned income they've ever had. They told me their business opportunity had given them a new sense of empowerment and hope for the future. They could pay their children's school fees. They could buy extra food. One woman proudly showed off the outfit she had bought—her first new skirt and top in ages. Then the president of the cooperative shared a Rwandan proverb: "If you don't know where you've come from, you won't know where to go." They doubly appreciated what they had because they had not only been through extreme poverty but had also faced the prospect of imminent death.

As I listened, it struck me that it wouldn't be a bad idea if I looked at my life with that proverb in mind. After all, Jesus has saved me from certain death. How can I forget where I've come from?

*Lord, help me to remember where I've been, so I can better
understand how blessed is the path You've paved for me.*
—JEFF CHU

JULY 3

*The Lord is my shepherd; I shall not want.... He leadeth me beside
the still waters.... I will fear no evil; for thou art with me.*
—PSALM 23:1–2, 4

My wife Beth, our son Jodie and I were on vacation in the mountains near Lake Lure, North Carolina. One day while we were hiking along the banks of the Broad River, we stopped to gaze at a series of small rapids cascading down to the lake. Suddenly I looked upstream and saw a mother mallard duck and five ducklings approaching the swirling rapids. The ducklings seemed like puffs of fluff, too fragile to negotiate the dangerous waters.

As they approached the rapids, the mother duck scooted in front of the ducklings and they swung behind her in single file. With determination, she led them over the first drop, watched each of them disappear underwater and bob to the surface, and then herded them to the shoreline and calm water. After a few minutes rest, she led the ducklings back into the swift current, down the next rapid and back to the safety of the still water. Slowly they made their way downstream, one challenging descent at a time.

That mother duck and her obedient ducklings have become a spiritual symbol for me. They remind me of the way God leads me through turbulent waters. When I'm anxious or afraid, I'd like to remember that God is in the river with me, guiding me over the rapids, one challenge at a time, and on to still water.

*Lord, when the currents become treacherous, remind me
that You are with me, guiding me toward safety and rest. Amen.*
—SCOTT WALKER

JULY 4

Thou hast given a banner to them that fear thee.
—PSALM 60:4

*I*n 2001, New Yorkers celebrated the 225th anniversary of the Revolutionary War battles of 1776 with a series of reenactments. I took my then-five-year-old son John to several of them. John loved the colorful uniforms, the lively fife-and-drum music and the demonstrations of musket firing and infantry tactics. And like most little boys, he was especially excited by the profusion of souvenirs offered in tents full of craftspeople and vendors.

The things that appealed to John didn't always fit our budget, but one that particularly fascinated him did: a set of miniature flags of the Revolutionary period. There was the First Navy Jack, showing a rattlesnake on a field of red and white stripes with the legend "Don't Tread on Me"; the Grand Union flag, with thirteen stripes and the British Union Jack in the upper left corner; and the "Betsy Ross" flag, with a circle of thirteen stars in place of the Union Jack. But the flag that caught my attention was the Pine Tree flag that had flown over the floating batteries in Boston Harbor: a green pine tree on a field of white, bearing the legend "An Appeal to Heaven."

I think those Massachusetts patriots had a point: To be at our best as a nation, we have to be aware that our existence as a country is dependent on the One Who rules all the nations. No matter how tall the building or how high the mountain from which our flag flies, heaven is higher still.

Father, as we honor Old Glory on this Independence Day, remind us that in our national life as in our personal life, You are always our Lord.
—ANDREW ATTAWAY

July 5

The Lord gave Job twice as much as he had before.
—Job 42:10

Words from the Sea, Day 1: Awe

*H*ere near our friends' house the shore is all rocks, with no place to walk. But a short path along the bluff leads to a long, sandy beach. Or it did, in other years.

Even before unpacking the car, John and I set out down that path, eager to stretch our legs after the five-hour drive. We were stopped short by an impassable jumble of rocks left by a winter storm. The blocked beach access, I thought, was just one more example of how cherished things can be snatched away. The recent death of a close friend had made me extra sensitive to any loss—like our dogwood tree back home, killed by invading beetles. Even the closing of a favorite bakery seemed part of the pattern.

A few days later we found a roundabout way down to the beach. Finally we could make our customary walk to the outlet, our reluctant turnaround point, a broad stream where a swamp emptied into the ocean. But... "Surely," said John when we'd walked for twenty-five minutes, "we should have come to the outlet by now!" But the beach stretched on unbroken; before us lay miles of sandy coastline we'd never before explored. The same storm that had blocked the bluff path had sealed off the outlet and opened a new walking route. When God takes away something precious, the ocean tells me, He sends another gift in its place.

Father, I have lost my friend. What new avenue
of love will You open to me today?
—Elizabeth Sherrill

JULY 6

There is the sea, vast and spacious.
—PSALM 104:25 (NIV)

WORDS FROM THE SEA, DAY 2: AWE

oday from the porch, the ocean is speaking to me about vastness—about a horizon stretching beyond the limit of sight. Our home in suburban New York is at the bottom of a hill. Except for a wedge of sky above the trees, everything you can see is close by. The lawn, some shrubs and the houses on either side make up the view. But here on the coast! To the left the shoreline curves away into the distance; to the right, on clear days, you can make out the low silhouette of an island. Everywhere else is a boundless expanse of water—blue or gray or silver—beneath the immense dome of the sky.

Reluctant to leave the porch this morning, I've brought a pad and pencil with me to write out my shopping list. It's a long drive to the nearest stores and, with the price of gas, we keep trips to a minimum. Bread, milk, eggs, paper towels...we're low on all these things. A birthday card. Suntan lotion. Laundry detergent. If I don't write it all down, I'll forget something. But somehow I don't pick up the pencil. Not yet. Not while my eyes are gazing at a world stretching to infinity. Not while my mind is staggered by the immensity of God's creation.

Of course, I'll make that list: food, cleaning supplies, a birthday card—these are the details of living that Jesus made important by living our daily lives with us. It's just that amid the thousand details there also needs to be time to exclaim with the angels:

Holy, holy, holy Lord!
—ELIZABETH SHERRILL

July 7

There the ships go to and fro.
—Psalm 104:26 (NIV)

Words from the Sea, Day 3: Connectedness

From the beach this afternoon I spotted a majestic schooner far offshore, tall white sails tilting in the wind. I watched it through binoculars till it was out of sight, bound, no doubt, for Newport. Newport is nearby, at least by water. By land it's a long, slow, twisting route following the coast. And watching that schooner skimming straight to its destination, I suddenly saw the ocean not as the place where roads end, but as the open highway that first connected the earth's far-flung people. Long before reliable roads were built, the sea and the rivers flowing into it were the principal route for conquest, trade, settlement.

Three months earlier I'd also stood on a beach watching boats at sea. The sea was the Gulf of Thailand, and the graceful women walking past spoke a language I didn't know. We give names to particular stretches of water—South Pacific, Indian Ocean, North Atlantic—but, of course, it's all one ocean, one great waterway circling the earth. It's twilight now, and I've walked down to the point to watch the setting sun lay a golden trail across the water. Maybe, I think, one of those Thai women is watching this sun rise over the ocean this very moment. Maybe she, like me, is murmuring a prayer to the Creator of land and sea.

Help me see all the people of the world, Father, held in Your single embrace as Your single ocean enfolds the earth.
—Elizabeth Sherrill

JULY 8

Let us not become weary in doing good, for at the proper time
we will reap a harvest if we do not give up.
—GALATIANS 6:9 (NIV)

WORDS FROM THE SEA, DAY 4: PERSISTENCE

t was warm enough this afternoon to pull off my shoes and go wading—gingerly. I hadn't gone barefoot in a long time, and stones and pebbles were hard to see in the swirling water. Every time I stepped on one, it hurt. Afterward I sat on the sand, letting my feet dry, watching the gentle rush and retreat of the waves, listening to the rattle of stones in the surf. Those stones, I thought, were like the hard, hurting things in my life: the job that wouldn't go right no matter how long I worked at it; the relationship that remained broken no matter what I did.

There's something mesmerizing about waves. Instead of getting up, I nestled deeper into the soft sand, hypnotized by the water's motion. Pressing forward and withdrawing, advancing and retiring, endlessly dragging the stones back and forth; all day, all night, through years and centuries, rolling the stones over and over. Making sand.

Of course! It was this ceaseless advance and retreat of the ocean, wave after wave, never stopping, never giving up, that had turned hard stones into the yielding sand where I sat. I stood up and started back to the house...to the waiting task, to one more effort at reaching out.

Whatever job confronts me, Father, let the waves
remind me that quitting is the only sure way to fail.
—ELIZABETH SHERRILL

July 9

There is the sea...teeming with creatures beyond
number—living things both large and small.
—Psalm 104:25 (NIV)

Words from the Sea, Day 5: Life

A few hundred yards offshore this morning, a whale broke the surface of the water. I saw its dark rolling back for only a single tantalizing moment. But the thrill of that brief sighting has had me thinking all day about life in the ocean. Evidence of it lined the beach where I went walking: quahog shells, mussels, slippers, limpets, periwinkles; shore creatures feeding on the ocean's bounty; tern diving for fish; a gull feasting on the carapace of a horseshoe crab; a flock of sanderlings chasing the retreating waves. People, too, were harvesting the sea's riches, from the man in wading boots casting for bluefish as I passed to the lobster catcher I watched as he checked his pots.

But other things were on the beach today besides signs of life. By the end of my walk I'd picked up two bottles, a plastic ring-holder from a six-pack, a deflated beach ball and the remnants of a Styrofoam cup. And this before the season here begins; where there's been, yet, no oil spill; where, though overfished and partly contaminated, the sea still yields a small but precious catch.

I thought of the satellite photo of our ocean planet that hangs on my office wall—a startling blue jewel in the blackness of space, the only place in the universe we know of with liquid water. *What have you done,* the ocean asked me, *with this unique creation, God's laboratory of life, His incomparable gift?*

Father, show me how to cherish, protect and preserve
the world on which You've lavished the water of life.
—Elizabeth Sherrill

JULY 10

You change them like clothing, and they pass away;
but you are the same, and your years have no end.

—PSALM 102:26–27 (NRSV)

WORDS FROM THE SEA, DAY 6: CHANGE

*T*he seascape here is never twice the same, not just from one day to the next, but minute to minute. Seconds ago the whole surface was pewter gray; now it shimmers like silver. It can be as smooth as the "glassy sea" of Revelation or a churning froth of whitecaps.

This morning I sat on the porch, watching long, slow swells roll in to explode against the large rock just offshore, now lashing the base of the rock, now shooting straight up, now cascading clear over the top, chasing away the cormorants who settle there to dry their outstretched wings.

No two encounters of wave and rock are alike. Yesterday an artist set up her easel on the beach. I watched as, with her watercolors, she captured a split second in a wave's onward rush, stopped it, held it motionless forever.

That's what I'm always trying to do, I thought, looking at the living ocean before me, *with the circumstances of my life.* As though stasis, things-as-they-are, were God's plan for His world. Everything in that world, of course, tells me the opposite—tells me that no created thing stays the same for long. And nowhere does God speak to me so clearly of His forever making all things new as here beside His ever-changing sea.

Help me rejoice in the newness of Your world today, Father, in the serenity
of knowing that You are the same—yesterday, today and forever.

—ELIZABETH SHERRILL

July 11

One thing I ask from the Lord, this only do I seek...
to gaze on the beauty of the Lord.
—Psalm 27:4 (NIV)

Words from the Sea, Day 7: Beauty

*T*he bedroom windows here face east. Through them come the sound of the surf, the salt air of the sea and, of course, around 5:00 a.m., the light of the rising sun. Usually I groan and reach for my eye mask. Today, though, a Carolina wren sang so urgently somewhere nearby that I threw off the covers, dressed and headed down the road to my favorite vantage point at the water's edge.

On the dunes the rugosa roses were in bloom. I caught their fragrance before I saw them—white, pink, maroon. The tide was ebbing, leaving behind a carpet of glistening stones. I sat on a flat-topped rock and watched the incoming waves rise, curl, spill over. For an instant, as each wave crested, the early sun shining through it turned it translucent emerald green.

Beauty—the sheer, extravagant beauty of God's creation is what the ocean is calling me to see today. Tomorrow we have to leave this house by the shore, and I've wondered how I can bear to say good-bye to the salt air and blue water. The ocean is speaking to me about just that. *Open your eyes!* it says. *See the beauty of a raindrop as well as the beauty of a wave, a chipmunk as well as a whale, the potted plant in your kitchen as well as a wild dune rose. You've learned to look keenly here by the sea; look as keenly back home.*

Let me never call unlovely, Father, anything You've made.
—Elizabeth Sherrill

He shall give thee the desires of thine heart.
—PSALM 37:4

*M*y husband Gene and I had to have our beloved seventeen-year-old cat Minnie put to sleep. Gene didn't want another cat, but after two catless years I adopted a shelter cat—without talking it over with Gene first. He grew to love Girl Friend, but we made a pact: I wouldn't rescue any more cats. But I kept having a dream: I go out the door and discover an abandoned kitten, and I lovingly gather it up and take it inside.

One hot summer morning, while watering my ferns out back, I heard a squeak. *Oh no, not another baby bird fallen from the nest!*

I checked the bushes and there stood a weary, unbelievably tiny, hungry kitten. *However have you managed to get into our backyard?*

Sitting in the middle of our kitchen floor, I fed the little thing and spoke softly to it. Girl Friend sauntered by and hissed. Gene bellowed, "What's that?"

Joy darted around my heart as though I were a little girl. I had no idea just how much I needed to find a kitten—and keep it. In time, Girl Friend and Gene adjusted.

The kitten was a gift from God, so I named the new addition to our family Grace. Amazing Grace—she once was lost but now is found. I call her Gracie. She's a constant reminder of how often God surprises us with the very desire of our hearts.

My Father, to think You created this world and
still cared enough to give me an abandoned kitten!
—MARION BOND WEST

July 13

And said unto them, It is written, My house shall be called the house of prayer....
And all things, whatsoever ye shall ask in prayer, believing, ye shall receive.

—Matthew 21:13, 22

My ninety-three-year-old mother was recently hospitalized with congestive heart failure. When I arrived at her bedside in the critical care unit, I was shocked and saddened to see that tubes were keeping her alive. Because of her curved windpipe (created by osteoporosis), her already weakened heart and her now-congested lungs, the doctors held out little hope that she would survive. But the doctors hadn't counted on the First Baptist Church, where Mother had been a member for more than fifty-five years.

When Mother was first taken in the ambulance to the emergency room, she asked my sister to call her home church and put her on their prayer list. The pastor later called us to inquire after Mother and offered to drive the one hundred fifty miles if she needed him. For the next several days, we kept in touch. I asked for prayer that we would not be required to make any decision about the life-support system. In addition to the prayer line, church members also prayed for Mother at the Sunday morning and evening services.

They must have prayed a miracle, because after four days, the life support was removed and Mother returned to my sister's house—weak, still congested, but on the road to recovery.

Thank You, Lord, for church congregations that pray and believe they will receive.

—Patricia Pingry

JULY 14

Thy kingdom is an everlasting kingdom, and thy dominion
endureth throughout all generations.
—PSALM 145:13

*I*t had been five months since my sister Maria died in her sleep, and now I was in the cemetery, sitting at her grave and remembering. Living in the same town, Maria and I were more than sisters; we were best friends. I always thought we'd have so much time together. I used to picture us grown old, sitting in lawn chairs at the neighborhood pool, talking about our grandchildren. Then, without warning, the future I'd looked forward to was gone. All that seemed to remain was this little plot of land.

My mother and I had done our best to make it joyful. We'd planted flowers and decorated the grave with a garden gnome, an angel statue, cut flowers, seashells and sand from our family vacation spot on Cape Cod. The cosmos had grown tall and burst with blooms in shades of pink and white. As I sat, thinking about Maria, I began to pluck the spent flowers from the stems. Maria had often laughed at my lack of knowledge about them. Was it only a year ago I'd held up an iris bulb and asked her which way it went into the ground? Collecting the cosmos' dead heads, I became filled with loss. *What if there is nothing?* I thought. *What if my sister is just gone?* Without thinking, I began to twist the dead blossoms in my hand, gripping them as I cried. Finally, I pulled myself together and opened my hands to see my palms covered with seeds.

I smiled at the much-needed message: Death is not the end. Like flowers, it holds the seeds of a new beginning.

Father, Your love is always there. Help me to feel
Your comfort, especially during times of sorrow.
—SABRA CIANCANELLI

JULY 15

Turn, O Lord, save my life; deliver me for the sake of your steadfast love.
—PSALM 6:4 (NRSV)

Like any adult of a certain age, I've had my share of existential crises: *Who am I? What am I doing here? Why does my car always break down?*

This last question came to me beneath my beat-up minivan. The way I figured it, even if I found a way to liberate the starter and revive the van, I'd only be breaking even. The van wouldn't run better; it would simply run.

"What's the point?" I said aloud.

As I turned the drive shaft to get a better angle for my ratchet, I heard it: the sound of the car moving...off the ramps... onto me.

Luckily, I had blocked the back wheels, so I'm still here to tell you this story. One false move—say, forgetting to block the back wheels—and my wife is picking out my funeral suit.

Breaking even is not, I repeat, *not* a bad thing. Life is a struggle, but it beats the options. Life is an opera full of joy and tragedy and swift scene changes and amazing, unexpected arias. And—get this—we're not the audience. We figure out the script as we go, singing our roles (no rehearsal) as best we can. And it isn't over till the fat lady sings...or the jack slips.

In my particular scene from my unique opera, I replaced the starter. It was the most joyful, blessed, break-even thing I have ever done.

Whether I'm at the footlights or in the wings, from the overture to the final curtain, my life is in Your hands, Lord.
—MARK COLLINS

July 16

Behold, I make all things new.
—Revelation 21:5

Probably it has to do with my senior citizen status, but I simply cannot keep up with the myriad of new equipment continually coming out to make me more efficient. A friend showed me something that looked like a lipstick tube smashed flat. "Our company's entire records are on this flash drive." She inserted it into her computer and information appeared "out of thin air," as my mother used to say about things she didn't understand. Mom would've been amazed at knowing cell phones are being used for talking, texting, taking photos, making movies and playing music.

My mind boggles when I try to imagine my words joining billions of other visuals and voices and sounds and radio/TV talk and pictures all swimming around out there in the ether of Earth's atmosphere. What keeps them from mixing? I often long for what we senior citizens refer to as the "simple days." I identify with the slogan, "Stop the world—I want to get off!" But a little boy helped put my wishes into perspective when I asked him, "What did you learn in Sunday school today?" He brightened and confidentially told me, "God is good and He loves us kids."

Dear Father, when I become bewildered with the many new inventions bombarding me, it's so comforting to know You will never be improved upon because You, Your Word and Your workings never go out of date!

—Isabel Wolseley

JULY 17

He shall gather the lambs with his arm, and carry them in his bosom.
—ISAIAH 40:11

The early morning phone call surprised me; my friend Laurie was on the verge of tears. "Gail, I'm beside myself. Nicole got her driver's license yesterday, so she's driving to school today—without me! I'm so worried. You've done this before..." She paused, helpless. As if on cue, Nicole, who is her oldest child, drove up, and Trina, my youngest, bolted out the door of the house for her ride.

I flashed back to Tom at sixteen learning to drive. Would I ever forget the near miss with the cottonwood tree? "Just start braking way before you want to stop, honey," I said as I dug my nails into the armrest.

Then I thought of Trina's recent icy spin that had sent her into a snowbank. No injuries, just minor dents. Oh yes, I'd done this before. How my prayer life had revved into high gear once my kids started driving!

"I know how you feel," I told Laurie. "Believe me! But Nicole's a cautious driver. She's not wild or reckless, right?"

"Right."

"She has a new car and good tires, right?"

Fewer sniffles now. "Right."

"She's even got a cell phone and her little brother watching the gauges with her."

"But I'm not with her..."

"Look, Laurie. Do what I did—give her to God. I mean, really picture it. See yourself holding Nicole in your arms. Got it? Now hand her over to God. He's holding her now. She's safe in His arms. We all are."

Laurie seemed to be thinking this over. "I feel better now."

"Good. Call me again when she gets home."

Good Shepherd, teach me to share the ways You comfort me. Amen.
—GAIL THORELL SCHILLING

JULY 18

Thou in thy mercy hast led forth the people which thou hast redeemed.
—EXODUS 15:13

Last July I stood in the backyard of my cousin's Michigan farmhouse and watched a noisy thunderstorm sweep eastward in the darkening night sky. Huge cumulus clouds bubbled and boiled as the winds rolled them into the stratosphere. Lightning flashes exploded inside mountains of clouds. The drumming power continued its incessant pounding from within until bolts of light burst out and stabbed at the land below. The mountains of clouds seemed held in the sky by the brilliant white stilts of lightning.

I began counting as the long silver stilts steadied the fluorescent cloud heads. At the count of two, distant thunder that had begun with a whispering rumble burst into a crash. I was safe; the lightning had grounded two miles away.

I blew out a breath of relief and glanced down at a hedge separating the lawn from a field of ripening grain. A tiny light blinked off and on as it bounced quietly on top of the hedge. It was a lonesome lightning bug bobbing along like a cork on a gentle sea.

That night I saw a demonstration of both the power and the gentleness of God, two gifts He gives me daily. He gives me power to walk the road of life with His guidance and uses gentleness in love and forgiveness along the way.

Thank You, Lord, for Your power and gentleness.
May the life I live reflect my thanks.
—RICHARD HAGERMAN

JULY 19

But as for me, I will look to the Lord.
—MICAH 7:7 (NRSV)

On our trip through the Grand Canyon, my husband Keith and I listened carefully to the lecture on avoiding scorpions. "A bite from the big black ones hurts pretty badly," the guide said. "The little gold ones can kill you." He told us to check our sleeping areas before going to bed and to avoid sticking our hands or feet into anything without looking inside it first.

"If I get bitten, you'll be the first to know," I warned Keith. "I couldn't suffer it alone."

In the middle of the night, I felt a sharp pain in the left side of my neck. I sat upright in my sleeping bag and grabbed the flashlight out of my shoe. Pain radiated from the spot, past my eye and into my head. *Lord, be with me,* I prayed. Just as I flicked on the light, the black scorpion skittered away. A black one! *Thank You, Lord!*

I yanked open my backpack and pulled out the ointment we carried for red ant bites. I applied it liberally to my neck, hoping it would bring some relief. The pain lessened a little, and I finally thought to wake up Keith.

"You handled all that alone?" Keith asked, surprised.

Not alone at all. Not by a long shot.

Lord, please help me remember that I never suffer alone.
—RHODA BLECKER

July 20

Call unto me, and I will answer.
—Jeremiah 33:3

Church has always been like home to me. But the letter had changed all that. Written and distributed by a local couple, the letter condemned almost everything my husband David and I had worked for and believed in.

On this particular Sunday morning, I sought solace in the "prayer place" I had set aside in our guest bedroom. "God," I prayed, "it's almost time to leave for church. I'm on empty. Alone. Confused. Are You out there, God?"

Be still. Wait. The words seemed to come from nowhere.

At church, I waited until everyone was seated for the early service and then chose a spot near the back. David sat up front, waiting to deliver the sermon. To his left, Stephen Nix, who leads the band in our early service, began to play a lovely tune.

"Listen to that still, small voice speaking to your heart," he began singing. "Telling you don't be afraid, you're not alone...." Then the chorus came: "He loves you, He knows you, He's calling out your name." I was swathed in pure love. My sorrow melted. I felt I could waltz in midair.

After the final hymn, as I made my way toward the front, I surprised myself by offering a smile and a soft "hello" to the sad-faced letter-writers.

Stephen and the band were gone, but the sheet music was still on the stand. I read each word carefully. And then my eyes fell on the title: "He's Calling Out Your Name," words and music by Stephen Nix. Copyright © 2000.

In response to my morning prayer, Stephen had delivered my Father's message to me at just the right moment.

God, thank You for giving Stephen the words I needed.
Make me the messenger to the very one who needs them now.
—Pam Kidd

JULY 21

So then, just as you received Christ Jesus as Lord,
continue to live your lives in him.
—COLOSSIANS 2:6 (NIV)

*I*t's not easy to bounce back and trust when you have lost a child. After our son Reggie died in an accident a few years ago, Rosie and I wanted to keep our younger son Ryan close, protect him and not let him go.

A couple of summers ago, Ryan participated in an internship program and was required to attend a national conference in Philadelphia. We thought he would be traveling from Mississippi with some of his fellow interns, but it turned out Ryan would be going alone.

We were fearful and stayed near the phone, waiting for him to call. Ryan telephoned from his layover in Atlanta, excited to tell us that a family friend had been on the plane with him, was going to the same conference and would accompany him all the way to the hotel in Philadelphia.

When Ryan called again to let us know he had arrived safely, we praised God for His goodness. We are still learning to walk in Colossians 2:6.

Lord, I know that You are our Lord every day. I ask
that You enable me to continue to live in You.
—DOLPHUS WEARY

JULY 22

Your beauty should not come from outward adornment.... Rather, it should be that of your inner self, the unfading beauty of a gentle and quiet spirit.
—I Peter 3:3–4 (NIV)

When Daniel, the youngest of our four children, was a little boy, we collected seashells together on a Florida beach that has become a part of our family history. Early morning beachcombing is always an adventure—you never know what the sea will have cast up overnight—and the kids always competed to see who could find the neatest shell. Each was looking for a sparkler—a conch or olive unmarred, unbroken and undulled by countless tumblings in the tide.

All, that is, except Daniel. A broken piece of pen shell, iridescent in the just-blooming sun, was as special to him as a shiny turkey wing or vivid pink bay scallop. In his eyes a shell didn't have to be in perfect condition to be a keeper, admired and treasured.

Too often, it seems to me, we reject—sometimes subconsciously—people and things because of their imperfections, forgetting that we ourselves have many blemishes. I once saw these words inscribed on a pulpit for the benefit of the preacher: WE WOULD SEE JESUS. With effort and practice, some people have learned to look beneath the surface and find Jesus in everything and everyone. We may not be able to see the hearts of others as He can, but we can try.

Sharpen my eyes and ears, God, sensitize my soul,
So I hear unspoken words, see the doughnut, not the hole.
—FRED BAUER

July 23

I was seated in church with my grandson Caleb, age five. He reached for the small pencil and envelope used for recording attendance and giving, and said, "This is so you can write, 'I love You, God.'" God wrote an entire book saying "I love you" to the human race. But not once did I ever think of scribbling those words on a pew envelope to be offered at the altar in blessing to Him.

My granddaughter Hannah, age seven, once sang me a song she had learned in summer Bible school about following Jesus. She paused midsentence to say, "I know how you turn back on the path to God."

"How?" I asked.

"When you read the Bible and pray and obey the commandments...and then you stop."

Her explanation was so stark and pure I felt myself squirm. I had been experiencing a season of struggle regarding those very issues. I needed a jolt. I found myself backing away from that abrupt edge, the "stop." I wanted once again to open my Bible and pray and have a heart to obey—to move forward on the holy path. I missed saying, "I love You, God."

*Jesus, in the pages of my Bible, I find Your reassuring promises
telling me I can start following Your path anytime.*
—CAROL KNAPP

JULY 24

And a little child shall lead them.
—ISAIAH 11:6

*E*veryone was stunned by my daughter-in-law Cheryl's death. How could this happen? How could her husband Paul and their eight children bear such wrenching grief? How would Paul manage, with four children still at home, ages fourteen, nine, seven and five? He was working long hours, and the four grown children were living on their own, with full-time jobs. There were no easy answers and so many hard decisions that no one had ever expected to make.

Robert and I went with Paul, Cheryl's brother Steve and Amy (age fourteen) to the mortuary to help make arrangements. Together we chose a casket and a time and place for the funeral. We talked with the minister, chose Scriptures, music and a poem, and arranged for Cheryl to be buried next to her mother.

In the afternoon, my daughter Karen and the older children went to buy a new dress for Cheryl and picked out a pretty cross pendant with lavender stones to match.

While they were gone, five-year-old Kayla sat down by me and started telling me about the school supplies her mother had bought for her. My heart ached for my granddaughter, who was starting kindergarten next week without her mother. And I thought, *Kayla doesn't fully realize the terrible thing that has happened.*

Then her soft blue eyes looked up into mine and she said, "You know, Grandma, I won't see Mommy anymore because she died. But she still loves me, and she can see me from heaven." In that moment, some tight place in me was released, and I hugged Kayla and affirmed that what she had said was true. By the grace of God and with the help of a child's pure faith, I trust that Paul's family will make it through this tragedy.

O Holy Spirit, grant us faith to bear our grief.
—MARILYN MORGAN KING

JULY 25

As the hart panteth after the water brooks, so panteth my soul after thee, O God.
—PSALM 42:1

"Pam, the canoe's ready!" David called from the patio of our lake cabin.

"Who said anything about a canoe?" I called back, not moving from my comfy chair in the cool recesses of the house.

David slid open the door and looked at me, perturbed. "This morning you were lamenting over how long it's been since you've had a ride in the canoe. Now I've pulled it out of storage, cleaned it up, dragged it down to the lake... and I'm waiting."

It was hot outside—sweltering, actually. And I was immersed in a good summer read. I was perfectly happy lolling in cool comfort, but I had, as David said, "lamented," so I didn't really have a choice.

A few minutes later, we were gliding out into the lake. I sat in the front and David paddled in the back. The lake was as smooth as silk. The sky was iridescent blue. The only sound was the swish as David pulled the paddle in and out of the water. Up ahead a blue heron skimmed so near the surface of the lake, we could see its wing tips touch its reflection in the water. It was enough to set me to praying, silently thanking God for the beauty that stretched out in every direction.

"Gosh, David," I said finally, "this feels so good. It's exactly what I needed. You lured me away from the lazies, and I appreciate it."

The truth is, with thermostats and storm windows and air-conditioned cars, it's easy to miss whatever waits, at this very minute, outside our windows and beyond our doors. It might be a symphony of night sounds, twinkling stars or a morning sunrise. Is the wind blowing? Is a gentle rain falling? Whether or not you and I think it, sitting in our comfort zones, our souls long for God and for the beauty He created. Look! Listen! He waits!

Father, within Your presence, I find a perfect peace...and I praise You.
—PAM KIDD

And every one that heareth these sayings of mine, and doeth them not,
shall be likened unto a foolish man, which built his house upon the sand:
And the rain descended, and the floods came, and the winds blew,
and beat upon that house; and it fell: and great was the fall of it.
—MATTHEW 7:26–27

The children's sermon quiz was "What is the shortest verse in the Bible?" "God is love" was my first thought. The answer: "Jesus wept," in the passage that describes Lazarus being raised from the dead (John 11:35). That got me to wondering how short a devotional I could write. Here's my attempt.

Last year we decided to remodel our Indiana lake cottage that has been in the family since 1910. I wanted to save as much of the original building as possible, but the carpenter balked. "Putting up new walls over an old foundation won't work," he advised.

When I hesitated, he asked if I knew what happened to the guy who built his house upon sand. His point made—we both knew the parable told by another carpenter, or maybe more correctly, a carpenter's Son—a new footing was poured.

If you build your house (your life) upon rock (God's Word) and not upon sand (temporal things), Jesus told His listeners, you will be safe and saved from all winds and floods (forces that would separate you from God's love)—now and forever. That's the short version of a very long truth.

> *Help us, Lord, to see the big picture,*
> *Eternity's part in this life's mixture.*
>
> —FRED BAUER

July 27

*I have come into the world as a light, so that no one
who believes in me should stay in darkness.*
—John 12:46 (NIV)

I've had to make some difficult decisions in my life, but one of the hardest was the decision to come back to Mississippi. When I left as a young man, I vowed never to return. But I felt that God was calling my wife Rosie and me back to Mendenhall. We had to put our own wishes aside and answer that call. Even after twenty-five-plus years of working in this impoverished rural community, it's a decision I have to renew often.

Recently, someone asked me, "Dolphus, do you ever feel like leaving Mississippi?"

"Yes," I replied, "I think about leaving from time to time."

"How often do you think about leaving? Once or twice a year?"

"No, I feel like throwing up my hands and quitting about once a week."

"Then why do you stay?"

"Because my heart tells me that God wants me to stay," I answered. "Whenever part of me feels like giving up, in my spirit I know that being faithful to Him is far more important than my personal desire to escape problems and frustrations."

*Lord, even when I'm sure I've had enough, give me the strength
to keep on going and to keep on trusting You.*
—Dolphus Weary

JULY 28

And they shall be mine, saith the Lord of hosts,
in that day when I make up my jewels.
—MALACHI 3:17

Sixteen miles south of the Montana border on Interstate 15 is a crossroads named Spencer, Idaho, where rock hounds dig for ugly round rocks called "vugs." The outer layer of a vug has lumps that look like warts on a toad, but inside some of the vugs is a layer of hydrated silica, thin as a plastic produce bag, that is the base for a brilliant gem called a fire opal.

Hours of water-cooled grinding removes the ugly outer layer of rock to expose the fragile gem layer and a black backing-stone glued onto it. Then another delicate grinding process exposes an almost invisible layer of multicolored spots, which is covered with a clear quartz cap. The cap makes the kaleidoscopic spots sparkle like lights on a Christmas tree, and the ugly rock becomes a flashing opal.

While I worked with these gems to make earrings for my wife and daughters, I decided I was like the opal. I have an ugly outer layer of envy, pride and selfishness that covers a fragile layer of gem-quality faith placed inside by God. When God grinds on my outer layer of self-centeredness, I become heated and irritated as the abrasive trials wear away my ugly exterior. But finally a layer of faith appears. God caps it with the forgiveness of Christ, and it flashes and sparkles with the truth of the living Savior.

If you ask God, I know He will cap your jewel of faith also and reveal the true beauty of what He created in you.

Lord, let my faith flash like the fire opal.
—RICHARD HAGERMAN

JULY 29

*And what is the exceeding greatness of his power to us-ward
who believe, according to the working of his mighty power.*
—EPHESIANS 1:19

*I*t was something I had intended to do for ages. Finally, at age eighty-one, I figured it was time. I took a train for the hour-and-a-half ride to Smithtown, Long Island, where Sue Nunziata, historian of the First Presbyterian Church, met me. I had written ahead saying that all I wanted was to see inside the centuries-old church where my grand-uncle Edward Abbey had been the pastor. Sue had other ideas.

"Liz and Bill Ewing are waiting to meet you," she said, "and Brewster Lawrence, an old-timer, is taking us all to lunch."

I was happy to think of Mom—could it have been a century ago?—traveling by train from Indiana for all the good times she told me about. I remembered well the tall, bewhiskered Edward Abbey at the time that Mom, my two brothers and I were his guests in 1934. He died the following year, but he was quite alive when I again saw his church. It was built in 1826: white clapboard, Federal style, with a steeple reaching up in three balustraded stages to a weather vane. I saw him as the dignified shepherd standing at his pulpit, high up on a white rostrum, looking over his seated flock, the doors to their pews securely closed.

Liz Ewing had a surprise for me: the record of church christenings. There I was, a year old, with Dad's and Mom's names as double proof. They had brought me from Kentucky for the event.

"I was around at the time," Brewster Lawrence said, "but, sorry, I don't remember your christening."

"That's okay," I said, "but it's good to know it happened."

*The living memory of my christening is gone, Father,
but the records, like the effects, are still there.*

—VAN VARNER

JULY 30

Sing praises to the Lord, O you his faithful ones, and give thanks to his holy name.... Weeping may linger for the night, but joy comes with the morning.
—PSALM 30:4–5 (NRSV)

*T*woke up feeling depressed. I could think of no reason for it, yet my usual cheery outlook for the day was missing. After breakfast I sat down in my prayer chair. *Lord, I'm feeling kind of down today. Please help me find a better attitude.*

Whoosh! A dragon belched fire right over our house. I knew there was no such things as dragons, but that's what it made me think of. *Whoosh!* I jumped up and ran outside. Hanging about fifty feet above was a hot-air balloon, its red, orange and yellow stripes glistening in the sunlight. A man and a woman waved to me over the edge of the gondola.

"Hello down there!" the man called.

"Hello!" I yelled, waving back.

The man turned and tugged at something that released a small plume of flame inside the balloon. *Whoosh!* The balloon lifted higher into the air and drifted away.

"Have a nice day!" the woman called.

I raised one arm in farewell. "You too!"

I watched until the balloon became a speck in the distance and then walked, smiling, into the house. I went back to my prayer chair and said out loud, "Thank You, God! That was a unique answer to prayer!" With spirits lifted as high as that balloon, I continued my morning meditation.

Lord, thank You for unexpected events that bring us joy.
Today I'll watch for an opportunity to lift someone else's spirit.
—MADGE HARRAH

JULY 31

"In this world you will have trouble. But take heart! I have overcome the world."
—JOHN 16:33 (NIV)

*W*hen I'm on the mountaintop, giving advice to those in the valley is easy. Bible verses work well when things in life are on the up and up. But when the valley experience comes to me, how can I best handle it?

In May 1995, a charitable foundation we had been depending on for our ministry in Mendenhall, Mississippi, was accused of fraud. We had participated in its matching grant program, believing there were anonymous donors who would match any funds we invested with the foundation dollar for dollar. When the truth finally surfaced, I went into a two-week depression. I didn't want to talk to people because I felt I had let down so many who had trusted in our integrity.

Then several things happened that turned me around. One was a devotional time centered on John 16:33. Peace grew in my heart from knowing that God was in control and that He provided all we had and all we would need. Then I thought about all the ways God had guided us down through the years. The words *I won't complain* quickly came to mind. I continued to repeat those words over and over.

The members of our board of directors called to assure me they were standing with me. And then I wrote to all of our donors to let them know what had happened. We received only four negative responses. We still have not gotten all our money back, but I do know more than ever that God cares about our ministry. And if I trust in Him and stay close to Him in prayer, I need not be afraid to move forward.

Lord, help me to know that You are concerned about all that happens to me.

—DOLPHUS WEARY

August

Let the word of Christ dwell in you richly.
—COLOSSIANS 3:16 (NRSV)

*O*n a high mountain slope above our cabin in Colorado stands a grove of bristlecone pines, kin to the famous bristlecones of California. With their twisted trunks and bearded cones, they are purported to be among the oldest living things on earth, some of them as old as two or three thousand years.

My husband Larry and I hiked up to that grove of pines one day, and I placed my hand against the trunk of the thickest tree. I imagined that tree standing there, solidly rooted through two thousand years of winter storms, spring rains and summer sun, ever since Jesus was born. It gave me a feeling of connection, as though I was reaching back through time to become a part of Jesus' world.

Back at the cabin, I picked up our Bible, sat down on a chair near the fireplace and opened to the middle of Matthew. I read once more the parables, the prophecies, the drama of the Crucifixion and Resurrection. Then came Jesus' last message before He ascended into heaven: "Lo, I am with you alway, even unto the end of the world" (Matthew 28:20).

Connected to Jesus? Yes! His words, strong and enduring through two thousand years, stand firmly rooted in the assurance of His love. For me. And for you.

Father, I face this day with confidence, because I know
You are with me now and forever.
—MADGE HARRAH

AUGUST 2

Weeping may endure for a night, but joy cometh in the morning.
—PSALM 30:5

*S*omeday this, too, will be a pleasure to recall."

When I was about twelve years old, I came across that saying, copied it down and taped it to my desk drawer. Many years later that same desk was loaded onto a moving truck, headed for our new home—high on a hill, with no yard, less maintenance and fewer rooms. We were simplifying. When the truck pulled up to our new home, the driver walked slowly into the empty kitchen, hat in hands, and said, "Mrs. Kidd, I have some bad news. We didn't know about the hill when we packed the truck...and I'm afraid the load shifted." He looked like he was going to cry.

We walked out to the truck as one of the crew struggled with its back door. As the door slid open, I peered inside. It was as if someone had taken all our furniture, housewares, books and clothes and put them in the spin cycle of a huge dryer. There were boxes filled with bits of broken glass; legs were separated from tables; bureau drawers were scattered about. I was holding back hysteria as I returned to the house and began telling the men where to put the furniture. In came my childhood desk. I gently pulled open the top drawer and there was that same old saying taped inside. *Of course*, I thought, *we wanted to simplify and we just got a little extra help.*

Later that evening, the owner of the moving company appeared, a grim expression on his face. I'm sure he anticipated a lawsuit. But my husband and I had agreed: This move was a new beginning. "Everything's fine," I said.

Father, give me the gift of perspective so I can face setbacks with good humor.
—PAM KIDD

August 3

They have ears, but they hear not.
—Psalm 115:6

I just read an article about the options that will be available on cars of the future, and I'm fighting back yawns.

Why don't carmakers give us something we really need? I don't want windshield wipers that sense moisture and turn themselves on. I can tell when it's raining, and I don't like "options" that take away the most important option of all, my control of the car. I'd like to see them design things like:

1. A heater that I could leave on low while I shop, so I could return to warm seats and clear windshields.
2. A horn for the rear bumper, so I could beep at the children playing behind me in the driveway or warn the tailgater to back off.
3. A foot-operated dimmer switch, so I don't have to take my hand off the wheel to dim the lights. My first car had this, back in the 1950s.
4. Radio knobs bigger than raisins.
5. A thinner steering wheel, so I don't feel like I'm wrestling a boa constrictor when I turn the wheel.

What applies to carmakers applies to me, of course. Before buying that expensive gold watch for my wife, maybe I should ask her what she really wants. It could be that she'd rather have a new sewing machine.

How nice that we have a Father in heaven who urges us to tell Him our needs and wants, even though He already knows what they are.

Thank You for respecting our wants and needs, Lord.
—Daniel Schantz

AUGUST 4

Bring joy to your servant, Lord, for I put my trust in you.
—PSALM 86:4 (NIV)

When my husband Joe, our daughter Sarah and I were in Italy a couple of Augusts ago, we took a tour of a vineyard in the Tuscan countryside. On the way, our bus passed through the lush green countryside and then began a long, winding climb up a steep hill to a beautiful old manor-turned-winery. As we peered out the windows at the vineyard, we were shocked. The ground was rocky and powdery dry, and the vines appeared thirsty and stressed.

Our bus stopped at the top of the hill where the winery stood. Inside the sprawling building our guide led us downstairs into a cool, musty cellar containing giant wooden casks of aging wine. She explained the lengthy process of making fine wine, and then she revealed why the vineyard looked so dry: The most stressed vines make the best wine.

That started me thinking about the previous summer, when I was struggling to recover from an operation during which I nearly died. In the first difficult days of recovery, I wondered why God had allowed the surgical blunder that left me fighting for my life. I had been thoroughly prayed for before and during the surgery, so what was God doing? I didn't feel Him near; all I could do was cling to His Word.

Now here I was a year later, fully recovered and traveling with a magnified appreciation for everything. My marriage was richer, I'd learned amazing lessons of God's faithfulness, and I was grateful for even the smallest things.

The past year has seen grievous times too, such as the loss of several precious friends. But I've learned that hardships can add robustness to the flavor of simple blessings and sweetness to the unchanging goodness of God, even when I don't always understand the way He works.

Faithful Father, when life deals me difficult times, let my harvest
be a deeper, richer, more thankful dependence on You.
—MARJORIE PARKER

AUGUST 5

"I will not leave you orphaned; I am coming to you."
—JOHN 14:18 (NRSV)

I opened my eyes to total blackness. I had to go to the bathroom now! My feet slammed onto the floor. *Why is the bed so low? Oh yeah, we're in Fairhope, Alabama, in a B&B.* I sat very still and listened—nothing. Feeling my way, I remembered a recent doctor's visit. "You've lost a third of your sight in six weeks," the doctor had said. Or was it hearing? I felt a wave of terror. If I lost both my hearing and my sight, I'd be alone. A familiar Voice whispered, *Keith, can you hear Me?*

"Yes, Sir," I said very relieved. "I'm glad You're still with me."

Don't worry. I'll always be with you. But what will you do if you can't see or hear?

"Maybe You could help me work out a code to tell my family I'm all right. Maybe I could figure out how to help people like me surrender to You, so they wouldn't be alone."

How did you think of that in the midst of your own fear?

"Well, Sir, remember in 1956, after my mother's graveside service when I realized I was alone? You asked me, *What are you going to do?* "I said, 'Maybe You can show me how to introduce other lonely people to You.'"

So that's what your work has really been about.

"Yes, Sir, I guess so."

Then I heard a concerned familiar voice outside. "Keith, are you all right?" It was my wife Andrea.

"Yeah, I'm okay."

"Can't you find the light switch?"

I smiled in the darkness. "Yeah, honey. I just did."

Lord, thank You for sending the Light to guide us all the way home to You.
—KEITH MILLER

AUGUST 6

"For man looks at the outward appearance, but the Lord looks at the heart."
—I SAMUEL 16:7 (NASB)

This summer I volunteered to teach a Bible study at a women's shelter. Initially it sounded like fun, but I'd begun to dread it. How would I be able to relate to the women? I drove to the shelter in the sweltering afternoon sun. Inside, stifling heat greeted me. The air conditioner repairer hadn't come, though none of the women complained. They invited me to eat dinner with them—hot dogs and watermelon. We made polite conversation at the worn Formica table.

Then we went into the tiny den for the Bible study. At first it was too quiet, just the sounds of the oscillating fan and women clearing their throats. I sat down on the braided rug with a few of the others. I'd been a Sunday school teacher for fifteen years, so I'd carefully prepared a lesson. As I stared at my handwriting, I knew I couldn't teach from my notes. Instead, I told them the truth. I shared the struggles in our family—drug addiction, abusive relationships, mental illness and jail time. I told them some people in my family had come close to homelessness.

After I opened up with them, they opened up with me. Several had drug histories and most had been in abusive relationships. God's sweet Spirit began to move among us. When it was time to leave, I asked one of the women to close with a prayer. Every single word of her prayer was for me, for my family, for our needs.

Oh, Father, bless that woman for her great kindness.
—JULIE GARMON

AUGUST 7

Jesus wept.
—JOHN 11:35

*M*y brother Davey and I loved to hear stories of our father's childhood in the mountains of Tellico Plains, Tennessee. Daddy was one of those kids who are happiest while roaming the woods and swimming the rivers and riding horses deep into what is now the Cherokee National Forest. He tolerated school for the sake of football and sat in the back row in church so he could take off his Sunday shoes during the last hymn and dash out the door for the day's adventure.

He told us many tales of being roped in for Sunday school. When he was asked to memorize Scripture, he'd always be ready with the same verse. "The shortest one in the Bible," he'd say with a smile. "'Jesus wept.'"

I was devastated when Daddy died suddenly in his early sixties. In the days after the funeral, I'd often go out to walk and think, trying to make sense of his early death. That's when I remembered Daddy's favorite Bible verse. "Jesus wept," not for Himself, but for others, for us. *Of course,* I thought. *In all this sadness and despair, Jesus weeps with me.* Eventually my season of mourning passed, but the verse nested in my spirit.

Years later, a neighbor, wounded by a broken relationship, took her own life, and Jesus wept. While I watched helplessly as a loved one fell into an unwholesome situation that ended in disaster, Jesus wept. And when the unimaginable happened and a good friend's baby died, Jesus wept. In a fallen world, the applications of Daddy's "shortest Bible verse" are endless.

So the next time you experience pain—an ache in your body, a hurt in your heart, suffering in your spirit—take hold of a little barefoot boy's favorite verse and remember you are not alone. God is near. When you weep, He weeps with you.

Father, no tear escapes Your notice. When sorrows come,
join my tears to the tears of Your Son.
—PAM KIDD

AUGUST 8

I have called daily upon thee, I have stretched out my hands unto thee.
—PSALM 88:9

*S*tark terror. That's what I felt on this sunshiny morning as I tramped on the North Carolina beach. I shaded my eyes and looked out at what long-ago sailors had dubbed Cape Fear. Its ferocious currents had made it a graveyard of ships.

Battling my own private shipwreck, I walked to a spit of land by the swirling ocean. I sat in the shade of a dune and pulled a sandy, soggy, year-old note from my jeans pocket. "Keep your chin up. We're praying for you," it said. A few weeks before that note arrived, my husband and I had separated. After thirty-one years, I was on my own, with no job, no career, no confidence. The note, signed by several friends, had been a lifeline. Many readings had left it creased and coffee-stained.

I hadn't sunk: I'd gotten a job, and I was paying my bills. Best of all, Whitney and I had gone into counseling, and our marriage was mending. Soon I would move back home. But on this morning, on Cape Fear, the good news was washed away by terror. I stared, trembling, at the ocean crashing on rocks. My toes curled into the sand as if looking for something solid to grip. "Life is so uncertain," I whispered. "Who knows what our future will be?"

A gust of sea air rattled the paper in my hand. I read it again and again, until its truth stilled my fear. *The real lifeline is not in the note,* I thought. *It's tied around me in unbreakable cords of prayer.* I reached for that lifeline and felt a tug from the One Whose hold on me is as certain as the ocean's on the sand. The fear left.

Lord, thank You for the lifeline of prayer.
Help me use it to reach out to others.
—SHARI SMYTH

AUGUST 9

The Lord is good to all, And His mercies are over all His works.
—PSALM 145:9 (NASB)

*T*t was the end of a long day, and I was just blocks from my apartment when I remembered that my wife would be home late and I had to get dinner for my stepdaughter Mara. Too tired to think of anything else, I picked up a pizza and hurried home. When I opened the door I immediately remembered the other item I was supposed to pick up: mousetraps.

"Make it go away!" Mara was shouting, her legs curled up under her on the sofa. On the floor, a mouse scurried about. For the past few days, this animal had been wandering around, terrorizing Mara and puzzling our two dogs.

The pizza got cold as I lumbered back and forth, trying to scoop the mouse into a shoebox. "Mara, it's just a mouse," I said for the millionth time.

"I—hate—mice," she replied simply but firmly.

I sympathized with Mara, but I'd developed a soft spot for this singularly bold and clueless creature. I'd "forgotten" to pick up traps for days.

The mouse finally vanished under a bookshelf, and Mara and I ate our cold pizza. Later, I went out again and found a hardware store that sells humane traps. I dropped in a piece of pizza crust, set the trap door and hoped for the best. Around 3:00 a.m., I was awakened by a small rattling sound. I'd caught the mouse!

Our apartment is just a few blocks from a park. The streets were empty, and the walk there was oddly pleasant. I gave the trap a shake, and the mouse ran off to its uncertain future.

From mice on up to people, God gives all of us our roles to play in life. Most of the time, we're all just feeling our way in the dark, relying on His grace. Maybe that's one reason God has such a soft spot for us too.

Lord, may Your mercy teach me to be merciful—even to mice.
—PTOLEMY TOMPKINS

AUGUST 10

And God said, Let us make man in our image, after our likeness:
and let them have dominion over the fish of the sea, and over the fowl
of the air, and over the cattle, and over all the earth,
and over every creeping thing that creepeth upon the earth.
—GENESIS 1:26

hen, forty years ago, we were preparing to leave Ohio to move to New Mexico, an acquaintance said to us, "I can describe Albuquerque in one sentence: Grass is a status symbol." That was true then, when everyone in this desert city, including us, worked to keep our lawns green and well trimmed. But the population of Albuquerque exploded through the years, and we now have a water shortage. More people have turned to xeriscaping, which means doing away with grass and creating landscapes out of colored rocks, gravel and native plants that require little water.

I've noticed that the people around me are becoming more aware of the need to preserve other natural resources too. They're buying fuel-efficient cars; recycling their metal cans, newspapers and plastic products; helping to protect endangered species; and finding ways to cut down on the pollution of our air and rivers. I think when God gave us dominion over all the earth, He didn't mean we had the right to exploit and destroy His handiwork. I think He meant for us to be responsible caretakers of His creation.

Thank You, God, for this beautiful world! I'll look
for more ways to help protect our environment.
—MADGE HARRAH

AUGUST 11

*"Do not fear, for I have redeemed you; I have
called you by name; you are Mine!"*
—ISAIAH 43:1 (NASB)

*B*eau is my ninety-pound golden retriever. Every day we greet the new morning together and each night we take long walks. I guess you could say we're best friends.

Tonight as I write these lines, Beau is sprawled on the study floor next to my desk. Outside, a thunderstorm rages, and Beau is fretful and nervous. Bad weather releases the ancient wolf in Beau, and he seeks shelter and security. Twice in the past five minutes he has stood up and placed his wide muzzle on my leg, demanding that I ruffle his ears and pat him on the head. And when I stop, he lifts his paw for me to hold. He can't be touched enough.

I guess I'm a lot like Beau. When I walk through my own storms, God just can't be near enough to me. I, too, want to be touched and feel God's big hand grasp mine. I need reassurance that God is bigger than the storm.

Tonight as I help Beau through his troubled moments, I'm reassured that God's love and care for me dwarfs my own compassion. Though sometimes I don't feel God's hand on my shoulder, He's always there. And He has promised me there's no storm He and I can't live through together.

Dear God, help me to feel Your presence this day. Amen.
—SCOTT WALKER

And he said unto me, My grace is sufficient for thee.
—II CORINTHIANS 12:9

*I*n Florida my wife Shirley and I attend a Sunday school class made up of mostly senior citizens—some very senior. There's Art from Pennsylvania, Paul from Michigan, Ralph from Iowa and Bill from New York, to name a few. All are about ninety, give or take a few months. Each one has spent a lifetime in the church, and each brings a wealth of secular and spiritual experience to the class. Sometimes we stay on the Bible lesson for the day, but no one objects to a few detours. Their stories are full of faith principles that add to our discussions.

Bill, who taught the class for many years, said something one Sunday that I haven't forgotten. Someone brought up a particular horrendous deed and wondered if the sin could be forgiven. "Of course it can," Bill replied. "We serve a God of second chances. And remember, with Him, sin knows no size." *Sin knows no size.* That's a tremendous truth. Whatever our offense, none exceeds God's grace. As amazing and unlikely as it sounds,

Our Father's grace knows no bounds.
—FRED BAUER

AUGUST 13

Do good...hoping for nothing.
—LUKE 6:35

*J*ust home from the office, my husband walked into the kitchen with a big smile on his face.

"What's up?" I asked.

"The funniest thing happened to Barb today," David answered. "She stopped for a quick lunch at a fast-food restaurant, and while she was in the drive-through waiting for her turn to pay, the girl at the window said, 'The lady in front of you just paid for your lunch. She said to tell you to have a good day!' You can't imagine how happy that made Barb."

The more I thought of Barb's adventure, the more it reminded me of God's grace: a gift utterly undeserved, joy undeserved, blessings undeserved. An idea ripened in my mind.

"I've got a great idea," I told David after dinner, my face brimming with mischief. "Why don't we go out for a quick ice cream?" His eyes lit up.

In the drive-through, David explained our mission to the cashier. "We want to pay for the people behind us," he said.

"Are you sure? It's fourteen dollars and two cents."

"I'm sure," David answered, handing her a twenty.

We felt like pulling into a parking place and enjoying the surprise, but we knew instinctively that watching would somehow break the spell. Grace is best when you aren't expecting anything back. But as we pulled out of the parking lot and onto the street, we started to laugh. We laughed all the way home.

Oh, Father, the sheer joy of sharing Your grace is all I need. Thank You.
—PAM KIDD

AUGUST 14

Be joyful in hope, patient in affliction, faithful in prayer.
—ROMANS 12:12 (NIV)

I love to knit. Many *Daily Guideposts* readers know that and, over the years, have joined me as the needles click to knit wonderful little sweaters for needy children all over the world. I've knitted blankets too, for each of my four grandchildren. When I heard about the pending arrival of the fifth, I began her blanket, choosing a very pretty but difficult pattern. As I knitted, though, my world grew darker. I underwent electroconvulsive therapy. Much of my short-term memory vanished, but not my ability to knit.

The blanket grew longer in squares of alternating pattern. And as I had so often in the past, I began to pray the stitches. Knitting the plain-stitch squares, I prayed for hope, prayed for my vanished self and prayed to stay alive. With the purl-stitch squares, I prayed for the unborn Madeline, that she would make a safe journey into a world where she'd be happy, healthy and grow up unshadowed by depression.

There is a strain of heredity in depression, and I panicked at the thought of bequeathing it. But as I recovered—little by little—I felt a quiet faith, built on hundreds of rows with thousands of stitches, that Madeline, her brothers and her cousins would grow up not only depression-free but also in a world where new treatments would conquer the demon. The pale green blanket became a blanket of hope. And I was there, smiling, to wrap Madeline into its folds.

Thank You, Jesus, for sharing our pain and for the hope
and healing You bring to so many.
—BRIGITTE WEEKS

August 15

Let anyone with ears listen!
—MATTHEW 11:15 (NRSV)

Of the five senses God gave us, His gift of being able to hear seems to trigger most of my memories. I think of things like:

The distinctive shrill whistle of the Rock Island train—headlight urgently flashing—as it roared past our place in a symphony of sound. The swaying cars clatter-clattering on metal rails, the smokestack making a staccato phuff-phuffing, the mammoth engine plaintively chuch-chuch-chuching into the distance.

The whump-whump of a carpet beater when my mother dangled and then whacked rugs over a clothesline to dislodge dirt during her twice-a-year house cleanings.

The pawk-pawk-puh-dock from the chicken house when a hen was bragging about having deposited a fresh egg—a day's work for her.

The hypnotic tick-tock-tick of the parlor's dignified mantel clock. Counting its sonorous bong...bong, I could tell the time without looking.

The rhythmic squeak-squeak of the porch swing. It was nearly drowned out by the nightly drone of the locusts' zoo-ree, zoo-rees or the chatter of passersby who simply dropped by on hot summer evenings without calling ahead.

And then there are sounds I can still hear today but only in near silence: faint rustles of cottonwoods startled by a breeze, plips of surfacing fish, contented eep-eeps of baby birds nestled for the night.

It makes me wonder if one of the reasons Jesus spent time alone was so He could rest surrounded by the solacing sounds He couldn't detect in the midst of a noisy crowd.

It's hard to hear still small voices—including Yours, precious Lord—when bedlam abounds. Show me a corner where I can bask in luxurious quietness.
—ISABEL WOLSELEY

AUGUST 16

O Jerusalem, that bringest good tidings, lift up thy voice with strength;
lift it up, be not afraid; say unto the cities of Judah, Behold your God!
—ISAIAH 40:9

*M*ost mornings I log on to my computer at work, open the e-mail program and just start hitting the delete button. Hot stock tips, instant loans, online degrees, "genuine faux" watches, rapid weight loss programs, cyber casinos—all kinds of junk e-mail clutter up my in-box.

I rarely open up any of this junk. That's because I've gotten pretty good at identifying them by the subject line. Some of them are pure gibberish: "President's Marsupial Plan" or "Bulk Rag Injection." Some are a little more insidious: "Security Notification" or "Order Delivery Status." Some border on the sinister: "Your credit has been accessed!" But I usually see through their tricks and unmercifully delete them.

The other day an e-mail from an unknown source popped up on my screen with the subject line "God Loves You."

"Yeah, right," I muttered. "I wonder what God loves so much that He wants to sell it to me." I hit DELETE with a mixture of annoyance and satisfaction.

A day later it was back. I deleted it again. This time I felt a little uncomfortable; I don't like deleting God. *That's what they're counting on*, I thought. They probably wanted to refinance my mortgage if I would kindly hand over my Social Security and bank account numbers. *I didn't just fall off the turnip truck, you know.*

A couple of days passed and there it was again: "God Loves You." I hesitated, finger poised above the DELETE key. *I'm going to regret this*, I thought, certain I was being suckered. I opened it.

Nothing—just a blank white screen. No pitch. No product.

God loves me.

The Internet is an interesting place, and I'm not sure I could even tell you *where* it exists. But one thing is sure: Certain messages always get through.

Thank You, Lord, for the reminder that Your love
is everywhere, even in my in-box.
—EDWARD GRINNAN

August 17

A time to plant, and a time to pluck up that which is planted.
—Ecclesiastes 3:2

*B*lue flax, newly transplanted from a friend's yard, fluttered by the mailbox as I stared dumbly at the letter from my landlord of five years. "Therefore, you must find another rental before September 1."

I shook my head in disbelief. Just a few months earlier the same landlord had invited me to choose new carpet and plant a garden. All spring I had removed sod, forked loam, fertilized and planted gifts from my friends' gardens. Now the delphinium, lavender, lilies, tulips, daffodils and veronica would stay behind. I'd be gone before the painted daisies, grown from seed, showed their colors.

Leaving my garden was the least of my worries. Where would I go? Rentals were few, and my job search hadn't turned out the way I had hoped. After twenty-three years in my cozy community, why was everything falling apart now?

Or was it? For several years I had pondered relocating two thousand miles back east to my native New Hampshire to keep closer tabs on my frail parents, who were now in their eighties. Was this the right time?

Within days, pieces of the transcontinental move clicked together: I would live at my parents' summer place in New Hampshire, just an hour away from them, and teach at a nearby junior college. Carol, my friend since college, would drive back with me. I would keenly miss my community and my garden, but I knew my parents needed me nearby.

Minutes before departing, I dug up the English rose I'd planted just weeks earlier. "Rosie" would travel with us and begin a new life in New Hampshire too. As I started the car to begin our journey, Carol slid in and offered me a nosegay plucked from my now abandoned garden. She smiled.

"Something pretty for the trip—and seeds for your new garden."

Lord of creation, help me trust Your time, not my own.
—Gail Thorell Schilling

AUGUST 18

His dominion shall be from sea even to sea, and
from the river even to the ends of the earth.
—ZECHARIAH 9:10

I was totally wiped out, and not even the nice clean hotel room with its sparkling view of the Rocky Mountains could revive me. The week before, I had been to Seoul, South Korea, to celebrate the fortieth anniversary of the Korean edition of *Guideposts* magazine. Then it was back to New York, up to Massachusetts and finally out here to Colorado for a jam-packed conference.

I threw my luggage on the bed and began transferring fistfuls of clothes to the dresser and closet. From the side pocket of my suitcase I tugged a pair of walking shoes I'd brought along in the now unlikely event that I might want to go for a hike, and tossed them into the bottom of the closet. As I did, caked-on dirt went flying all over the newly vacuumed carpet. *Oh no.*

I got down on my knees and swept up the dried mud with my hands. I was about to toss a handful into the trash can by the desk when I stopped and stared at the dirt in my palm—Korean dirt. I'd last worn these shoes on a tour of a historical Korean village, one of the many tourist spots to which my gracious host Mr. Go took me. Afterward, we'd gone to the border with North Korea and in a drizzling rain stared through the high fence at the forbidding demilitarized zone. We had bowed our heads and said a prayer.

Maybe it was the jet lag, but suddenly I was overwhelmed by astonishment at how small our world really is and what little it takes, even a clump of dirt, to make me feel connected.

Father, cradle this small world of ours in Your hands,
and keep us safe and connected to You.
—EDWARD GRINNAN

AUGUST 19

A wise man will hear, and will increase learning.
—PROVERBS 1:5

The wild country outside of Caribou, Maine, had called my dad and me back for a second year of fly-fishing. My brother-in-law Ben had turned our adventure into a threesome. But the fishing turned out to be terrible, and a succession of dreary days dampened our spirits. When I awoke to the sound of rain pelting the roof of our little cabin, my impulse was to pull the covers over my head and sleep till noon.

"No way am I going out in that slosh," I said.

Dad shook the foot of my bed. "Brock," he said, "sometimes the best fishing is in the worst weather." Begrudgingly I put on my waders, loaded up my fly vest and headed out to the river. I left Ben upstream and crab-walked my way into the current. Soon I was caught up in the calm rhythm of fly-fishing. I enjoyed the feel of the cast as the line rose in graceful loops and then unfolded forward to land on the surface of the water. All at once my fly was enveloped with a slurp, my line tightened, and my reel began to scream. The trout had to be huge, and if I fought too hard too fast, it would snap my line. If I was going to land it, I would have to chase it downstream.

"Ben," I hollered, "bring your net! I need some help!"

I fought that fish for almost fifteen minutes, and with Dad and Ben's assistance I finally got it in. A beautiful eighteen-inch brook trout, the biggest any of us had caught.

But the biggest catch of the day came at dinner when Dad said, "I hope you'll remember that God can use the bleakest day to deliver His gifts." And how!

Father, no matter how dreary the day, You're always ahead of me, waiting.
—BROCK KIDD

AUGUST 20

A person's steps are directed by the Lord.
—PROVERBS 20:24 (NIV)

One of the things I love best about being a grandmother is reading books to my grandchildren. Isabelle Grace is still in the board-book stage. These sturdy books are short and simple, with thick pages perfect for little fingers. Sometimes I read Isabelle longer books with more text and detailed pictures. Usually they have too many words for her liking, and she turns the page before I'm ready. Occasionally, though, a picture intrigues her and she stares at it long after I've finished reading. But one thing is certain: Isabelle is in charge of turning pages. If I forget and flip forward, she emits a squeal, as only a two-year-old can: "Isbee do! Isbee do!"

A few days ago, after Isabelle had gone home, I held the book we'd been reading and thought about how much Isabelle enjoys being the one to set the pace, the one to say when it's time to move forward in the story, the one who determines when a new scene comes into play. Often I behave like Isabelle, wanting to set the pace for my life. I complain that good times go by too fast. I question why the hard times linger. I want the sunshine-filled pages to stay open forever and those fearsome storm-filled ones to whiz by in a blink. Of course, I'm not the One turning the pages.

I'm old enough to know that grief and illness, disappointment and rejection have their merits. I learn more in shadow than in sun. Still, it's a challenge to surrender control and embrace the pace set by the Author of our lives and cheerfully let Him turn the pages.

I'll keep my hands off, Lord, and let You take charge
of my life—page after page after page.
—MARY LOU CARNEY

AUGUST 21

And I heard a voice from heaven saying unto me, Write, Blessed are the dead which die in the Lord from henceforth: Yea, saith the Spirit, that they may rest from their labours; and their works do follow them.

—REVELATION 14:13

Outside my father-in-law's room, I heard a hospice nurse say, "We usually die the way we lived." I've held on to what she said, specifically the word *usually*. Usually, as in "not always." That means there's still a chance I won't die the way I lived: in traffic, in lines, looking for my daughter's soccer shoes ("No, Daddy, the red ones"). I won't die working on my car, filling out forms, watching stupid reruns. I won't die simply waiting...waiting...waiting...

Once, on a beach in Avalon, New Jersey, my father-in-law told me this joke: "I want to die like my great-great-grandpa: peacefully, in his sleep. Not screaming like the passengers in his wagon when he drove it into the river."

I laughed when he told it to me, and that's how I want to go: eyes closed, head back, the sun on my face, throat full of happiness at the sheer absurd joy of it all and hoping the Lord's sense of humor is way more merciful than just.

Lord, help me to live even the smallest of moments with my eye on eternity.

—MARK COLLINS

"The Lord will guide you always; he will satisfy your needs
in a sun-scorched land and will strengthen your frame."

—ISAIAH 58:11 (NIV)

*M*y husband's best friend Norm fell off the roof of his house. Complications from his injuries set in, and he wasn't expected to live through the night. Distraught, Norm's family gathered at the hospital. Not wanting to intrude on their privacy, Wayne and I felt there was little we could do but pray as we waited for word. Feeling the need to do more, Wayne asked me to contact our church to ask if one of the pastors could go to the hospital and pray with the family. The assistant pastor went and reported back that he'd met the family, shared the Gospel and prayed with them. He told us how grateful they were for his visit.

Later, when we got the news that Norm had miraculously survived the night, Wayne and I were overwhelmed with joy. But when I mentioned our pastor's visit to Norm's wife Sharon, she sounded confused. No one from the church had stopped by to visit or pray with them. We learned that the pastor had met with a different grieving family. As it happened, their family member had died that night.

Some might say that our assistant pastor made a mistake, but I don't believe it. God sent our pastor to the people who needed Him most.

Thank You, Lord, that You know our needs
and are always ready to meet them.

—DEBBIE MACOMBER

AUGUST 23

Beloved, let us love one another.
—I JOHN 4:7

*M*y husband John and I were uneasy as we drove into the manicured country club in Hershey, Pennsylvania. After all, we were coming to interview the notoriously unapproachable Ben Hogan, "the Texas Iceberg," whose machinelike performance on the golf course made him what many still consider the greatest player ever. How would a man famed for stony-faced remoteness respond to our questions?

We'd come to ask him for his secret. How, we wanted to know, had he made his astounding recovery from a near-fatal car crash? Perhaps, we thought, it was the iron self-discipline he'd acquired teaching himself to play golf—swinging a club till his hands bled. Or perhaps it was his legendary concentration, shutting out every thought but getting well, as he'd shut out the distraction of the fans trooping behind him from hole to hole.

When the accident occurred, doctors said he'd never walk again. Incredibly, just three years later, he was back on the links, beginning to reclaim the career that would make him a legend.

We were met in the clubhouse by a short, trim, 130-pound man with a slight limp and, instead of the scowl we were steeled for, a welcoming smile. For an easygoing two hours we chatted about what had made the comeback possible. It did take discipline and focus, he agreed.

"But mostly," he said, "it was the letters."

They'd come by the thousands, from housewives, office workers, students—all with essentially the same message: "We care about you, Ben! We're praying for you."

"Before those letters came," said Hogan, "I told myself I didn't care whether people were for me or against me. To win, I thought I had to shut the spectators out. To find suddenly that you have thousands of people rooting for you...why, I just had to get better!"

A terrible accident, surgeries, pain—and a gift bigger and longer lasting than any of them.

Bestower of blessing, help me discern the gifts You wrap in darkness.
—ELIZABETH SHERRILL

AUGUST 24

For it is by grace you have been saved, through faith—
and this not from yourselves, it is the gift of God.
—EPHESIANS 2:8 (NIV)

t was the final day of a summer missions trip with my high school youth group, and we had some free time to explore the Mexican town where we were staying. That afternoon in the central plaza, my friend Steve took out his guitar and started playing, and the rest of us sang fragments of any song we could remember. Our repertoire included "The Star-Spangled Banner," "Amazing Grace" and a couple of rock songs. Our cacophony drew many curious glances from the townspeople, and to our delight a few passing tourists threw money into Steve's open guitar case.

By the end of the concert, a group of raggedly dressed children had gathered around, staring in wide-eyed amazement at the pile of pesos in the guitar case. Hoping to make them smile, we took the money to a corner store where we purchased nine cans of soda. Eight of the children jumped for joy when we handed them the drinks, but one little girl wouldn't take it until I spoke to her father. Thinking that the free soda must come with strings attached, he asked me in Spanish who had given it to her. I replied with the first words I could think of: It was *"un regalo de Jesus Cristo"*—a gift from Jesus Christ. He nodded slowly at the little girl, and she drank excitedly.

Two months later I began my freshman year of college, quickly involving myself in a long list of activities. As I reached the brink of burnout, I remembered that man on the plaza and saw how much of my life had become an attempt at proving I was worthy of God's love. I took a deep breath and reminded myself that His love is *un regalo*, no strings attached.

Lord, thank You for loving me unconditionally.
—JOSHUA SUNDQUIST

AUGUST 25

"And I will cause showers to come down in their season;
there shall be showers of blessing."
—EZEKIEL 34:26 (NKJV)

I don't want to go to this picnic," I growl to my wife. "It's hot, I'm tired and I don't want to meet people." I was in my usual start-of-school mood, made worse this year by a hot summer that burned up my garden.

About a hundred of us are crammed into the picnic shelter at Rothwell Park—faculty, staff and their families. The tables are crowded with fragrant foods and sparkling drinks, but the air is heavy and everyone seems tired and grouchy.

Suddenly, thunder—distant at first, but now exploding like cannons on a battlefield. Lightning crackles like enemy gunfire and children run to their mothers. Rain begins to fall so hard it feels like we've camped out under Niagara Falls. Strong men lift tables of food and carry them to the middle of the pavilion, and we huddle around them. Children are sucking their thumbs and crying, while parents try to comfort them: "The angels are bowling," they say. "The Devil is just having a fight with his wife."

At last, the rain slows, and tiny boys and girls race out into the showers, screaming with joy, and then scamper back inside when lightning flickers. Soon we are all eating, laughing, rejoicing at the cool air and refreshing rains.

My face is wet, but not with rain. I'm sitting off to the side, reflecting on God's grace. I'm counting my blessings: the cool rain, beautiful children, good food, great co-workers and God's providence. I'm grateful for ears that can hear thunder and for eyes that can see the kindness on the faces of my co-workers. Suddenly I'm no longer afraid of the start of school.

Thank You, God, for knowing just when to send the rains of blessing.
—DANIEL SCHANTZ

So he went down and dipped himself seven times in the Jordan...and his flesh
was restored like the flesh of a little child and he was clean.
—II KINGS 5:14 (NASB)

A few years ago I experienced clinical depression. Before then I'd been strong and dependable, the kind of person people turned to for help. I'd prided myself on my self-sufficiency. That horrible year my mother visited almost daily to check on me. I hated her coming and I hated her leaving.

Today I found a notation she made in my Bible. She wrote, "For Julie, August 26, 1994." Mom prayed for my immediate healing and noted her prayer right next to God's command to Naaman the leper to be dipped in the Jordan River seven times.

I desperately wanted my healing to happen on the very day she prayed. That way I'd never have to tell anyone. I could maintain my image: Julie, the strong one. I just knew God would fix me instantly, like Naaman. But that wasn't God's plan at all. The opposite happened: I got worse, much worse. I stopped sleeping and eating, and cried most days.

On November 11, 1994, I finally saw a doctor. The doctor prescribed an antidepressant, and I saw a counselor. I wasn't healed my way, in secret or quickly. Very slowly, God directed me to seek help from others. In His perfect way, He dipped me in the Jordan River seven times and healed me.

Oh Father, thank You for Your healing! You restored me from my point
of complete brokenness at just the right time and not one day sooner.
—JULIE GARMON

August 27

"Having eyes, do you not see?"
—Mark 8:18 (nasb)

One of my colleagues was getting blinding headaches. Each morning she'd be fine, but by the end of the workday she could barely tolerate the sight of her computer screen. Finally we cajoled her into going to see an eye doctor. It turned out her vision was horrible: Everything was blurry. "I thought," she told the ophthalmologist, "that was just the way the world looked."

The day after she got her first-ever pair of glasses, I asked her how things were looking. Her face lit up, and the words rushed out. Everything seemed magical, from the leaves on the trees ("So many!") to the words on her computer screen ("So sharp!"). Even our concrete office floor had had its dullness wiped away: The boring old slab suddenly had, in her rejuvenated eyes, dozens of shades of gray.

In my mind that's a little like what the Bible can do for me. To see life through a biblical lens is to put on new glasses, which can refresh how I see the world around me and give me perspective I didn't have before.

Lord, You're the one optometrist Who can connect my eyes to my soul.
—Jeff Chu

AUGUST 28

"It was not you who sent me here, but God."
—GENESIS 45:8 (NASB)

 'd been picking the wild grapes from those vines along the veranda, but before I made jelly from them I thought I'd stretch out on the sofa for a short nap," my elderly mother explained as she recalled the details of that day on the phone. I could just see her on the old maroon sofa, slippers kicked off, glasses folded on the paper stand, purple grape juice staining her bib apron.

"I don't know how long I slept," she went on, "but when I really woke up I was already halfway across the street on my way to Helen's house." Helen was another senior who lived kitty-corner to Mom in the little village. Helen had lived alone since her husband was hospitalized. "I felt so foolish," Mom continued. "I was wearing my slippers and apron, and I didn't even have my glasses on. I thought for a minute I should go back home and change, but something told me I was needed."

Helen invited her in. Just as they were about to enjoy a cup of tea together, Helen's phone rang. "Hello? Yes, this is Helen speaking. No, I'm not alone. A neighbor just dropped by unexpectedly."

As Mom watched, Helen suddenly sat down, her face ashen. Replacing the receiver with trembling hands, she looked at Mom with tear-filled eyes. "That was the hospital calling. My husband just passed away."

Suddenly Mom knew why she had come and Who had urged her on.

Lord, help me to follow through faithfully on Your nudges.
—ALMA BARKMAN

"I the Lord do not change."
—MALACHI 3:6 (NIV)

*W*hen I was a child, tent revivals held by traveling evangelists came along at least once every summer. The wooden folding chairs, the sawdust floor, the breeze under the tent flaps and the birds in the rafters are still alive for me, as are the powerful images of the preachers themselves.

There was the musician who played a jumble of instruments, including the marimba and the musical saw. His wife sang. The words of one song especially stand out:

Wonderful grace of Jesus,
Greater than all my sin.
How shall my tongue describe it,
Where shall its praise begin?
Taking away my burden,
Setting my spirit free.

Then there was the chalk artist who sketched his sermons on a huge spotlighted canvas. Every night a different picture poured from his fingers. The one I remember best was a narrow, dirt road that ran through the cross and empty tomb and ended in the bright lights of eternal life. And there was the poetic evangelist with the bigger-than-life, gravelly voice. Every night he thundered out a different theme with the same solution woven through: "When despair knocks, send Jesus to the door." "When doubt knocks, send Jesus to the door." "When temptation knocks, send Jesus to the door."

Today those tent revivals have gone the way of black-and-white television. They're miles and years removed from my busy, more complicated world. Yet, the same simple, undiluted gospel message still holds: "Grace greater than all my sin" rescues me and keeps me on the path to eternal life.

Lord Jesus, thank You that Your power is still the answer
to temptation, despair and doubt.

—SHARI SMYTH

AUGUST 30

I understand more than the ancients, Because I keep Your precepts.
—PSALM 119:100 (NKJV)

The label on my chainsaw says, "Do not attempt to stop chain with hands." Just one more silly product-warning label. Like the one on an iron: "Do not iron clothes while they are being worn." Or the sleeping pills that warn, "May cause drowsiness." Then there's the sunshield for the car that says, "Do not drive with sunshield in place." And the warning on a wheelbarrow: "Not for highway use."

Doubtless these warnings are there to protect their makers from lawsuits, but I suspect many of them are based on long experience with lunatic customers. Someone probably did try to finger-brake a chainsaw or push someone down the highway in a wheelbarrow. Impatient drivers probably have left the sunshield in place and peeked over it. And I have no doubt that some "Odd Couple" bachelor has tried to iron his shirt while wearing it.

To modern ears many of the laws of God probably sound just as silly as those warning labels. "Do not swear," "Do not steal" and "Do not commit adultery" seem like sensible requests to me, but not to everyone. Not anymore.

But I'm grateful to a heavenly Father Who anticipated what lunatics people can be and gave certain behaviors a strong warning label.

Thank You, Lord, for the warnings along the way.
—DANIEL SCHANTZ

AUGUST 31

*For lo, the one who forms the mountains, creates the wind, reveals
his thoughts to mortals, makes the morning darkness, and treads
on the heights of the earth—the Lord, the God of hosts, is his name!*
—AMOS 4:13 (NRSV)

I woke up this morning in a motel, feeling exhausted from two weeks of traveling. Now, as my husband Larry headed the car toward the Colorado border, I sat listlessly staring out the window at the Kansas landscape. I felt so drained I'd skipped my morning prayers. *Maybe we should just give up the rest of our trip and head for home,* I thought. Our car topped a rolling hill and I looked off across the prairie, startled by the sight of dozens of tall silvery towers with rotating windmill arms. They marched across the countryside in all directions, looking like drum majorettes twirling batons.

"Wind farm," Larry said.

I'd heard of those wind farms, and I'd read that just one of those windmills could generate enough energy to power hundreds of homes. Here were at least a hundred windmills. I sat in awe, thinking about that. Wind. A nonpolluting source of energy and power. You can't see it, but it's always there, available to everybody.

"Okay, I get the message," I whispered and settled back in the seat, focusing on my morning prayers. Soon I felt the renewed energy that comes from connecting with the Higher Power.

> *Heavenly Father, keep my spirit open today
> to the power of Your guidance and strength.*
> —MADGE HARRAH

September

"It is enough for the disciple that he become like his teacher."
—MATTHEW 10:25 (NASB)

I received a surprising faith boost through my job selling baked goods at the farmers' market. I had a tent and tables to set up, heavy racks of bread to load and unload, long hours standing in the weather-of-the-day and waves of people eager to hear me explain my wares. Mothers came with children to buy their favorite cookies. Men stopped by on their lunch breaks to pick up pepperoni rolls. Summer customers wanted sweet breads for the cabin or buns for the outdoor grill. Autumn shoppers purchased scones to go with morning coffee and savory loaves to have with soup. One woman preparing a Greek dinner for friends bought the spinach feta; a man on a bicycle liked his granola with raisins; a curmudgeonly man counted on his sourdough.

Somewhere in the middle of my job, the joy hit me: the unexpected joy of serving people, matching the right breads to their needs and watching them walk away satisfied. I formed a new picture of the Son of Man, exuberant in sharing God's message, excited to serve others: Jesus providing wine for the wedding guests in Cana (John 2:1–11), touching the hand of Peter's mother-in-law so the fever left her (Matthew 8:14–15), giving sight to a man born blind (John 9:1–12), restoring life to a twelve-year-old (Luke 8:40–42, 49–56), welcoming children into His arms (Mark 10:13–16).

How Jesus must have celebrated with the recipients of these wonderful works! What joy He must have felt every morning, anticipating the great things He would do, the words of life He would teach!

Jesus, like You, let me be jubilant in serving.
—CAROL KNAPP

Where will you leave your wealth?
—ISAIAH 10:3 (NASB)

SMALL CHANGE FOR BIG CHANGE! read the sign over the large plastic bottles placed along the front of the church.

In each of the six bottles was a cardboard mailing tube, and on the tubes smaller signs that read PENNIES FOR PROCLAIMING, NICKELS FOR NURTURING, DIMES FOR DISCIPLINING and QUARTERS FOR CHRIST'S KINGDOM.

It was Missions Outreach month at our church, and the idea was to emphasize stewardship by encouraging the Sunday school children to come forward and drop their offerings into the appropriate bottles.

On Sunday the children trooped up the aisle while an enthusiastic nine-year-old thumped out the offertory on the piano. She was soon accompanied by the sound of dozens of coins popcorning into the plastic bottles.

As the children milled about, a tall, awkward teenage boy stooped to help a toddler whose pennies were clasped in sweaty little hands. An older sister directed her kindergartner brother toward the nickel bottle. A mother slipped out of her pew to go up front and suppress the unbridled enthusiasm of two siblings, each determined to donate to the same bottle at the same time. A grandfather showed his tiny grandson how it was done by dropping a coin into the quarter bottle.

Even as "the people were restrained from bringing any more" (Exodus 36:6, NASB), a dawdler plunked in one last dime and walked back down the aisle with a satisfied grin.

The missionary speaker smiled and addressed the children. "You start by giving your pennies to the Lord, and then one day we hope you will give Him your lives."

Lord, I dedicated my life to You years ago, but have I shortchanged You in the stewardship department? Help me to be a more cheerful giver.

—ALMA BARKMAN

SEPTEMBER 3

And yet shew I unto you a more excellent way.
—I CORINTHIANS 12:31

*C*hange can be frightening. Years ago I was laid off from my job as a first-class machine operator. This wasn't just a temporary layoff, it was permanent. Getting a new job would mean relocating to another city or taking work on the evening shift.

I was about to accept the evening shift when my wife Ruby said, "You're thirty-nine years old, Oscar. Don't you feel it's time you used your college education? The night job is okay, but it's a dead end. Do you want to work nights for the rest of your life? Don't you want to grow? Pray about it."

Her words startled me because moving up would mean having to take an exam. What if I fail? How will I study? I hadn't been in the classroom for sixteen years. I prayed, took the exam...and was offered a new job as a mechanical tester in engineering.

At the interview, though, the supervisor said, "You have no experience. You'll have to start as a trainee." A trainee? That would mean an initial fifty-percent reduction in pay! How will we manage? Have I made the right decision? What if things don't work out all right?

"Trust God," Ruby insisted.

As it turned out, I loved my new job. Within months I was given a raise, and then along came a project with unlimited overtime. Soon I was making as much as I had before, and over the years that new pathway led me to technical writing and then management. I will always thank Ruby for her suggestions. All I needed to do was take a risk and work hard. The rest was in God's hands.

Lord, You pointed the way. Then You stepped away and waited for me to follow.
—OSCAR GREENE

*Listen, my beloved brothers and sisters. Has not God chosen the poor
in the world to be rich in faith and to be heirs of the kingdom
that he has promised to those who love him?*

—JAMES 2:5 (NRSV)

Each year my husband Larry and I drive a thousand miles to attend the Orr family reunion, which is held at the Ozark Prairie Presbyterian Church outside Mt. Vernon, Missouri. This small brick church was built by Larry's impoverished but stalwart Scots-Irish ancestors after they immigrated to America from northern Ireland in the early 1870s. The church is a replica of the one the family left behind in Aghadowey and has been in use ever since it was built.

Each reunion begins the same way. Everybody stands and sings, "Faith of our fathers, living still in spite of dungeon, fire and sword. Oh, how our hearts beat high with joy whene'er we hear that glorious word!"

My heart beats stronger, too, as I share those words with the family members who carried their faith across the ocean to America so long ago and have now passed it down through six generations.

Faith. What an inheritance to give one's family!

*Father, today I will share my faith with someone
who may not know the promises of Your Word.*

—MADGE HARRAH

SEPTEMBER 5

"You shall have to clear out the old to make way for the new."
—LEVITICUS 26:10 (NRSV)

*E*ndings seemed to come at me all at once. During just one spring my two-year term as president of the parents' association at my children's school ended, seven years of teaching my daughter Maria's Sunday school class ended when she moved into the confirmation program, my son Ross graduated from high school, and my weekly Bible study ended when our leader moved to another city. Everyone seemed ready to move on except me. How could God expect me to say good-bye to all these facets of my life at the same time? Friends I'd made through volunteering, the contributions I'd made to the life of the school, even my Bible study were part of my identity. *This is who I am*, I thought.

But as a little time passed, new opportunities opened up out of the old. The school hired me to work part-time, allowing me to strengthen many of the friendships I'd made and forge new ones. I was offered the opportunity to teach a Sunday school class once a month, a good fit for my working schedule. I started attending regular Sunday morning Bible classes, learning about God's Word from new teachers and new classmates, many of whom I'd never met. Nothing replaces having my son close by, but I feel a new kind of delight hearing about the fabulous musical experiences he's having in college in Nashville, Tennessee, none of which would have been possible if he hadn't been ready to move on.

I've learned that many of life's endings really are beginnings; you simply have to look a little farther down the road and know that God has something more in mind.

*Dear Lord, give me courage to let go of the familiar
and embrace the plans You have for me.*

—GINA BRIDGEMAN

September 6

Blessed are they which are called unto the marriage supper of the Lamb.
—Revelation 19:9

*B*eryl was in church today. I was surprised. Pete, our deacon, told me the other day that she can rarely get out of her apartment. She's ninety-nine years old and frail. When he took communion to her, he said she just looked at the bread in her lap, wondering what to do with it. How would she act during communion this morning? She stared around the church as if seeing it for the first time, which is certainly not the case.

I hated to think of her getting old. She and her daughter Carmen have been bulwarks in the congregation ever since we joined twenty-five-years ago. They were always so warm, welcoming our newborns, monitoring the boys' growth, celebrating their baptisms and confirmations, rejoicing in the milestones of our life. For years they have been the church's unofficial greeters.

Communion came. Beryl rose unsteadily. She was in the second row. The whole congregation was focused on her. Carmen took her hand, and they walked slowly to the front. Beryl paused, confused. Carmen didn't even have to look around. Another woman was right behind. She offered an elbow, and Beryl took it. All at once, Beryl seemed like a bride in a wedding, confident of where she was and what she was doing.

She took the bread and dipped it in the cup. She smiled. She returned ever so slowly to her seat.

"Send us out in the world in peace," we prayed, "and grant us strength and courage to love and serve You." I was glad I wasn't going out into that world alone. In Christ, I would be with Beryl and she would be with me.

We are never lost when we are with You, Lord.
—Rick Hamlin

SEPTEMBER 7

And the vines with the tender grape give a good smell.
—SONG OF SOLOMON 2:13

*W*hen I was a boy, I used to help my mother pick grapes from the canopy arbor that stretched from our back porch out to the shed. We would pick three or four washtubs full of the heavy clusters, and my mother would transform them into jelly.

She would crush the grapes in a colander, cook them and then pour the hot, sweet liquid into crystal-clean jars. I loved playing with the opalescent bricks of paraffin she'd melt and pour on top of each jar to seal it. Soon the whole neighborhood smelled like wine.

My parents and grandparents raised their own food and gleaned the goodies that nature served for free: nuts and berries, wild plums and apples, even weeds such as dandelions and lamb's quarters. Grandma didn't have twenty-five brands of commercial jelly to pick from, nor thirty-five brands of bread to spread it on. She was grateful just to have food, any food! And she knew her dinner didn't come from Sam Walton or Mr. Smucker, but from the Heavenly Gardener, the Creator of every good thing.

When I sit down to breakfast, I need to reflect on the real source of my bounty. Back of the biscuit is the wheat, and back of the wheat is the sun and the rain. Back of them all is the providence of a generous Creator.

I see Your loving hand, Lord, in everything I bring to my lips.
Make me as generous with others as You have been with me.
—DANIEL SCHANTZ

"Lord, forgive!... For your sake, my God, do not delay,
because your city and your people bear your Name."
—DANIEL 9:19 (NIV)

*B*ible study was over and I rushed out to buy some food for a funeral luncheon. If I hurried, I'd just have time to get it there by noon. I zipped through the store, aware that the peace I'd felt during the Bible study was slipping away and impatience was surfacing.

I was barely able to restrain myself and slow down behind the wobbly old lady in front of me in the prepared foods aisle. Tense and anxious, I finally arrived at the checkout line. I was tempted just to write my check in silence without greeting the checker, but I forced a hello and a smile. It wasn't until I jumped back into my car that I knew my battle to behave was worth it: I still had my Bible study name tag on! What if I'd let my impatience be known along with my name?

Contrite, I realized that, with or without a name tag, there's Someone I'm always representing. In my hurry to do a good deed, I could have undone something just as important: my witness.

Lord Jesus, as Your disciple, I bear Your name. Help me
to be a good witness to You in every part of my life.
—MARJORIE PARKER

September 9

*"Look at the birds of the air; they do not sow or reap or store
away in barns, and yet your heavenly Father feeds them."*
—Matthew 6:26 (nkjv)

I've been a serious birder ever since I took a college course in ornithology. Dr. Everett Myers, my professor at Bowling Green State, predicted that if anyone studied birds for just a season, "they would fascinate you for the rest of your life." He was right.

Today, I was watching a downy woodpecker on the maple outside our kitchen door. It was hunting for insects. When a woodpecker climbs, it does so with its feet together and its tail feathers beneath. All woodpeckers use their stiff tails for support as they climb up. If they were to head downward, they would lose their footing.

Not so with nuthatches. After the downy left its perch, a white-breasted nuthatch took its place and began foraging for food. The herky-jerky nuthatch first went up the tree and then came down, able to move in either direction at will because of its strong legs and feet. Unlike the woodpecker, it places one foot higher than the other to keep its balance.

Jesus must have been a bird-watcher. He said that not even a common sparrow falls without God's knowledge (Matthew 10:29) and that "foxes have dens and birds have nests, but the Son of Man has no place to lay his head" (Matthew 8:20, updated niv). His point in both cases was that our all-knowing heavenly Father is aware of everything that happens. He knows our needs, supplies them and sustains us. But He expects us to do our part. As someone insightfully noted, "God may feed the birds, but He doesn't put food in their nests."

*We thank You, God, for always being there,
For assuring us daily of Your constant care.*
—Fred Bauer

SEPTEMBER 10

Mine eyes are ever toward the Lord.
—PSALM 25:15

*E*arly in September 2005, heart-wrenching stories from survivors of Hurricane Katrina appeared on television. Some victims were barely able to speak; others were openly angry. Many detailed how such a horrific experience might have been avoided. Some placed blame on the lack of preparation and the disorganized response. Their reactions were understandable; after all, they had just lost everything.

Then, on September 8, I watched yet another survivor on television. Her hand rested on her canine companion, a beautiful German shepherd. He sat erect, his eyes fastened on the woman he loved, respected and trusted. The woman didn't seem aware of the microphone the reporter held close to her face while explaining that she was blind and had barely escaped with her life and her guide dog. Along with thousands of others, she'd waited for days on a bridge in New Orleans to be evacuated. "How do you feel about all this?" the reporter asked her.

Her face positively glowed. She smiled and, to my amazement, she sang her response to the reporter's question: "Oh, Jesus, oh, Jesus, I know You care! Oh Jesus, oh Jesus, I still trust You."

Oh, Lord, help me keep my eyes on You, no matter what.
—MARION BOND WEST

September 11

Surely goodness and mercy shall follow me all the days of my life.
—Psalm 23:6

 t's the most enduring image I have of life in New York City in those days right after 9/11. The weather, it must be remembered, was gorgeous. Clear, bright and sunny, while smoke rose from a pit downtown. The streets near our offices on 34th Street were almost empty, making it possible for fire engines, ambulances and emergency vehicles to rush to and from a site newly christened Ground Zero.

Posters were being put up on streetlamps with images of the missing. Little shrines of candles and flowers were assembled in parks and squares. But most of us went to our jobs, trying to do our work. At lunchtime I headed out to pick up a sandwich, and I noticed a stern-looking policeman on the corner of 33rd and Madison. That's how our police officers usually look, brusque and businesslike.

Just then a woman, clearly distraught, bumped into him. At any other time they would have backed away from each other in horror. Instead, the policeman gently put his arms on her shoulders and looked into her eyes as if to say, "Are you all right?" After a minute she nodded: "Yes, I'll be all right." And she went on her way.

It was a reminder to me that the brusque New Yorkers I live with have caring souls. Much of the time you don't know it. People are in a hurry, going about their business. But at that terrible moment we looked into each other's eyes and discovered how much goodness was there.

I shall not forget, Lord, all the goodness You have put in Your people.
—Rick Hamlin

"I have been sent to speak to you and to tell you this good news."
—LUKE 1:19 (NIV)

The gray-haired man sat quietly fishing off the dock at a small Minnesota lake on a cloudy August afternoon. We exchanged greetings. I would have moved on had he not spoken softly, "I come here to think about the Bible, God's Word."

I felt drawn to talk with him, and I learned he had been an officer in the South Vietnamese army during the Vietnam War. Twice he'd been injured by land mines. Fragments of shrapnel in his arm still caused him pain.

At war's end, he was thrown in jail by the North Vietnamese regime. He endured horrendous conditions for ten years. Often there was no food or medicine. Many of his fellow prisoners died.

Upon his release, he returned home to what little family he had left. He felt empty inside and without hope. Then he read two words on a sign displayed outside a church—"Good News." He didn't know what the Good News was, but he knew he needed it.

He went alone to the church the next Sunday and heard the good news of Jesus Christ. The faith he found that day eventually led him to pastor a Vietnamese congregation in the United States.

I'd walked out on the dock that day feeling alone and discouraged. God used a fisherman to remind me that the Good News is never old news.

Jesus, no matter what other news clutters my day,
it's always a Good News day with You.
—CAROL KNAPP

SEPTEMBER 13

For the Lord God is a sun and shield.
—PSALM 84:11 (NASB)

*M*y husband Rick and I are building a log house in the woods. It's been a long time coming. We started thinking about it twenty-five years ago, even before we were married.

As soon as we put the FOR SALE sign in the front yard of our current house, I started writing daily lists for Rick. I had a plan, the best plan, the logical way things should happen.

Last night, we visited our home-in-progress. I like to go every few days so I'll be surprised with the changes. Normally, I use these visits to keep Rick on task. But last night a different line of thought nagged at me. *Why don't you try not to ask any questions this time? Don't ask him if he scheduled a framing inspection. Don't ask how soon he can plant grass. Don't ask if he's ordered the wood-burning stove. Trust. Be quiet.* As we walked around, I let go just a little and didn't prod.

We drove off in the September sunset. Without talking, I reached over and laced my fingers through Rick's as we looked at the orange-pink glow of the disappearing sun.

"God did a pretty good job of the sunset tonight, didn't he?" I said. And the thought came: *Even without my help.*

> *Father, You created the sun and the entire universe.*
> *Surely You can orchestrate the details of my life too.*
> —JULIE GARMON

SEPTEMBER 14

That they may dwell in a place of their own....
—II SAMUEL 7:10

The weather-beaten old house stood tall and straight.

"What in the world does John want with this old relic?" I asked John's mother Lana as she pulled the car in front of it.

"It has great potential," she told me, "and it cost him next to nothing."

"But he can't move his wife and baby into that!"

"Of course he can't right away, but he's fixing it up. You want to look in the back windows and see what he's done?"

We drove around to the back, which looked even worse than the front. Lana saw her son's car in the yard and said, "He's already here. We can go inside!"

Grudgingly, I stepped out of the car, skirting the weeds and the scrap pile. I let Lana go ahead of me onto the porch. When it didn't cave in, I followed tentatively. When she opened the back door, I gasped, "Oh, that's beautiful!"

I was looking into a bare room whose walls were a fresh, gleaming white. Lana began to point out where the sink would be, and the stove, and the washer and dryer. I followed her into a long, wide room, shelved on all sides.

"What I wouldn't give for a pantry like that!" I exclaimed.

The tour continued through the dining room with a fresh coat of blue paint, a wide hall where a mahogany post supported the handrail of matching stairs, and into an open room with a floor covered in newspapers. Two walls were painted to match the dining room and in the middle of the floor stood a round baby-walker, waiting for a baby.

"It's so like a human life," I told Lana when we were in the car. "Sin gets hold of a soul and beats it down until it's without hope."

Lana added, "Then God steps in with His patience and gentle love..."

"...And changes it into a wonderful treasure," I said, finishing the thought, and the promise.

Father, help me never to lose sight of Your wonderful power to beautify my life.
—DRUE DUKE

For the bread of God is he which cometh down
from heaven, and giveth life unto the world.
—JOHN 6:33

Thumbnail cubes of bread are arranged on a gleaming silver tray. There's a hush in the sanctuary; piano music drifts from the altar as the tray is passed down the rows.

I reach for my own small piece. It is light and feathery in my hand. Silently, I acknowledge my sins before the One Who died for them. Hope flickers in my heart like the flame of the Communion candle. Maybe next time I will be more careful in my choices. For now it is enough to slip the bit of bread in my mouth, remembering the sacrifice of my Savior.

Until last Sunday, this had been my usual Communion experience. What made that day different was, for the first time, I was responsible for preparing the Communion bread. The night before, my husband had brought me two loaves of French bread. I pulled out the cutting board, picked up a knife and began to trim the crusts off the loaves. As I performed this simple task, I became acutely aware of what I was doing and why.

Then I thought about the other things these loaves might have been used for—a party snack dipped in seasoned sour cream, a side order smeared with butter and served with pasta in a restaurant, lunch for ducks on a pond. Instead, this bread would be fed to hearts famished for forgiveness and longing for God's hope and healing in their lives.

As I watched the bits of bread disappear from the tray at Communion that Sunday, I felt a new awe: God's Son gave His body on the cross and called it the Bread of Life. Such bread is not to be handled casually.

Lord Jesus, You left us the comforting, sustaining imagery
of bread to represent Your broken body. May my reaching for it—
and for You—be always genuine and never routine.
—CAROL KNAPP

SEPTEMBER 16

The one who guards a fig tree will eat its fruit.
—PROVERBS 27:18 (NIV)

The last time Dad had been to church he had driven his car and walked into the service on his own. This time we pushed him in a wheelchair after a difficult recovery from stomach surgery.

We headed straight for Dad's customary place in the sanctuary—a special bench in a small alcove near one of the side doors. Dad had helped put the bench there seven years earlier when my mother needed a wheelchair after a stroke. Now Mom was gone, and it was Dad in the wheelchair and me beside him on the bench.

When I picked up the hymnal, I worried that Dad might not be able to read it. But as I handed him the book, I was surprised to discover it was a large-print edition. As Dad's voice joined with mine in song, thankfulness came over me for the unknown person who had put it there.

I felt the solid bench underneath me. Dad's years of faithfulness to Mom during her disability had become the means through which God, in turn, showed His faithfulness to Dad. Dad had been there Sunday after Sunday, making the bench a comfortable place for disabled people to worship with their families, never guessing that someday he would need it himself.

I suppose that's the way it is with those who faithfully serve and give. They never guess the ways in which their acts of kindness will be returned to them in their own time of need.

Dear Father, thank You that our small acts
of faithfulness have a way of returning to us.
—KAREN BARBER

"For I know the plans that I have for you," declares the Lord.
—JEREMIAH 29:11 (NASB)

*M*y husband Gene and I had to stay over for two nights after a conference in Montrose, Pennsylvania, to get reasonably priced flights home. "What will we do?" I wailed. "Everybody's gone now."

"Maybe God has special plans just for us," Gene said.

"Like what?" I asked, arms folded. "We don't even have a car."

"Want to walk uptown?"

When I was growing up in Elberton, Georgia, my friends and I walked "uptown" to the square almost every day. But I hadn't done such a thing in almost fifty years.

As we approached the tiny town nestled in the hills, I felt as though we had walked into a Grandma Moses painting. The two-story Victorian houses we strolled by had beautifully manicured lawns, huge ancient trees and neat picket fences. At the Montrose Country Store, Gene rocked in a chair by the door while I browsed inside. Across the street at a pet store, four little kittens followed us around. We enjoyed lunch at a sidewalk café and ordered double-scoop ice cream cones, finishing them off while walking around the square. As we walked back to the conference ground, Gene reached for my hand.

That night we were the only people in camp. A soft rain became a lullaby; after it stopped, we listened to the crickets and frogs. There was no television, not even a radio. We weren't expecting any phone calls. "Why don't I read to you?" Gene asked.

"Okay."

Gene picked up his Bible and read several psalms. The gentle rain started again and I drifted off to sleep anticipating tomorrow.

Oh, Father, when will I learn to trust Your lovely plans for me?
—MARION BOND WEST

SEPTEMBER 18

I will sing of the Lord's great love forever.
—PSALM 89:1 (NIV)

ot long ago I heard our son Ryan talking on the phone in his room. He'd gone through a lot over the course of the year—a wonderful trip to Germany, a week at a Young Life camp in Georgia, the loss of his older brother Reggie in a car accident and his seventeenth birthday in July. He was a young man now, and I wondered how much longer his mother and I would be the defining influences in his life.

I walked past Ryan's room and saw him on his knees, the phone in one hand, a Bible in the other. Later I asked him about it.

"Dad, I was talking to one of my friends," he said. "She was having some difficulties, and I was encouraging her with Scripture."

Wow! Ryan had been practicing what we had been teaching him all his life. I wanted to praise God.

Now, whenever I start to wonder if my children—or anyone else—is really listening to me, I remind myself that if I'm faithful and share the truth as best I can, our heavenly Father will accomplish all He wants to accomplish through me.

Father, help me to do my best to be faithful and entrust the rest to You.
—DOLPHUS WEARY

On the day of prosperity be joyful, and on the day of adversity consider; God has made the one as well as the other.
—ECCLESIASTES 7:14 (NRSV)

*W*hen our son lost his job, he and his family moved in with us. Our daughter, also jobless, joined us too. Then my parents and my husband Larry's mother became ill, so Larry and I took turns traveling to Missouri to help them. When our parents' illnesses were pronounced terminal, our children moved out of our home and Larry and I brought in our parents, whom we cared for over the next ten months as they died, one by one. Sometimes I felt besieged, like Job, and questioned God's purpose.

Then I heard a motivational speaker talk about attitude. She said, "When you face adversity, do you wallow in misery and whine, 'Why me?' Or do you examine the problem while asking, 'What good can come from this?'" She added that it's possible to grow and change for the better because of the pain we experience, but we have to choose to do so.

"All right, God, help me see the good in this," I prayed.

So He showed me. During the months our children and grandchildren lived with us, we developed a closeness that will stay with us the rest of our lives. When our parents lay dying, our children came often to visit them, creating new bonds of love.

Time of adversity? No, a time of togetherness, with one another and with God.

Thank You, Lord, for the troubled times that strengthen our souls and help us grow.
—MADGE HARRAH

There is neither Jew nor Greek, there is neither bond nor free,
there is neither male nor female: for ye are all one in Christ Jesus.
—GALATIANS 3:28

I was having dinner with Peter, an African-American friend, and as we discussed a criminal case with racial overtones that was causing a ruckus in the New York City media, my mind flashed back to the late 1950s and an incident from my childhood.

My parents had taken me along on a business trip to Roanoke, Virginia. One night when they had a function to attend, they left me in the care of an African-American babysitter at our hotel. I had my heart—and stomach—set on a real Southern-fried chicken dinner, and I wanted to be served at a swanky table by a tuxedoed waiter rather than order room service.

The babysitter took me down to the hotel restaurant, where I was addressed as "sir" and ceremoniously ushered to a table draped in white linen by a window. Alone.

I glanced behind me: My sitter was standing with the maître d', pointing to something on the menu and then at me. He nodded. Then she went outside and kept an eye on me through the window while I ate my Southern-fried feast in solitude.

I was puzzled, to say the least, by why she couldn't sit with me, and later I asked my mom about it. "Sometimes we don't treat each other the way God wants," she said. "But things are getting better."

I looked across the table at my friend Peter as he scanned the menu. Things have gotten better. They aren't perfect, but they are not as bad as they used to be. Mom was right. Little by little, I believe we are learning to treat each other the way God wants.

Father of us all, teach me to reach out rather than pull back,
to include rather than exclude, to trust rather than fear.
—EDWARD GRINNAN

SEPTEMBER 21

Because you knew that you yourselves had better and lasting possessions.
—HEBREWS 10:34 (NIV)

Last year my diseased hip joint was replaced with a titanium ball-and-cup lined with ceramic. Just twelve weeks after the surgery, I was in Colorado, skiing without pain for the first time in years. Then I started taking stairs two at a time, something impossible just last fall. A few weeks after that, I was chasing my wife Joy around the park on her five-mile daily walk/run and almost keeping up. And finally, just last summer, I went on a six-day solo canoe trip to the Boundary Waters Canoe Area Wilderness in northeastern Minnesota and carried all my own gear, including the canoe, as if I was twenty again.

Then I went for my six-month postsurgery checkup. The doctor told me everything was looking great, and if I was careful, my new hip would last a good twenty or twenty-five years.

Now that made me think. Even with the best results, this great technology is going to wear out; I am going to wear out. Maybe not next year or in the next ten years, but someday I won't be able to take the stairs two steps at a time or carry that canoe over the rocky trails. As good as I feel now, it won't last forever.

So I asked myself, what does last forever? I decided to make a list and found it was a pretty short one, with nothing material or physical on it: Faith lasts. Love lasts. Hope is the fuel that keeps them both burning. Character made out of integrity, generosity and kindness lasts too.

Now mind you, I'm still going to exercise this bionic hip and all my other parts to keep them moving as long as possible, but I've decided to exercise the things on my list too. Because, as I understand it, I get to take those with me when I leave the hip behind.

Lord God, thank You for the wisdom You give doctors to heal and help, and for the opportunities You give me to grow and thrive into eternity.
—ERIC FELLMAN

SEPTEMBER 22

For we walk by faith, not by sight.
—II CORINTHIANS 5:7

Life is hard for the poor folk of rural Mississippi, and African-Americans are among the poorest of those poor. To help the children of the rural poor break the chains of poverty and racism, Mendenhall Ministries founded Genesis One Christian School. The school has always been close to my heart, and I was happy that my son Ryan had a chance to attend it. So I was glad that our foundation was able to support a new ministry headed up by Mrs. Kincaid, a former teacher at Genesis One.

When I told Ryan I was going to visit Mrs. Kincaid, he was eager to go with me. We drove about forty miles from Jackson, Mississippi, to the little town of Morton, and then about two miles farther out into the country. When we came to a two-story house, Ryan said, "Daddy, that's the one we're looking for." We got out and knocked on the door.

Mrs. Kincaid came to the door and greeted us, giving Ryan a big hug. She invited us in and told us about the things she was doing. "Since I left Genesis One four years ago," she said, "I've been operating a day-care center here. But what this community really needs is a school like Genesis One, and I'm going to start one. I don't know where the money will come from, but we've already broken ground for the new schoolhouse. Do you see that freshly graded space across the road? I'm trusting God to get it built right there."

It's always a good idea to approach a new project or a change in my life with careful thought and prudent planning. But there are times when, after thought and prayer, we have to have the courage to follow our vision, work hard to clear the ground and trust God to "get it built right there."

Lord, give me the courage to walk out in faith to answer Your call.
—DOLPHUS WEARY

And the peace of God, which passeth all understanding,
shall keep your hearts and minds through Christ Jesus.
—PHILIPPIANS 4:7

As I boarded the plane, I was surprised to find that the passenger behind me was one of my students. Carrie and the rest of the University of Pittsburgh women's soccer team were flying home from a game in Philadelphia. We chatted and then returned to our respective books. I acted calm and collected, which really is an act for me, because I'm a tad fearful of flying. Make that more than a tad.

I hadn't noticed how overcast it was until we climbed into a thick bank of clouds. Despite the weather the flight was smooth and my pulse rate was nearly normal. I thought about trying to sleep and then I looked outside.

It was sunset above the clouds. The sun—ninety-three million miles away but looking mighty close—spilled out like an exploded orange across acres and acres of white, puffy canvas. Here and there little cream-colored waves peeked above the others, frozen in a vermillion ocean. And because we were flying west, the sunset hung in there, suspended, like an encore performance that never really left the stage.

"Carrie," I whispered behind me, "Carrie, look!"

Carrie was already at the window, as awestruck as I. For a moment, we weren't student and teacher; we were both students of good fortune, struck dumb by this amazing treat...a divine wonder that, like the peace of God, "passeth all understanding."

I finally relaxed because I now knew that the firmest, surest support is not visible. We're held aloft by faith, on a long, sometimes worrisome, but always wondrous journey where we're always heading home.

Thank You, Lord, that all of us, all of our lives, are held in place by this
ridiculous, ineffable mix of clouds and sun and divine wonder.
—MARK COLLINS

SEPTEMBER 24

Do not fear, for I am with you, do not be afraid, for I am your God.
—ISAIAH 41:10 (NRSV)

*W*e were having supper in our cabin in the mountain village of Platoro, Colorado, when a loud pounding on the door brought us out of our seats. It was Myron Eckberg, our neighbor from up the road. "A cabin at the lodge is on fire!" he cried. "Bring as many buckets as you can find."

My husband Larry and our daughter Meghan grabbed buckets from under the stairs while I collected jackets from the coatrack. The three of us, along with Kayla, Meghan's eight-year-old daughter, jumped into our truck and bounced over the dirt road toward the lodge, a quarter-mile away. When we arrived, we saw a line of people passing buckets of water to each other from the nearby river, their bodies silhouetted against the flames that shot up into the gathering darkness. A friend ran to meet us, explaining: "We've called the fire station in the valley, but the fire truck won't get here for at least another forty-five minutes."

Larry and Meghan rushed off to join the bucket brigade. I kept Kayla with me and gathered other children around me as their parents arrived carrying their own buckets. A cold wind sprang up. I knew the water carriers must be freezing in their soaked clothes, but they kept on going. "Protect them, Lord," I prayed. "Please don't let anyone get hurt."

By the time the fire truck arrived, the first cabin had collapsed, but the water-soaked cabins on either side had been saved. Best of all, no one had gotten hurt. My heart filled with gratitude for the courage and generosity of the people of the town, and I breathed another prayer: "Thank You, Lord, for good neighbors."

Heavenly Father, please help me today to be a good neighbor to everyone I meet.
—MADGE HARRAH

September 25

Follow me.
—Matthew 8:22

Last January I was ordained as an elder at Hillsboro Presbyterian Church. I've attended Hillsboro since my father became its minister when I was nine months old. To be an elder alongside him and to serve the church that is my extended family has been my lifelong dream. Now my opportunity had finally come.

Soon it was time for the annual elders' retreat. I'd always wondered what my father did when he was gone from us for this weekend event and now I'd find out. The retreat combined devotions with thoughtful reflections on our faith and on our responsibilities as Christians. "Let's talk about God's way," my father said on the final morning. "How would our world look if we actually lived as Christ taught?"

As the discussion picked up, the distinction between the world's way and God's way took on a vivid meaning as it became increasingly clear that what we are urged to do as a church and as elders and members differs wildly from the way the real world works. Imagine taking God's way into the world where we work and play and live together—loving people regardless of our differences, forgiving quickly and without reservation, caring for the sick, feeding the hungry, welcoming the stranger, being thankful for the day at hand.

I wondered if God wanted us all to be His elders, whether ordained or not, and to take His teachings seriously. Maybe He's counting on us to make His way and the world's way one.

Dear God, help me to reflect Your way in everything I do.
—Brock Kidd

"The Lord himself goes before you and will be with you.... Do not be afraid."
—DEUTERONOMY 31:8 (NIV)

Late in the baseball season a couple of years ago, I ran across the story of Jackie Mitchell, "the girl who struck out Babe Ruth." Jackie was seventeen years old in 1931 when, signed to a minor-league baseball contract with the Chattanooga Lookouts, she struck out Ruth and Lou Gehrig in an exhibition game. Prior to the game, many fans said Jackie couldn't possibly handle such legendary hitters. But that didn't stop her. Determined to use the physical gifts God had given her, Mitchell faced her fears and succeeded, continuing to play exhibition games in an all-male sport for several years.

That story inspires me now because I'm facing something I'm not sure I can do. I was asked to teach Sunday school at the Spanish-speaking mission church begun by our congregation. I agreed to assist another teacher in a class of fourth- through sixth-graders, but then the leader called, desperate—she had no one to teach the two- to four-year-olds. By myself, with the youngest kids? That's not exactly my strength. And they don't speak English.

I wanted to say no. What was I getting into? Then I remembered feeling the same fear years before when my daughter had asked me to teach her Sunday school class. Yet God had given me the tools to succeed. Now, as then, I feel Him saying, "Trust Me. I will be faithful to you." So, like Jackie Mitchell, I'm ignoring all the reasons why I can't do it, stepping on the mound and giving it a shot. I'll let you know how it goes.

Give me what I need, Lord, to do this job right for You.
—GINA BRIDGEMAN

September 27

You have been my help; Do not abandon me
nor forsake me, O God of my salvation!
—Psalm 27:9 (nasb)

About twenty years ago I began corresponding with a woman I'll call Ryan. We didn't actually meet until about five years ago, when she moved to the Atlanta area. We met for lunch and occasionally dropped each other notes. After a while she mentioned almost casually in a letter that for some time she'd been sleeping in her car.

Her needs were overwhelming. My initial reaction was to put some distance between us, but I tried to do the best I could for her. I made countless calls trying to find her a place to live and help of some kind. I continued to write to her, enclosing what assistance I could. It's very difficult to share the little happenings of everyday life with someone who's living out of a car.

Ryan always answered my letters in her beautiful handwriting, insisting that God was meeting her needs. When her children were small, her minister-husband had left them. Later, a horrific storm had taken away her house and belongings. But she insisted that God was still with her and took care of her. "I'm sleeping in the Waldorf Astoria of parking lots! A policeman—or maybe he's an angel—watches over me." One note said, "What you sent was just what I needed today." *What about the other days?* I wondered. My help was so insignificant and my sense of discomfort so great that I thought about not writing. Then a letter came. "I don't tell people how I live anymore," Ryan wrote. "They are too uncomfortable with my situation and turn away."

Whenever I had read the story of Jesus' Crucifixion, I had always felt anger at the disciples who ran away and hid. *I would have been there with John and the two Marys,* I had thought, *not hiding in the courtyard like Peter.* Now I knew better. I went to my typewriter and wrote, "Dear Ryan..."

Lord, as I stand with those who are troubled, I am standing at the foot
of Your cross. Help me to not turn away from them. Amen.
—Marion Bond West

SEPTEMBER 28

If I take the wings of the morning, and dwell in the uttermost parts of the sea;
Even there shall thy hand lead me, and thy right hand shall hold me.
—PSALM 139:9–10

*B*ardsey Island is a small but very sacred site just off the end of the Llyn Peninsula of North Wales. It's a quaint and peaceful isle of monastic ruins, grazing sheep, a beckoning lighthouse, a sturdy mountain and a profound silence braided with the unhurried sounds of the sea.

Even though our group of twenty-four pilgrims has traveled thousands of miles over land and sea and spent two weeks on the Llyn Peninsula leading up to our Bardsey crossing, we have been told we might not be able to make it to the island. Everything depends on the wind, the sea and the grace of God.

Yet here we are! As we begin our two days of silence on the island, I find an inviting space by a stone wall where I can sit in the grass overlooking the fields and the infinite sea and just let myself sink into being. As I release the many small concerns of my daily life, I feel myself, by grace, gradually entering into the great Oneness that is beyond naming. Some time later, I notice I'm gazing deeply into a single blade of grass that is ready to spill its seeds, and I see that it's a mirror of its Creator.

How could there ever be a place where God is not? The Holy One is in the mountain and the creek across the road from our house, in the wide open spaces of the Great Plains, in the magnolias and soft sounds of the South, on the sandy beaches of the coastal shores, even in the sparkles of ground glass in the concrete of a great city.

Yes, even there, Beloved One, and even here.
—MARILYN MORGAN KING

SEPTEMBER 29

And he shall turn the heart of the fathers to the children,
and the heart of the children to their fathers.

—MALACHI 4:6

It was the third anniversary of my father's death, and by the accounts of the grief experts I should have been over it and getting on with my life. Instead, I found myself rehashing snippets of the final two-and-a-half years of Dad's life, the sharp decline he'd taken physically and mentally after my mother passed away. Gone was Dad's quick wit, his ability to spin a hilarious tale, the way he challenged the contestants on *Jeopardy!*

I also yearned for one of Dad's hugs. For try as I might, I couldn't recall a time in those last years when I knew for certain he loved me. *Dementia stole Daddy from me, God.*

I dined alone that night at a restaurant and lamented the secret place in my heart that only a father's love could fill. Just then, I spotted a man and his little girl sitting shoulder-to-shoulder in a red vinyl booth, coloring a picture on a placemat. The girl, maybe three, reached for one of her daddy's French fries. The man tugged on the girl's blonde pigtails. *I used to have pigtails like that, God.* Happy, bouncing ones with pretty grosgrain ribbons. Back when I was Daddy's girl.

Suddenly a warmth started at the top of my head and traveled to the tips of my toes—the warmth of a father's love. Dementia, you're the great deceiver. My daddy never stopped loving me.

Thanks to a daddy and his little girl, my God-finds for today, I found my father again.

Daddy's living with You now, Lord. Would You
please tell him how much I love him?

—ROBERTA MESSNER

For thus saith the Lord God, the Holy One of Israel; In returning and rest shall ye be saved; in quietness and in confidence shall be your strength.

—ISAIAH 30:15

I'm supposed to be at work in an hour. I haven't felt well for the past few days, so I have a legitimate excuse to call in sick. And so many things happened last night and this morning.

Last night I saw God's work in a harvest moon. I'm sure I didn't say that aloud—"Hey, kids, wake up! I know it's forty-two degrees outside, but come see God's work!" Instead I stood there watching it, bright and round like a child's new ball, just staring and shivering.

Last night I had a dream. I was a kid again, sitting on the dryer and watching my mom (alive again!) as she loaded sheets into the ancient Kenmore washer. She was humming a Tony Bennett song, "I Wanna Be Around."

This morning I awoke with Grace, our six-year-old, asleep on my chest. Her small, round head was against my ribs, her long hair like a blond waterfall around me. I got up late, because I didn't want to wake her.

I know I'm supposed to be about the Lord's business, but maybe today I'm supposed to do that business in a different way. Of course, when I do call work, I won't tell them any of that.

Lord, thank You for the days when sickness slows me down just enough to see the signs of Your presence around me.

—MARK COLLINS

October

OCTOBER 1

*The cup of blessing which we bless, is it not
the communion of the blood of Christ?*
—I CORINTHIANS 10:16

I am comfortable with the way certain things are done in the kind of church I've gone to all my life. When we serve Communion, for example, the basket of bread comes around, followed by the cups of grape juice, while music plays. I sit and pray and reflect. I love this time.

I went to a Christian retreat center recently. After the Sunday worship service, Communion stations were set up in the front and back of the auditorium. We were to stand in line and, once at the station, take the bread from a basket and dip it into the wine while the man and woman in charge of the station whispered, "This is Christ's body broken for you. This is Christ's blood shed for you."

I felt uncomfortable taking Communion this way. *Do I dunk the bread a little or a lot?* I worried. *When they speak the words to me, do I thank them? Do I respond in any way? If I don't, will they think I'm rude?*

The sermon was very moving that morning, the music particularly beautiful. If not for their bothersome way of administering Communion, it would have been a perfect service. I walked up to the station and dunked the bread, not too long and not too short, saying nothing. I walked back to my seat with the wine-soaked bread and prayed, annoyed that I wasn't going to get to enjoy this Communion the way I usually do.

That's when God intervened. He allowed some wine from my piece of bread to drip into my palm. The image and feel of the wine on my hand was more than I could bear. I cried under the weight of my sin as I felt the price Jesus paid for me with His blood on the cross. Communion had never been this powerful before.

Lord, sometimes I have to get out of my comfort zone to really feel Your power.
—DAVE FRANCO

OCTOBER 2

I trust in God's unfailing love for ever and ever.
—PSALM 52:8 (NIV)

On vet's orders, our cat Nickel was temporarily sporting a brand-new lampshade collar and she was running into trouble negotiating the terrain in the living room. Every time she tried to step from the hardwood floor to her favorite carpet, the bottom of the collar would catch on the rug's edge. One step forward and Nickel was nose-to-carpet, lampshade firmly planted on the ground. She backed up, ready to try again and land facedown, when I gently lifted the collar. A moment later, Nickel was curled in her favorite spot on the rug, gazing at me, trusting and content.

It amazed me that she didn't blame me for her predicament. Our other cat, Antimony, is not so forgiving. But while "Tim" is the family skeptic, Nickel seems to have faith that I'll look out for her.

When I had taken her to the vet a week earlier, even as they had her stretched out on her back for the ultrasound, completely vulnerable and in pain, she looked at me with that same quiet trust. After her operation to remove a bladder stone, she resisted taking her pills and picked at her stitches, but didn't hold it against me when I forced her to swallow the pills and took her back to the vet for new stitches and the lampshade collar.

Soon enough Nickel learned to lift her head when navigating around obstacles and to swallow her pills without too much fuss. Eventually the collar and stitches were gone, but the trust was still there; I am her protector.

Nickel reminds me daily that I'll find comfort and peace in trusting in my Protector. Whatever obstacles I face, even if I feel "nose-to-carpet" and helpless, God is looking out for me.

Heavenly Father, I turn my eyes to You with a trusting gaze.
I know You will always guard me and guide me. Amen.
—KJERSTIN WILLIAMS

OCTOBER 3

"Do not fear;...I have summoned you by name; you are mine."
—ISAIAH 43:1 (NIV)

*I*n the four weeks I'd been at Dennis Junior High, this was the first time I'd ever been in the office. Now I stood there, bright drops of blood falling onto my white tennis shoe, unsure what to do. Request permission to call home? Ask to see the nurse? Get a late pass to homeroom?

Suddenly, Miss Pigg, the dreaded Dean of Girls, appeared beside me. I gripped my finger tighter as I stuttered out the explanation. "The car door—I slammed it on—it's my f-finger!"

"Oh, Mary Lou, let me see!" she said, bundling me off toward the nurse's office.

I don't remember what happened at the nurse's. No doubt she bandaged the cut responsible for the small, crescent-shaped scar on my index finger. What lingers most vividly about that whole experience is the fact that Miss Pigg knew my name. I was stunned that this woman, whose reputation was based on detentions and calls home to parents, had taken time to find out about me—the new girl in school. Miss Pigg's compassion was something I hadn't heard about from the other kids.

It's pretty easy to think of God the way I thought of Miss Pigg: a powerful being watching our every move, just waiting for us to make a mistake. But God is much bigger than that stereotype. He's compassionate as well as just. And what's more, He knows us all by name.

Let me come boldly to You, Father, with my hurts and heartaches—and my mistakes. Mend me and forgive me and send me out to do Your will.
—MARY LOU CARNEY

OCTOBER 4

I will sing praise to thy name, O thou most High.
—PSALM 9:2

*M*y husband Robert and I recently attended a weekend program exploring the relationship between dreams and the soul. It's a subject of interest to both of us, because we share our dreams over breakfast and travel together on our spiritual journey.

"I just don't know how to get to my soul," one of the participants told the leader.

"I'll give you the best way I know," he replied. "Take a praise walk in nature. That'll get you there." Then he suggested that we all go outside and take a walk, each one going a separate way, and just notice and give thanks for all we see.

The retreat house in southern Colorado is surrounded by wilderness and majestic canyons. I chose to walk eastward on a winding path that took me upward on rocky ground. Looking around, I praised God for the panoramic beauty of the surroundings.

Next, I found a shady place under a canyon overhang and sat down. At first I just sat quietly, breathing in the beauty of the green grass, yellow-leafed trees, ground-hugging plants, and boulders large and small, unmoved by human "fixing." As I sat there, I thought I heard a bird. The gentle wind seemed to whisper, "Yes, it's hiding in a hole in the canyon wall." Sure enough, within a few minutes a beautiful bird with a black-and-white tail flew out of its canyon home, soaring above me, filling my heart with birdsong and praise.

Great Creator of all that is, thank You for mountains and rivers and golden leaves, for green grass and tiny ants, and for the "impossible" flight of honeybees. Oh yes, and for canyon birds singing and soaring into listening hearts.
—MARILYN MORGAN KING

OCTOBER 5

The Lord is the One who holds his hand.
—PSALM 37:24 (NASB)

his morning I was reading Psalm 37. The psalmist is wrestling with his own humanity and admitting his share of mistakes. With a wisdom that comes with age, he concludes, "Rest in the Lord and wait patiently for Him; ...Do not fret, it leads only to evildoing. ...When he falls, he will not be hurled headlong; Because the Lord is the One who holds his hand" (Psalm 37:7–8, 24, NASB).

As I read these words, I remembered a moment when I was a small child, walking through a large public market in the Philippines with my father. It was very crowded and people pressed relentlessly against us. Suddenly I became frightened that I would be separated from my father and hopelessly lost. Just then my dad's big hand came down and grasped mine. His grip was so firm I was sure he wouldn't let go of me, that I was safe because he was with me.

As I've watched my life unfold, I've discovered that no matter how much I fail or how many boneheaded decisions I make, God will never let go of my hand. As King David wrote near the end of his inconsistent life, "Just as a father has compassion on his children, So the Lord has compassion on those who fear Him" (Psalm 103:13, NASB).

Dear God, thank You for being my Father
and not letting go of my hand. Amen.
—SCOTT WALKER

OCTOBER 6

According to the kindness that I have done unto thee, thou shalt do unto me.
—GENESIS 21:23

W hen I got the letter from the "no-account loser," I hardly knew what to think. At least that's what he called himself, "a no-account loser living in a patched-up trailer." He was writing me to ask how he might improve his life.

In the midst of what my husband David was fondly calling "Pam's kindness kick," I knew I couldn't simply ignore the letter and lay it aside. Kindness demanded a response. First, I took some time to ask God to help me with my reply, and then I sat down and began to write: "Dear Robert, in your letter you write, 'There must be some way I can be a more worthwhile person.' I've been thinking about that and finally I realize there is only one answer: You already are."

I encouraged him to talk to God about the person he would like to become. I reminded him that God delights in his efforts and can't wait to see what he might do next.

One letter followed another, and soon Robert was sharing his life story with me, offering me a window into worlds I hadn't imagined. He sent thoughtful scientific and philosophical articles for David and me to read. We began exchanging favorite books. And the nature of our correspondence was beginning to change. In the beginning I was Robert's cheerleader. Now he was cheering me on too. When I felt blue, Robert was the first to point me to the bright side, and when David and I traveled to Africa, it was good to know that Robert was praying for us twice a day.

In the beginning I reached out to Robert out of a commitment to being kind. In the end I gained a friend.

Father, thanks so much for being You...and for returning
what I offer others tenfold back to me.
—PAM KIDD

"For no word from God will ever fail."
—LUKE 1:37 (NIV)

A few years ago I was feeling trapped and helpless, facing issues I couldn't resolve. I decided to visit an older friend, Tom Parrish, and glean his life-earned wisdom.

As we talked in his study, Tom walked to his bookshelf, thumbed through a small book and handed it to me. "Read this page," he said.

Glancing at the cover of the well-worn book, I saw it was *Gitanjali*, a collection by the Indian poet Rabindranath Tagore. As I read the opened page, printed words became an epiphany:

> I thought that my voyage had come to its end at the last limit of my power—that the path before me was closed, that provisions were exhausted and the time come to take shelter in a silent obscurity.
>
> But I find that thy will knows no end in me. And when old words die out on the tongue, new melodies break forth from the heart; and where the old tracks are lost, new country is revealed with its wonders.

Suddenly I knew that though I might be powerless, God is not. And though my vision might be limited, God sees beyond the horizon of the universe.

Advent is the season that calls us to reflect on the incarnation of this age-old truth: "Nothing is impossible with God!" The birth of Jesus reveals for all time that God is with us. And as the apostle Paul wrote, "If God is for us, who can be against us?" (Romans 8:31, updated NIV).

Father, give me the faith to believe that "when old tracks are lost, new country is revealed." Amen.
—SCOTT WALKER

OCTOBER 8

The word is very near you; it is in your mouth and in your heart.
—DEUTERONOMY 30:14 (NIV)

For as long as I can remember, I've loved words. I'm especially fond of little sayings, quotes that form the backbone of my personal and spiritual life. That's why I put a large piece of glass on my desk and promptly began to stick words underneath.

On any day, without even moving my chair, I can be motivated by these words, printed in black on a faded piece of yellow paper: "You are going to do something great today!" Victor Hugo offers me advice for tough times: "Have courage for the great sorrows of life and patience for the small ones." James 1:17 (NIV) reminds me, "Every good and perfect gift is from above." A cute piece of Mary Englebreit artwork encourages me: "Do Good. Avoid Evil." Mother Teresa, ever the model of Christian charity, tells me, "Love is a fruit in season at all times and within reach of every hand." And when I'm tempted to skip lunch, Kobi Yamada's question jars me into making better choices: "Be good to yourself. If you don't take care of your body, where will you live?"

I'm grateful for the power of words in my life. I'm especially grateful for the Word that became flesh and dwelt among us, inspiring and challenging us. And I'm grateful, too, for the wisdom and humor that words bring me.

Which reminds me, did I mention my favorite quote? "All a girl really needs is the right pair of shoes." Advice from (who else?) Cinderella.

Today and every day, Lord, let my words be inspired and directed by You.
—MARY LOU CARNEY

OCTOBER 9

Why art thou cast down, O my soul? ...Hope thou in God.
—PSALM 42:11

*M*y birthday that Sunday was not lining up to be much of a celebration. I hadn't received any phone calls or cards, and my gift was one of those practical ones for which husbands are famous and wives don't appreciate. My hints about going out to eat had fallen on deaf ears. A birthday cake was nowhere in sight.

The one highlight of the day would be at church. Our pastor asks the congregation to sing "Happy Birthday" to anyone whose birthday falls on a Sunday. And so I waited expectantly through the announcements, waited through the opening hymn, waited while the pastor mentioned another birthday coming up the following day.

And then he began his sermon.

How could he be so forgetful? I felt slighted, overlooked, disappointed. *Why do people take me for granted, Lord? Especially today of all days!*

A few minutes later, an old hymn, "Be Thou My Vision," redirected my focus. Two lines in particular spoke directly to my soul: "Riches I need not, nor man's empty praise, Thou mine inheritance, now and always."

But, of course! How could I be so forgetful as to overlook God's blessings during the past year, let alone a lifetime? Even as I closed the hymnbook and placed it back in the rack, I could feel my heart beginning to celebrate a happy birthday.

Thank You, Lord, that the upside of down times is that You
use them to put things into their proper perspective.
—ALMA BARKMAN

Therefore shall ye lay up these my words in your heart and in your soul.... And thou shalt write them upon the door posts of thine house, and upon thy gates.
—DEUTERONOMY 11:18, 20

*S*ome years ago, when my wife and I moved into a new building on Chicago's North Side, I noticed our next-door neighbor touching a small metal object on her doorpost as she left her apartment.

What's that? I wondered.

As weeks passed, we became acquainted, and one morning over coffee I summoned up the courage to ask about it.

"Oh," she said, putting down her cup, "it's a *mezuzah*. Hebrew for 'doorpost.' Inside is a small scroll of parchment with Scripture from Deuteronomy 6:4–9 and 11:13–21, an affirmation of our faith in God, to keep His words in our minds and hearts, as He commanded."

"*Hmm,*" I said, impressed. "At first I thought it was some kind of security device."

She smiled. "In a way, it is."

Lord, I don't have a mezuzah *on my doorway, so remind me, before I step out into the world, to stop a moment to ask You for Your guidance and protection.*
—RICHARD SCHNEIDER

Let my prayer be set forth before thee as incense.
—PSALM 141:2

*I*n 1992, Anna and Nelson Tabirian fled the embattled Armenian city of Yerevan and found safe haven in Darmstadt, Germany, where we were blessed to have them as neighbors. Although Anna and I laughed and chatted while our children played together, a trace of sadness always shadowed her face.

One day, her voice quavering, she told me about her elderly parents in Yerevan. They were experiencing food shortages, they had no electricity, and they were in need of medical treatment. Wringing her hands, Anna said, "Oh, Mary, I have such great fear for them."

I sympathized with Anna's anxiety for her family far away. I had just learned that my mom was experiencing paralysis of her left arm. The doctors were unable to diagnose the problem, and I longed to be with her.

A few days later I described to Anna the beautiful Russian church in town. To my surprise, Anna exclaimed, "Oh, I must go to this church today, this afternoon." When she returned from church, her face was beaming. "I have been so afraid," she confided, "but today I prayed and lit a candle. Somehow I know my family will be safe."

When Anna left, I found myself worrying again about my mom. The latest report was that her problem could be neurological and she needed to see a specialist. Then I remembered Anna, her peace and the dark cloud of worry that had vanished. She had left her fear with the candle burning quietly in the church.

I should have asked Anna to light a candle for Mom. *Wait! I can do it here, right now.* I lit a little candle, put it on the kitchen counter and whispered, "Oh, Lord, please help Mom find the right doctor. Please be with her."

As I went in and out of the kitchen that day, I relinquished a little anxiety each time I noticed the flickering flame. Then, at night, I blew out the candle and watched the rising smoke. With it, like Anna, I left my need in God's faithful care.

Lord, thank You for the little things, like a candle,
that remind me of Your providence.
—MARY BROWN

OCTOBER 12

Be of good courage, and do it.
—EZRA 10:4

*T*he Sunday-school lesson today was about taking risks. In the course of the hour, the class cited examples of Bible characters who took a chance: Abraham, who followed God's command to "go from your country...to the land I will show you" (Genesis 12:1, updated NIV); David, who stepped forward to battle the giant Goliath; Moses, who courageously led the Israelites out of Egypt; Daniel, who defied a king and risked death in the lions' den; and Peter, who left his boat when Jesus called him to walk on the water.

The common thread in each of these stories is trust in God. What keeps us from acting when we face challenges? Sometimes we aren't sure it's God's voice we're hearing and we hesitate. Sometimes we're afraid we'll fail or look ridiculous, fearful of what others will think. But when it becomes clear God wants us to go in a certain direction and we don't, that's disobedience. Noah's neighbors probably thought he was nuts when he started building an ark. *A flood? Forget about it.* Jonah heard God's call, disobeyed and became fish food.

What is God calling you to do today? To make some change in your life that will demand courage? Prayer is always my first port of call when tough decisions are required. Speaking of ports, I'm reminded of the seafarers' axiom that observes, "Man was not made for safe harbors." Or as a friend of mine says upon leaving, instead of "Take care," "Take risks."

> *Lord, renew us even as we grow old, Give us*
> *a zest for life and make us bold.*
> —FRED BAUER

Blessed is the man whose strength is in You,
Whose heart is set on pilgrimage.
—PSALM 84:5 (NKJV)

This has not been a good week. Things did not work out as I had hoped, and the past few days have brought disappointment and discouragement. No matter how mature and experienced I become, these "days in the valley" do not become easier.

I went for a long walk this morning. Stepping out into a clear, crisp autumn day, I slipped a small Bible into my coat pocket. As I walked, I flipped open my Bible to Psalm 84:5–6 (NKJV): "Blessed is the man whose strength is in You, Whose heart is set on pilgrimage. As they pass through the Valley of Baca, they make it a spring; the rain also covers it with pools."

The Valley of Baca is associated with weeping. Indeed, the word *Baca* is derived from the verb *bakah*, "to weep." Reading these verses reminded me that to follow God is to be on a long journey—a pilgrimage—that traverses all kinds of terrain. We wind our way up mountains and down steep valleys. There are deserts and ocean vistas. We experience moments of laughter and weeping, excitement and boredom, comfort and pain, birth and death.

I began my walk this morning in the depths of the Valley of Baca. But the Bible reminds me that I do not walk alone. God can change my tears of disappointment into refreshing springs and the dismal rain into pools of pleasure.

Dear Lord, help me to remember that wherever I go,
I'm on a pilgrimage with You. Amen.
—SCOTT WALKER

OCTOBER 14

Love one another deeply, from the heart.
—I PETER 1:22 (NIV)

*E*mily is Caucasian; the Johnsons are African-American. They got to know each other about twenty years ago when they attended the same church. As Emily's health began to fail, the Johnsons cared for her. Emily now has Parkinson's disease and lives in an assisted-living facility. The Johnsons take her to church, to the doctor and wherever else she needs to go.

My wife Rosie and I visited the Johnsons not long ago and observed how tenderly they care for Emily. We saw them gently put her in a wheelchair and take her shopping, patiently listening to her whispers as she told them what she wanted. We moved from one aisle to the next in the store as she slowly read the labels on the cans. The kindness the Johnsons display toward this woman is truly phenomenal. No one pays them to do it; no court or agency assigned the job to them. They were moved by God to walk beside a person in need.

As I saw this, I was reminded of I Peter 1:22: "Love one another deeply, from the heart." Here was deep agape, reaching out and caring for a friend, and here I was observing it from a historical barrier of race—no boss, no employee, only God's kind of love.

Lord, help me to grow in Your love, so I can always
be ready to reach out and care for a friend.
—DOLPHUS WEARY

OCTOBER 15

Unto thee will I cry, O Lord my rock; be not silent to me: lest,
if thou be silent to me, I become like them that go down into the pit.
—PSALM 28:1

*S*ome years ago my wife and I were walking down the street with our baby daughter tucked in the crook of my arm. She was a hundred days old at the time and folded into my elbow like a football. Suddenly she twisted out of my grasp and sailed off into the air. For a chilling second she was falling headfirst between us toward the concrete sidewalk. Without thinking I shot out both hands, juggled her for a second, and clutched her to me in such a spasm of horror and relief that she began to sob and I had to hand her to my wife, who was shaking.

I dreamed about my baby's headlong flight for weeks afterward. I dreamed about it every night. The dream never varied: I was walking down the street with her on my arm, she twisted away and I didn't catch her, and she died.

I talked about this dream to my wife many times. She never lost patience with me. One morning she listened to me recount my nightmare again. After a moment of silence she said, "If you hadn't caught her, we would be in hell," and she was right.

I've thought since that we are often at the lip of hell, and a Hand comes and fends off the fire, and mostly we don't even see, let alone acknowledge, that Hand. But for a minute this morning maybe we should, for there are many hells and they are all too real and so many of our brothers and sisters now and in the past are seared by evil. So we kneel and pray, and then rise and make ourselves arrows of light against the leering dark.

Dear Lord, two words, and I say them with all my heart
and bone and verve and fire: thank You.
—BRIAN DOYLE

OCTOBER 16

"Do not fear, I will help you."
—ISAIAH 41:13 (NASB)

*E*arly this morning, I sat in my easy chair by the upstairs window of my study. I quietly watched as shadows lifted and the sun cast soft light on a new day—a fresh set of challenges and opportunities.

For a moment I sat with my tattered study Bible closed. Then I turned to the book of Isaiah and thought how often I have reflected on this ancient prophet's words. Each Christmas I relish hearing Handel's "Messiah," listening spellbound as the tenor soloist sings from Isaiah 40:1–2: "Comfort ye, comfort ye my people, saith your God.... And cry unto her, that her warfare is accomplished, that her iniquity is pardoned." Isaiah reminds me each Advent that God is always in the process of bringing peace and forgiveness into our world.

Jesus quoted from Isaiah more than any other portion of Hebrew Scripture. Jesus immersed Himself in the words of this great prophet and was shaped by his spirit and insight. As I opened my Bible, my eyes fell on these words: "For I am the Lord your God, who upholds your right hand, Who says to you, 'Do not fear, I will help you'" (Isaiah 41:13, NASB).

How much did I need to hear these words this morning! I needed to be assured that I will not have to make my way through this day alone; that there is a Father Who loves me, Who holds my hand, Who assures me I won't have to succeed by my own strength and ability.

I wonder how many times Jesus took comfort from these words? How many early mornings found Him reflecting on His day and quietly intoning these words: "Do not fear, I will help you"?

> *Dear, Father, help me to believe You are with me,*
> *and help me to grasp Your hand. Amen.*
> —SCOTT WALKER

Your Father knoweth what things ye have need of.
—MATTHEW 6:8

*H*ello...anybody home?" I knew his voice long before I made it to the door. The loud pounding was him, knocking on the door with his elbow because his big arms were always full of groceries. Ministers and their families can know some lean years. But like clockwork, just when our pantry was looking bare, Daddy would appear, his car loaded down with treats that our budget would never allow. In he'd come, filling the house with his enthusiasm, spoiling our children Brock and Keri, taking us all out to fancy restaurants. He was so proud of my husband David and of the things we accomplished in the church. As we near the end of this phase of our lives, I can't help wondering what Daddy would say to us if he were here.

We've been at Hillsboro Presbyterian Church for thirty-seven years. When we came, I was in my early twenties and Brock was nine months old. Keri was yet to be born. We've grown up with this church; we've seen it expand from fewer than fifty members to more than seven hundred. We've been here for every birth, baptism, wedding and funeral. I know it sounds crazy, but in this ending I sense a beginning. The future seems a bit like a bare pantry at this point, but I wait, fully expecting a knock at our door.

I wait for our Father, with His arms so full of hopeful tomorrows, He has to knock with His elbow.

Father, I wait. But with You, I know I never have to worry.
—PAM KIDD

OCTOBER 18

When thou passest through the waters, I will be with thee;
and through the rivers, they shall not overflow thee.
—ISAIAH 43:2

*T*was driving through a rainstorm in upstate New York one Friday last spring, headed east on Route 23 toward my house in Great Barrington, Massachusetts. Millie, barely a year old, was curled up in the back of the Jeep in her dog bed. There was a crack of thunder, and lightning slashed at the Berkshire Hills ahead. Then, negotiating a curve beside a nearly overflowing swamp, I felt the wheels slip from under me. Foolishly, I must have hit the brakes instead of steering with the skid. We veered off the road toward the swamp, and all of a sudden we were airborne.

The Jeep rolled once, twice, bouncing crazily down an embankment, so fast and so violently my mind had no time to register it. We landed wheels down in the swamp a good twenty feet from shore and in about three feet of water. Mud and ooze caked the windshield. The passenger's side roof was crushed; water sloshed over the floorboards. *Millie!* I undid my seatbelt, pushed the door open and waded to the back of the Jeep. She was trembling with fear but otherwise unharmed. I popped the hatch. "Honey, you're going to have to learn to swim," I muttered, easing her out into the water and steering her toward shore, one arm under her belly. She struggled to keep her chin above the muck and paddled heroically. "Good girl!"

Cars had pulled over and people met us with blankets and looks of amazement. One woman, a total stranger, hugged me and said, "It's a miracle you survived. I saw the whole thing. An angel was watching over you and your dog." I was aware of very little when the Jeep flipped over. But Someone was in control.

I have no doubt now, God, that in my greatest need You are closer than ever.
—EDWARD GRINNAN

OCTOBER 19

He that received seed into the good ground is he that heareth the word,
and understandeth it; which also beareth fruit, and bringeth forth....
—MATTHEW 13:23

*O*n our visit to China, our tour guide to the Badaling section of the Great Wall, northwest of Beijing, was a young woman whom I'll call Sarah. She spoke nearly flawless English, and she was well-trained in the history of this twenty-five-hundred-mile-long structure.

After the others in our party left to scale a distant part of the wall, my wife Shirley and I stayed behind with Sarah in one of the lower watchtowers. There we talked about all sorts of things, including religion. Her parents were practicing Buddhists, she told us, but "like most young people, I am not a believer." Then Sarah asked a question I wasn't expecting: "Are you Christians? And if so, why?"

I took a deep breath, knowing our party would be returning soon. How do you answer such a question in five minutes? I began by saying I grew up in a community of believers, so it was easy for me to accept Jesus as my personal Savior, sent by God to proclaim His Word, which is recorded in the Bible. I went on to tell her Christians believe in a personal God, one Who guides them, one Who hears and answers prayers, one Who is all knowing, all powerful, always present, one Who loves unconditionally, one Whose mercy and grace are limitless.

"It must be very comforting," Sarah replied. I nodded. By now our group was returning and that was the end of our conversation. I wonder if our little talk planted any seeds.

Remind us, Lord, that Your words fell on hard ground—and soft,
Those with eyes who saw and those who blindly scoffed.
—FRED BAUER

OCTOBER 20

For I am convinced that neither...rulers...nor powers...will be able to separate us from the love of God in Christ Jesus our Lord.
—ROMANS 8:38–39 (NRSV)

I got up feeling a bit lethargic. The Indian summer skies had gone gray, my house was cold, and I felt a sense of futility over what was happening in our world. I fixed a cup of coffee and headed dully for the computer. I had mail; Rocklin, a college student in Changchun, China, had checked in.

Hi, Anti Bee. This is Rocklin. Hopefully there is my face in your mind. I'd met Rocklin a year and a half before when I visited my youngest son in China. Blake was teaching conversational English on a college campus. Rocklin was seventeen, lonely, suffering from a lifetime of emotional neglect, but he made Blake his friend and spiritual mentor. I inherited some of that role simply because I'm Blake's mother. Hearing from Rocklin through the wonder of technology, my lethargy vanished, not just because I enjoy hearing from him but because he reminds me that on the far side of the world, in a communist country, amidst millions of people, God found this young man and gave him to Blake and me to nurture and support and pray for.

Lethargy, gray skies, a sense of futility—what are these when Rocklin reminds me that through the chaos and fear God calls us by name. *Yes, Rocklin, there is your face in my mind, for you are proof that nothing—neither rulers nor powers—can separate any of us from the love of God.*

Dear God, keep me focused on Your power and love, remembering that amidst the chaos of our times, You hold everyone's faces in Your mind.
—BRENDA WILBEE

October 21

The joy of our heart is ceased; our dance is turned into mourning.
—Lamentations 5:15

he early sun was dancing through my kitchen as I checked e-mails on my laptop. The words I had been dreading flashed across the screen: "Prince is gone."

Prince lived in rural Zimbabwe, in a one-room shack with a bed and a glow-in-the-dark star that hung from the ceiling. Like thousands upon thousands of children, he had AIDS. His mother and brother had already died; his father, also HIV positive, was doing his best to make sure his son had at least one meal a day. After our first meeting I came back to Nashville, Tennessee, loving this little guy. I wondered how I might make things better for him. Books, I thought, and food. I e-mailed Paddington, who directs our work with AIDS orphans in Zimbabwe. Yes, he said, he'd make the long journey to Prince's village to look out for him. On our next trip to Africa, we took Prince gifts from America: a windup radio, a flashlight and a soft blanket of his very own. By the time I received the news of Prince's death, many people knew his name, and his sweet smile had fueled interest in our work in Zimbabwe.

Think of Prince gazing at his plastic star and me in my comfortable American home. Only a very clever God could have put us together and engineered the gifts that followed: For Prince, food, books, a windup radio, and the knowledge that a great many people had come to love him and that his life mattered. For me, a chance to follow God's call, to touch His hand and to share the depth of His laughter and His tears by loving a little guy named Prince.

Father, in my dancing and in my weeping, let me be one with You.
—Pam Kidd

OCTOBER 22

Therefore encourage one another and build up one another,
just as you also are doing.
—I Thessalonians 5:11 (NASB)

*I*t was dinnertime, and I had just whizzed into the drive-through to pick up a cup of coffee and a cheeseburger on my way home from work. But something told me the homeless man rolling a dolly loaded with suitcases and blankets around the parking lot needed the sandwich much more than I did.

I slid into a parking spot and then tiptoed toward the man, who was now kicking a restaurant-sized peanut can. I barely breathed as I listened for the rattle that would mean another meal for him. Nothing.

As I handed him the bag containing the cheeseburger, I was filled with a sense of self-satisfaction that I instantly abhorred. "This is for you," I announced, glancing into his bloodshot gray eyes. "God bless you." As soon as the words rolled off my tongue, I hated the way they seemed to distance us even more. Instead of meeting the man's gaze, I focused my eyes on the collar of his tattered jacket, raised high against the cold.

Ever so gently, he held my hand until at long last our eyes met. Then he brushed his hand against mine and, as if granting me the key to the universe, responded: "God bless you."

In that moment, one of God's eternal truths took up residence in my heart: Every one of God's children—rich or poor, young or old, educated or common—has equal access to the heavenly Father and can freely offer His blessings to another.

Thank You, Father, for those who unknowingly point me to You.
—Roberta Messner

OCTOBER 23

*S*ome years ago we entertained someone in our home who had experienced one of those life-after-death episodes. While others demanded specifics ("How does heaven look?" "Do you see people you know?"), my son Brock's question was different: "Does God have a sense of humor?" he asked hopefully. I understood perfectly where Brock was coming from. If God doesn't have a sense of humor, most of us are in big trouble.

But something tells me we're safe. After all, God made giraffes and teenagers and avocado seeds. Each had to be created with a chuckle of mischievous delight. And think about what nice pencil holders ears make, and how ugly ducklings and even uglier caterpillars are born to soar on magnificent wings. Brock, however, was thinking of something else. Religion in the South sometimes takes on a harsh tone. Some see God as a hard disciplinarian, intent on separating the worthy from the unworthy. A few weeks earlier, in the throes of a painful divorce, Brock had received an angry letter from someone who fancied himself as a sort of heavenly judge.

Believing that God is like a good Father, I have to disagree with that unhappy letter writer. The fathers I know laugh a lot when they are with their children. They love hearing their stories. They pick them up when they fall. No matter what kind of mistakes their children make, fathers love them just the same. So I wasn't surprised when our guest looked straight at Brock and said, "God pulls for us. He suffers with us. And you can bet that when we laugh, He laughs with us!"

Father, laugh with us as often as You can.
—PAM KIDD

*"As for me, I would seek God.... He does great things
and unsearchable, marvelous things without number."*
—JOB 5:8–9 (NRSV)

On my street, the chestnut trees by the creek all let go at once, and there is a steady rain of hard fruit the size of tennis balls. On windy days, my children and I hear the nuts falling from our house, and we amble down the street and watch from a safe distance as the heavy green nuts leap from the trees. We take home handfuls and burnish the lovely brown nuts, and my young sons throw them at each other and at their sister until I insist they desist and put the boys to bed, but not the sister, who is a teenager and so never sleeps.

I work the nuts through my fingers like fat oily coins and consider the parallels between chestnuts and children. Both are wrapped in soft pebbly skins. Both have stubborn centers. Both gleam when polished. Crows are fascinated by both.

I watch the gangs of crows in the street flare and hammer and bicker and chortle among the shards and scraps of nuts and then go kiss my sons and nod to my daughter, who deigns, for once, to nod back. Her nod this evening seems like a blessing beyond price to me, for she has been sharp and sassy and supercilious, and I grow weary of being the tree from which she must carve her independence. But tonight she nods to me: a subtle message, a silent prayer, a fleeting gift. And we know all gifts are fleeting; yet they come to us all day and night, an ocean of generosity from the One Who made and makes everything that is.

*Dear Lord, I ask this one crucial, necessary, nutritious primary gift:
Will You help me just see and smell and hear and taste and touch
Your unimaginable sea of miracles every moment? Please?*
—BRIAN DOYLE

*His divine power has given us everything we need for a godly life through
our knowledge of him who called us by his own glory and goodness.*
—II Peter 1:3 (NIV)

*O*ur grandson Little Reggie stays with us every weekend. When he was three, he said to Rosie, "Grandma, I don't want to wear these clothes. I want to wear the kind of clothes Pops wears." (Pops is Little Reggie's pet name for me.) Rosie looked at him and asked, "Why do you want to dress like Pops?"

"I want to be like Pops," he said.

Little Reggie repeated his request over the next few weekends. Finally Rosie bought him a suit and tie. After he put on the suit, he said, "I want to dress like Pops because I want to be a preacher like Pops." We've heard Little Reggie share that wish many, many times since, and Rosie and I like to think of him letting that seed of faith grow and allowing God to use him to be a blessing for many. Tomorrow or ten years from now, his mind may change and he may have another goal for his life, but whatever Little Reggie grows up to be, we know God will give him everything he needs to do whatever work He has in store for him.

*Lord, help me to encourage the children in my life
to be the people You want them to be.*
—Dolphus Weary

OCTOBER 26

Don't be childish in your understanding of these things.
—I CORINTHIANS 14:20 (TLB)

*R*etirement brought an abundance of pleasure-filled days and new activities. I had more time for Bible study and organ practice. I enjoyed attending our grandchildren's school and sports events. Dressing in a stomach costume and talking to grade-school children about nutrition was a blast. I was even thankful for time to clean the basement and fish tumbleweeds out of the window wells.

But several months after I left work, food and fuel prices started to climb. My retirement fund shrank by forty percent in the weak economy. Freelance work wasn't as consistent as I'd hoped. As my bank account dwindled, I began to wonder about God's provision for my future. Then my husband Don and I stayed with our five-year-old grandson Caden while his parents attended a weekend conference. After his Saturday morning ice-skating lesson we had lunch at his favorite fast-food place. In the afternoon we went to his friend Noah's karate-themed birthday party. After that we spent two hours at Caden's favorite playground.

"You guys are sure taking good care of me!" he called from the top of the monkey bars. But when it turned colder and started to sprinkle, he begged for more play time and hid in a tunnel to protest our decision to leave. As I fished him out, God's truth hit me like the proverbial ton of bricks: Caden wasn't the only one in the family acting like a five-year-old. Retirement gave me the precious gift of time and freedom. I also had a warm house, nutritious food and an overflowing closet. Yet I complained that I might not have enough.

There is work for me to do in retirement: the vital task of maturing in faith and trust.

Loving and generous Father, thank You
for using a child to help me grow up.
—PENNEY SCHWAB

OCTOBER 27

You, Lord, are my lamp; the Lord turns my darkness into light.
—II Samuel 22:29 (NIV)

*H*ow I dread the onset of winter. The shorter days and increasing darkness trigger depression, and I often wake in the morning with a heavy heart, dreading the day. Lately I've felt on the verge of tears, stumbling at the edge of despair. When my emotions are like this, it tests my faith. I struggle to believe in God's love when I feel so awful.

But I discovered last week that one reward for dark winter mornings can be watching the sun rise. The murky sky was filled with heavy dark clouds, and I began enumerating my troubles: how I missed the long talks I used to have with my friend Barb who moved across country, and how I struggled with the challenges of parenting my two teenage children.

Suddenly the clouds began to reflect the sun's luminous shades of orange, yellow and pink. Soon they sent out radiant streamers of red and peach and purple and aqua.

Somehow, I thought, my dark emotions or troubles can serve to reflect God's light in a way I wouldn't otherwise see. Through my sadness and discouragement, perhaps *because* of them, the truth of God's faithfulness has a precious beauty. Maybe I don't feel any different, but the knowledge that He is with me and loves me becomes even more wondrous when I see His light on the dark clouds of life.

Oh, Lord, You are with me in my loneliness. Help me keep my eyes on You. Shine Your light into the dark corners of my life.

—Mary Brown

OCTOBER 28

I press on toward the goal to win the prize for which God has called me.
—PHILIPPIANS 3:14 (NIV)

For years I was in awe of the "hard" Bible study at my church. They met for an hour longer than my class next door, and when I'd peek in as I walked by, they'd be poring over the Bible with highlighters and marking pens. I'd heard they even had hours of homework each week! They seemed to know so much about the Bible. *I could never be like that*, I thought. *Where would I start?*

Then our son Ross, learning about the world's religions in a history class, came home with some questions I couldn't answer: Were the Gospels close to eyewitness accounts or written many years later? Did Jesus ever really say He was God? I knew I had to dig deeper into God's Word and find the answers to help Ross strengthen his faith. So I signed up for the hard Bible study, promising myself I'd attend the first day and see if I could handle it.

That was four years ago. Since then I've come to know God much better. But I've also learned a simple plan for facing intimidating situations, one that's worked for me whether it's taking a hard class, sticking to an exercise regimen or giving up a bad habit: *Go.* Make an effort to get started, even if it's only a baby step. *Stay.* Don't quit that first day; stick with it, even if you can't keep up. *Return.* Keep going back and making one more try. Soon all those "just one more day" attempts pile up, and you've made a lot of progress.

Stay close by me, Lord, so when I feel weak or my will begins to fail,
Your gentle nudging helps me press on.
—GINA BRIDGEMAN

OCTOBER 29

For we know that if the earthly tent we live in is destroyed, we have a building
from God, an eternal house in heaven, not built by human hands.... For while
we are in this tent, we groan...to be clothed...with our heavenly dwelling....
Now the one who has fashioned us for this very purpose is God.
—II CORINTHIANS 5:1, 4–5 (NIV)

Incredibly, years after our younger son and his wife lost their first child at birth, our older son lost his wife and their first child too. Kristen, due to deliver in two weeks, suddenly collapsed and died of an aneurysm. Their boy lived only ten days.

During Kristen's memorial service we learned how she'd affected others positively. These accolades were consoling; her life had been productive. But during the second memorial service we wondered, What about their baby's life? Had he made it through nine months in his mother's womb, plus ten days outside it, for nothing?

When a wise friend pointed out the verse above, the oppressive burden that had staggered us was partially eased. Although God makes each of us for the very purpose of spending eternity with Him, this baby boy simply had made it to his very purpose sooner than the rest of us.

Sometimes death seems purposeless, Lord, yet we are aware that in Your great
plan nothing happens that takes You by surprise. Help us to understand that
You, Who knows the end from the beginning, are always in charge.
—ISABEL WOLSELEY

OCTOBER 30

For He has not despised...the affliction of the afflicted; Nor has He hidden
His face from him; But when he cried to Him for help, He heard.
—PSALM 22:24 (NASB)

*A*n early autumn sun lit a pale sky at the retreat grounds. Most of the
trees had shed their leaves. An outdoor prayer labyrinth bordered
with stones curled toward a small tree. I sauntered along the winding path,
pausing to listen for a woodpecker and look at the sunlight in an oak's bare
branches. Halfway into the labyrinth, I spotted a browned oak leaf pocked with
holes. I picked it up and twirled it between my fingers as I walked. Through
its holes I could see glimpses of earth; when I lifted it toward the sky, I caught
pinpoints of blue; when I tilted it, the holes filled with flecks of sun.

These aren't holes, I thought, *they're windows. Through them I can see loveliness*
beyond the leaf. I made the leap from the leaf to my life. Recent battles over
choices and direction had left gaping holes. I understood the psalmist's cry: "I
am benumbed and badly crushed; I groan because of the agitation of my heart"
(Psalm 38:8, NASB). But hadn't new glimpses of God's love and mercy emerged?
Hadn't I seen how patiently He journeys with me (Psalm 138:8), how deep His
fountain of forgiveness (Psalm 86:5), how unshakable His power to sustain
(Psalm 55:22)?

An epiphany in an oak leaf: wounds becoming windows revealing God.

Father of lights, only You can open a window to reveal to me "the depth of the
riches both of the wisdom and knowledge of God!" (Romans 11:33, NASB).

—CAROL KNAPP

OCTOBER 31

Whosoever drinketh of the water that I shall give him shall never thirst.
—JOHN 4:14

*M*y husband George makes wonderful coffee. He takes great pride in its freshness and flavor, and keeps the pot scrupulously clean.

One rainy morning as he was drawing water from the tap, he gazed out the window and marveled: "Isn't it wonderful how water that falls from the sky, pure and clean, goes into the ground, seeps into the soil, and emerges clean again!" He plugged in the percolator and soon the fragrant aroma of coffee filled the room.

"Yes, but water is filtered as it flows," I said. "So by the time it reaches our faucets it is as clean and pure as the day it fell."

George sat down and opened the Bible. He leafed thoughtfully through it. The night before, we had gone to bed troubled about a number of things: the loss of one of his patients, a misunderstanding in the family. Now, pausing at the Sermon on the Mount, he read: "Blessed are the poor in spirit, for theirs is the kingdom of heaven."

George stopped. "Maybe our minds are like that water! So often filled with mud and muck as we try to find our way. We need a filter, something to cleanse us. That's why our breakfast Bible reading is important. The Bible cleans and purifies our thoughts."

I smiled. "Yes, Jesus said He is living water, George."

I knew we would have a good day.

Today, God, keep us pure in heart, mind and deed.
—MARJORIE HOLMES

November

November 1

Lord, thou preservest man and beast.
—Psalm 36:6

*I*t was a glorious day, and my family was gathered at my parents' house for a visit with my grandparents. My six-year-old son Harrison and my three-year-old niece Abby were playing in a pile of leaves in the front yard. As I watched Harrison frolicking, a dark cloud of worry fell over me. *How can I possibly give him everything he needs? Will he survive being shuffled from my house to his mom's? Is he doing all right?*

"Big Dad," Harrison asked my father, "why are the leaves still sticking to that tree?" All the other trees, except one, had lost their leaves.

"That's a red oak," my grandfather interjected. "We used to say God made red oaks for the squirrels."

"Why?" Harrison shot back.

"In the autumn the squirrels make their nests from leaves, but when the cold winds come, sometimes parts of their nests blow away. If you watch, you'll see squirrels coming to the red oak to gather new leaves throughout the winter when all the other leaves have disappeared."

"Hey, Abby," Harrison yelled as he ran toward the red oak, "come over here and look at this tree! God made it specially 'cause He loves squirrels so much!"

I looked up at the blue sky and thanked God for this great note of reassurance. If He had planned ahead for the squirrels, I was confident His plans were laid for Harrison and me and each one of His children. With a great "Whoopee!" I grabbed Harrison and made a dash for the leaf pile.

Father, let me live in the reality of Your love,
which reaches out far beyond my knowing.
—Brock Kidd

NOVEMBER 2

I will not leave you as orphans; I will come to you.
—JOHN 14:18 (NIV)

I've often wished for the special ability to comfort people as Jesus did. As a nurse in an acute care hospital, it was my job to give support to dying patients and their families and I often felt inadequate to the task.

On this particular morning, my patient Paul, a tall man with leukemia, had worsened during the night. A death-pallor lay on his handsome face, and he had drifted into unconsciousness. His wife Susan was bending over him, trying to coax him to open his mouth for a drink. "Paul!" she called to him. "Honey, can you hear me?" She put down her glass and cradled his head in her hands.

As I watched Susan, I prayed, *Lord Jesus, please comfort her and show me how I can help.* Suddenly, I remembered the hymnbook I had tucked into my large black purse. The previous day, Susan had told me about her husband's love for music, how, when he was well, he would sit for hours at the piano or organ playing hymns. So I had brought along a hymnbook, just in case.

I reached for my purse and pulled out the book. Handing it to her, I said, "Susan, do you think we could sing one of Paul's favorite hymns?" "Here's 'Amazing Grace,'" she said, "Paul's favorite." Then, turning to his unresponsive face, she said, "Honey, the nurse and I are going to sing for you."

"Amazing grace...," she began. Her voice quavered and broke in giant sobs. Then she took a deep breath and bravely continued, "how sweet the sound." But tears overwhelmed her again. She looked at Paul's face and managed to get through the song. Then she chose another hymn. This time there were fewer sobs. During a third hymn, I noticed her voice was becoming stronger.

For the next two hours we sang hymn after hymn. Staff nurses tiptoed in to check the machines, or to give medication. We scarcely noticed. What I did notice was a Presence in the room. Susan's anguished face had become relaxed and radiant. Then, with a voice full of confidence, she said, "Paul, this is not defeat. This is victory."

Help me today, Jesus, to be so in tune with You that I shall
be able to bring others the comfort of Your presence.
—HELEN GRACE LESCHEID

NOVEMBER 3

"I am the true vine and my Father is the gardener."
—JOHN 15:1 (NIV)

A mile from our house is a roadside restaurant in a spectacular garden setting. For years, on my morning walk, I've stopped to gaze over the hedge at beds of roses, peonies, asters—an acre and more of color changing with the seasons. *Who couldn't have a beautiful garden,* I've thought, *with the gardening staff they must have here!*

I'd always gone by too early to see any of them at work. Then one day, when I had to handle a big mailing project single-handedly, I didn't get out to walk till afternoon. As I passed the garden, a stocky middle-aged man came from the restaurant basement carrying a tray of begonias. Seeing me stop, he waved me inside the hedge. He had to spell his last name before I caught it: Joseph Csomor.

"Are you the head gardener?" I asked.

Mr. Csomor shook his head. "Just the assistant."

He'd come here from Hungary twenty-seven years ago, he went on. The restaurant had hired him as a cleaning man, but when he was through sweeping and scrubbing, he'd spent his free time digging around the roots of the potted geraniums that were the only flowers on the place. Seeing the geraniums thrive, the owner had let him plant some rosebushes out back.

My puzzlement grew as Mr. Csomor told how year after year he'd planted a lilac bush here, a marigold border there, until the garden became the showplace it is today. If he'd done all this... "Then what does the head gardener do?"

Mr. Csomor pointed a stubby finger skyward. "He makes the flowers grow."

When the job is a big one, Lord, remind me again that I'm "just the assistant."
—ELIZABETH SHERRILL

NOVEMBER 4

Beloved, since God loved us so much, we also ought to love one another.
—I JOHN 4:11 (NRSV)

*M*y husband Charlie and I spend Novembers in Sausalito, California, just over the Golden Gate Bridge from San Francisco. A dour café waiter there always remembers us, at least enough to give us a half smile. But last year when we walked in, he smiled broadly and hurried to greet us with a kiss for me and a handshake for Charlie. The bushy mustache that had hidden his perpetually downturned lips had vanished.

At first I thought it might have been the absent mustache that accounted for the change. Perhaps he'd been smiling all those years under all that hair. But, no, he couldn't stop talking and seemed happier to see us than in all the previous years put together.

Eventually a waitress clued us in: He was in love. He'd met a woman who not only loved him but refused to accept his glum disposition. She'd encouraged him to take up hiking, so he'd lost a few pounds.

Later, back in our rented cottage, we marveled at the change. "Look what love can do!" Charlie said.

That made me wonder: *Why aren't we all smiling like that waiter, rejuvenated and full of joy?* After all, God loves us in a way that human love can only shadow. Yet how often do I feel so utterly loved that I'm ready to change my life to reflect it? How often do I let the world know through my demeanor that I'm loved by the One Whose love redeems the world?

Not often enough. Still, tomorrow's only a few hours away.

Loving Lord, help me to feel and mirror the transforming power of Your love.
—MARCI ALBORGHETTI

NOVEMBER 5

"By me kings reign and rulers make laws that are just."
—PROVERBS 8:15 (NIV)

*L*iving inside the Washington, D.C., Beltway during the Election 2000 mess was an incredible experience. The media frenzy was so close it seemed to touch all of life. "Beltway fever," the irrational belief that everything important in the world happens inside the Beltway, was nearly out of control. Everywhere I went, people talked about nothing but the counts, recounts and court maneuvers.

Our little townhouse community has sixteen households, and among them twelve people work for the federal government or for a foreign government represented in D.C. All of them were on hold for five weeks, not knowing what direction their jobs and their lives would take. The fever began to infect my wife Joy and me in the form of uneasiness about the future, especially when some members of the media began to use the phrase "constitutional crisis."

Then one evening we had a dinner party that put it all in perspective. Our guests came from Africa, South America and the former Soviet Union. Soon the conversation turned to the election, and a precious woman who had escaped eastern Europe in the 1980s said, "You know, we are very afraid, especially because this is America."

"What do you mean?" I asked.

"The army is so strong and the weapons so powerful, there will be nowhere to hide when the troops come out," was her reply.

Joy and I started to laugh, until we saw how serious all our guests were. In many parts of the world, an election crisis means tanks and troops in the streets.

As we explained how our military is controlled by civilians, using President Kennedy's assassination and President Nixon's resignation as examples, our guests became more and more excited. "Truly, America is blessed," one said. "Only God could make such a system work."

Father, I am so blessed to live in a land free of tyranny and oppression. Make me thankful and more faithful to You Who gives this blessing.
—ERIC FELLMAN

November 6

Give the king your justice, O God.
—Psalm 72:1 (NRSV)

*W*ill your favored candidate win in the election? Although the outcome of the election may not be at all certain where you vote, this one fact certainly is: Some of us will vote with the majority and others of us will not. There will be winners and losers. And losing is hard.

That's why I'm using the advice given to me a long time ago, shortly after I became old enough to vote. I read Psalm 72 before I vote. It refocuses me away from winners or losers, or which candidate thinks most like me, or even about seeking God's favor for the politics of the one whom I favor. It's a prayer of values, not victory. Its focus is not power for one but justice for all, especially for the powerless; prosperity for all, especially for the poor; and peace for all throughout creation. And it is a prayer that the governments of the powerful protect and serve the legion of the powerless, not serve their own interests.

No matter how different my point of view is from someone else's, no matter what solutions I think are best for the challenges of society, on Election Day the psalmist again calls us to pray this prayer together for the well-being of all those created in God's image.

Grant me the wisdom and humility, God, to pray for our leaders and to work for my neighbors and to remember finally Whom we all serve.
—Jeff Japinga

NOVEMBER 7

The Lord is my shepherd.
—PSALM 23:1

The bleakness of the fall day was magnified by a slow, steady rain that merged asphalt and buildings into a gray, lifeless landscape. As I drove down one of the busiest streets in Nashville, Tennessee, the traffic crept along and then came to a standstill as the light in front of me went through a complete cycle from green to yellow to red. "I should've gone the back way," I muttered under my breath.

Just then a pedestrian caught my eye. He was walking on the edge of the sidewalk, swinging a white cane back and forth on the concrete. The blustery wind seemed to be blowing him a little off balance as he methodically searched for objects in front of him with his cane. Directly ahead was a telephone pole; he quickly tapped his cane and stepped around the pole as if he could see it. Still snarled in traffic, I watched him make his way forward, never missing a step, relying on his cane to show him the way.

The traffic began to move again, and as I pulled away I thought about what I'd just witnessed. That blind man finding his way on a rainy street was a sign that I could move in a more positive direction. I'd let myself become the victim of a dreary day, not seeing the Shepherd, staff in hand, Who waits to guide me.

Dear God, help me to remember that when I follow You,
goodness follows me.
—BROCK KIDD

November 8

"Do not be grieved, for the joy of the Lord is your strength."
—Nehemiah 8:10 (NRSV)

*S*aturday morning services had become kind of routine: We sang the same songs; we said the same prayers. Some of the joy and mindfulness had gone out of the worship, and most of us hadn't actually noticed we were only going through the motions. Then one Saturday a woman we had never seen before came to a service with our social action chairperson Clara. The new woman seemed nervous, despite the welcome we gave her. Clara explained that she had recently come over from the former Soviet Union, where she had not been allowed to attend a synagogue or even to admit openly that she had a religion.

Instead of having the Torah carried through the congregation before it was read, our rabbi had created a ritual of passing it from person to person. Each of us took the velvet-covered scroll from the person on one side of us and passed it to the person on the other. It all went as usual until Clara held out the Torah to the Russian woman. For a moment she was just frozen, staring at it. Then she reached out, hands shaking, and let Clara put the scroll into them. She slowly lowered her head over the Torah, cradling it, and silently she began to cry. Several minutes went by before she could turn and let the person on her other side take the Torah from her.

We were stunned, and as the Torah made its way through the rest of us and up to the platform for reading, our surprise became excitement. The Russian woman had reminded us of how precious the freedom to worship together is and that we must never let it become routine.

Help us never to take the privilege of honoring You
for granted, our God, and God of our ancestors.
—Rhoda Blecker

There is no authority except that which God has established.
—ROMANS 13:1 (NIV)

*E*lection year is a terrible time to live in Washington, D.C. Everyone gets caught up in politics, and often the rhetoric gets downright ugly. Friends who normally talk about everything with good humor get into heated arguments over the latest "talking points" or poll results. And because the federal government is here and employs so many of the residents, the local news is always about what is happening on Capitol Hill or in the White House.

My wife Joy and I serve as volunteers for the National Prayer Breakfast, which is a completely nonpartisan event. Like the military, our group is supposed to respect and serve to the best of our ability whoever is elected president. Often that's not easy.

On the Thursday before the last national election, some prayer breakfast volunteers were at lunch together. Everything was fine until someone mentioned a story from that morning's newspaper. Suddenly, battle lines were drawn and tempers started to rise.

Rapping a spoon loudly on the table, the senior member of the group got everyone's attention and then said: "Look, everyone calm down. There are two things we know for sure about the election. First, after all the uproar next Tuesday, we'll be back here next Thursday eager to do our best. And second, whoever is elected, God will still be in charge."

Lord, help me to remember that You are above all rulers and authority,
and to trust Your hand even when I cannot see Your purpose.

—ERIC FELLMAN

NOVEMBER 10

Behold, I stand at the door and knock. If anyone hears My voice and opens the door, I will come in to him and dine with him, and he with Me.
—REVELATION 3:20 (NKJV)

Recently I was cleaning out my overflowing attic, a painful task for a pack rat like me. There were lampshades, picture frames, extension cords, chipped knickknacks. But the hardest to sort were the boxes of memories: letters, drawings, trophies and yearbooks that belonged to my husband Whitney and our kids. *I can't throw out any of these,* I thought. One box had my name on it; I spent an hour sifting through it, memories pouring over me. At the bottom was a tattered picture of Jesus knocking at the heart's door. The picture had hung upstairs in the childhood home where I first heard Him call me.

I was six or seven and alone in our living room, sitting on the floor, staring dreamily through a window at a bare tree and the blazing blue sky, when the picture edged into my daydreams: Jesus, standing on a doorstep, suffused in light, scarred hand raised to knock. A thought, clear and bright as the day, came into my mind. *Wouldn't you like to ask Jesus into your heart?*

With a child's matter-of-fact faith, I got up, knelt by the sofa and prayed a simple prayer I'd learned in Sunday school. Nothing changed, yet everything did.

Fifty years later, in the semidarkness of my attic, I was caught again by the picture of Jesus and held by the reality of His long-ago call. Through all the memories, through the turning of seasons, the passing of decades, the shifting of locations, through sickness and health, through pain and joy and failure, even when I let Him wait outside the door while I went about my everyday busyness, His love has been with me—my Lord, my Savior and my lifelong Friend.

Lord, no matter what else falls by the wayside, gets lost or thrown out, You and Your love are with me forever.
—SHARI SMYTH

NOVEMBER 11

They will beat their swords into plowshares.
—ISAIAH 2:4 (NIV)

On an evening of troubling reports of unrest in the world, I sat down in my dining room, quite worried about my two oldest sons, who are in the military. After September 11, 2001, I had lost my sense of security and worried that we were heading for war.

Then my eyes fell on an old handmade brass lamp that had belonged to my grandfather. Grandpa had gotten the lamp after World War I from a fellow who had taken a surplus brass shell casing, welded it to a base and wired it as a two-bulb lamp. "Trench art" it's called, items such as vases and lamps made after World War I from leftover munitions.

The fellow who made Grandpa's lamp hadn't just changed the use of the shell; he had transformed its meaning by the decorations he painstakingly hammered onto the top of the casing. On one side he fashioned an American flag, unfurled proudly in the breeze, and on the other side he hammered a pair of doves perched on a leafy branch to symbolize peace.

Sitting there in my dining room as light glowed on the golden shell, I felt comforted by the message of the lamp, as if I were drawing strength from a past generation that had faced uncertainty with faith and trust, hope and prayer, courage and resourcefulness. The lamp bore testimony that all wars eventually end, and that in the Craftsman's hands, even an instrument of destruction can be remade to pour light and beauty into a troubled world.

Dear Father, I thank You that even in times of conflict I can find peace in affirming Your faithfulness and Your nearness.
—KAREN BARBER

November 12

I know what it is to be in need, and I know what it is to have plenty....
Yet it was good of you to share in my troubles.
—Philippians 4:12, 14 (niv)

One of the most comforting, reassuring, hopeful reasons I know to be an active part of a church community is the reassurance that when times get tough someone will be there to support you. Most of us have experienced that.

But what happens when the person who needs the care and support of the church community the most is the one who usually gives it? There was a time not long ago when a pastor friend of mine was in the midst of very difficult circumstances. Despite my own training in care for others, I often found myself tongue-tied around him. What if I said the wrong thing? Of all people, a minister would see through my words in a minute.

That worry had me walking on eggshells for a couple of weeks, until another friend of mine—a rough, gruff former army sergeant—set me straight. That morning, he marched right up to my pastor friend and in the midst of my careful, well-measured words, poked a finger in his chest and snarled, "What you need is just being normal. You come to my house Monday night and as many Monday nights as you want after that. We'll watch football." As he walked away, he stopped, turned toward me and said, "You too. Might loosen you up."

The gospel according to Monday Night Football isn't in the Book. Maybe it should be. For it teaches that the greatest gift we can offer a friend in distress is rarely fancy words or pious promises, but simply being there.

Grant, O God, that my life will be both faithful
to You and to those whom You love.

—Jeff Japinga

He was afraid and said, "How awesome is this place! This is
none other than the house of God; this is the gate of heaven."
—Genesis 28:17 (NIV)

*T*hurriedly opened the trunk of my car to throw in my suitcase, intent on getting to the hospital early enough to catch the doctors who were caring for my elderly father. I groaned as I saw the six short-sleeve shirts I'd taken from Dad's tiny closet at the nursing home. *Those should be taken to Dad's house, but I really don't want to go there*, I thought.

Going up the hill to Dad's empty house was depressing. It was hard to face the fact that he would never be well enough to live there again. I finally forced myself to go inside and ran back to the bedroom closet with the shirts as quickly as I could.

When I passed through the living room on the way out, I looked out the large window. The tree leaves had fallen and I could see Table Rock Mountain turning a golden pink in the early dawn. The rest of the mountain range was a smoky blue-gray, and a white mist curled along the valley below me. A thought formed clearly in my mind: *Sometimes you have to go places you don't want to go to see God's glory.*

There were other difficult places I didn't want to go that day. I didn't want to go to the hospital to deal with doctors and Dad's critical condition or to the nursing home to communicate my concerns about the gaps in Dad's care. But if God could send me up to a house I didn't want to visit to see a sunrise, He could show me His glory in all the other places I don't want to go.

Father, there are places I don't want to go today.
But if I must, please show me Your glory there.

—Karen Barber

NOVEMBER 14

Thy rod and thy staff they comfort me.
—PSALM 23:4

*D*usk was falling on an autumn afternoon, and I knew it was too late to take my golden retrievers Beau and Muffy out to run. But it had been a long day and I needed the exercise. Hurriedly putting the dogs in the back of my SUV, I took off for the Texas countryside.

When I unloaded Beau and Muffy near a friend's ranch, they exploded with pent-up energy, dashing across a cropped field and soon outdistancing me. The sky grew darker and the temperature dropped, but it was fun to run with the wind at my back, straining to keep the dogs in sight. Soon Beau and Muffy tired from sprinting and dropped back to lope along with me.

It was pitch dark as we reached a gate and turned to retrace our steps. Slowing to a walk, we watched the North Star rise in the sky, illuminating the frosted breath of man and beast. Suddenly the wild howl of coyotes exploded from a distant thicket and my dogs drew closer to me. Soon they were walking at my heels, finding comfort in the presence of a man they trusted.

I thought of the Twenty-third Psalm: "The Lord is my Shepherd, I shall not want." How often do I walk in darkness, unable to discern the future stretching before me? Dangers—both real and imagined—lurk in the shadows, and I grow anxious and lonely. Then, like my dogs, I seek the Good Shepherd, slow my relentless pace and settle down to follow Him.

Lord, help me to know that You are with me, that I do not walk alone. Amen.
—SCOTT WALKER

And, behold, the Lord passed by, and a great and strong wind rent the mountains, and brake in pieces the rocks before the Lord; but the Lord was not in the wind: and after the wind an earthquake; but the Lord was not in the earthquake: and after the earthquake a fire; but the Lord was not in the fire: and after the fire a still small voice.

—I KINGS 19:11–12

*D*o you talk to God?" an atheist once asked a believer.

"Oh, yes, all the time," replied the Christian.

"And does He answer you?"

"Certainly."

"In an audible voice?" the doubter pressed.

"No, in a still small voice that I hear with my heart."

"How do you know it's Him and not someone else?"

"Years of listening," the believer answered. "Years of listening."

Recently, I heard about a woman who wasn't sure God heard her prayers, so she asked the Lord to speak to her.

"What should I do with my life?" she asked.

"Visit the sick," God answered. "Help the poor, live in peace."

Startled to hear God reply so quickly and so directly, she muttered, "I...I was only testing."

"So was I," God returned.

Sometimes we pray so long about a problem that we fail to hear God's marching orders. Either that, or we are so intent on what we want that we don't hear what He wants. Spiritual listening requires stillness, faith and obedience. And real communication mandates pauses to let the other party get a word in edgewise.

Remind me, Lord, that my hearing clears
When I remember: one mouth, two ears.

—FRED BAUER

November 16

When anxiety was great within me, your consolation brought joy to my soul.
—PSALM 94:19 (NIV)

*T*he call from my wife Julee came in right before 5:00 a.m. She was in the Berkshire Hills where she was getting our house ready for a Thanksgiving family gathering. I planned to take the train up from New York City on Tuesday night, but now everything had changed.

"I fell down the stairs," she moaned. "The paramedics are here. It looks like I broke my collarbone. I'm going to the hospital."

"I'll be there as fast as I can."

"Call someone to come over and take care of Millie. She's hysterical."

Our young golden retriever had never seen a commotion like this. Who were these strangers and why were they taking Julee away? I threw some things in a bag, called our friend Chrissy to check on Millie and then go over to see Julee in the emergency room, and ran the few short blocks to Penn Station where I got a seat on the next train, due to leave in an hour's time. What a long hour it was, pacing outside the station, too distracted even to focus on a coherent prayer. *What if Julee needs surgery? What if it's worse than just a fractured clavicle?*

"The what-ifs will drive us crazy," I recalled a friend once telling me. *What if,* I suddenly reminded myself, *God is in charge, and I just need to step out of the way and calm down?* That's the what-if that mattered. Julee did break her collarbone, but she was going to be okay, and we had an interesting Thanksgiving with me doing the cooking. Millie was her joyous self once we were all reunited. *What if,* I reminded myself again a few days later as we waved good-bye to my family, *after all these years I just learn to let God take charge when I can't?*

> *Father, You never fail us in times of need.*
> *Next time I'll try to remember the most important what-if of all.*
> —EDWARD GRINNAN

NOVEMBER 17

I am like an evergreen cypress.
—HOSEA 14:8 (NRSV)

I brushed my hair over the sink this morning and winced. I'd loosened too many hairs and, yikes, nearly all of them were gray! *A new season of life,* I reminded myself as I walked into my bedroom, where the window gives me visual entrée into the branches of a large maple—now in November looking dead, though it's not.

A few hours later I heard a work crew on the roof, wielding blowers brought in to clear the gutters. This being a large rental complex, I have no maintenance responsibilities more taxing than sweeping my front stoop, so when the workers left I grabbed a broom.

Zealously swishing away dropped decaying leaves, I remembered the last time I'd raked a yard—my father's, peppered with maples, the autumn before he died. What a job! When my back hurt and blisters stung, I stopped to rest at the edge of a clean patch of grass, under a big evergreen, a white pine. Leaning on the rake, I looked at the tree: solid and majestic, not just being alive but looking alive—staying green—summer, winter, spring and fall, year after year. Yes, it shed cones that had to be picked up eventually—a few today, a few tomorrow. They were a little troublesome, but I didn't mind. I could appreciate their redemptive purpose as seed pods.

Of course, I'd complain if all the trees of the world were conifers. I love those springtime pastels and early autumn golds. But as the seasons of my life change, I feel more secure knowing that Hosea, God's prophet, said God was like an evergreen, not a leaf-dropper. Constant. Yesterday, today, tomorrow.

Lord, thank You for the constancy of Your being.
—EVELYN BENCE

"Very truly I tell you," Jesus answered, "before Abraham was born, I am!"
—JOHN 8:58 (NIV)

One Sunday before Thanksgiving, I phoned my mom to ask how she made her turkey stuffing. After giving me my annual tutorial, Mom exclaimed, "Guess who's coming for Christmas this year?" Mom hated the thought of anyone spending the day alone and often invited people to share the holiday. Before I could guess, she announced, "Jim and Eileen Connaker!" Hearing the names of my sister Sue's in-laws, I immediately pictured these jolly grandparents—Jim's dry humor and Eileen's lively laugh—and understood Mom's delighted anticipation.

Advent provides a good time to ponder the One Who is coming to all our Christmas celebrations. When Moses asked the Lord His name, God told him, "I AM THAT I AM" (Exodus 3:14). Now that's quite an answer! Who is coming this Christmas? The One Who exists before all. The One Who beyond all imagination or comprehension makes Himself known. The One Who contains all things yet cannot be contained by anything, Who takes on human flesh. God told Moses to tell His people, "I have watched over you and have seen what has been done to you in Egypt.... And I have promised to bring you up out of your misery in Egypt into...a land flowing with milk and honey" (Exodus 3:16–17, updated NIV).

In sending His Son, God offers to release me from bondage and lead me to a new land. Each day He calls me to begin anew my journey and experience more of His kingdom. Yet like the Israelites, I, too, easily settle for the slavery of this world's ways. What is my Egypt? What are my own afflictions or weaknesses? Where am I stuck? God knows and wants to lead me out.

Lord, please show me one step I can take this week to come closer to You.
—MARY BROWN

> *My brethren, count it all joy when you fall into various trials,*
> *knowing that the testing of your faith produces patience.*
>
> —JAMES 1:2–3 (NKJV)

There is an eighty-year-old violin repairer in Paris named Etienne Vatelot. Yehudi Menuhin, Pablo Casals and Isaac Stern were just a few of his clients. Though Vatelot says his hands are no longer steady enough to fine-tune instruments, his ear is still uncanny, able to diagnose problems—damaged wood, uneven fingerboards or the angle of a bridge, for example—for his trainees to fix.

I remember once visiting the shop of an old violin maker in New York City. He told me there were two elements that went into the making of a fine violin. The first was the wood. Fine instruments are made of north-side-of-the-mountain trees, he explained. "They have stood firm against winds and cold, and the bad weather has made them strong."

"And the second?" I asked.

"The touch of the master's hand," he answered with a smile.

People of faith, I've noticed, have often been seasoned by north-side-of-the-mountain trials and made stronger by their tests. And they, too, have been touched by the Master's hand.

> *Teach us Lord, not to ask for lighter loads,*
> *But greater faith for steep and rocky roads.*
>
> —FRED BAUER

NOVEMBER 20

I can do all things through Christ which strengtheneth me.
—PHILIPPIANS 4:13

*I*t was 7:30 on Sunday morning, and I was at church to play the piano for our worship band. I was rehearsing with them, struggling as I usually do, when our music director had an idea. "Dave, I want you to play like this," he said and then doo-dah-dahed. I gave him a deer-in-the-headlights look.

"Here, watch." He sat down and showed me. "I want you to do it alone before the band comes in, right at the beginning of the first song."

That's way too complicated, I thought. *I'll blow it!* "I don't think I can do that," I said.

"Yes, you can."

Rehearsal ended just as morning worshippers filed in. Only a minute was left before the service started. *Now's my chance,* I thought. *I have to tell him I need him to cut out my intro.* But just as I stood up to go over to him, one of the pastors caught up with him to discuss the service.

I sat at the piano and stared at the keys. *Oh, God, please don't let me blow it and look like a fool.* As I looked up, I caught the eye of one of the singers onstage with me. She must have read my posture because, without saying anything else, she mouthed these words: "Own it."

Suddenly I was ready to tackle the piece because I knew I was somehow called by God to be here at this moment, sitting on this piano bench. Therefore, my duty was to knock it out of the park. And if I didn't, I was to go down swinging.

So I played the intro, unafraid. It wasn't perfect, but it was mine.

> *Lord, that piece was mine only because it was Yours.*
> *Strengthen me to meet any challenge in Your service.*

—DAVE FRANCO

"Martha, Martha, you are worried and bothered about so many things."
—LUKE 10:41 (NASB)

*O*ur church had begun sponsoring a women's shelter. Carol, who managed it, told the congregation she wanted someone to invite her gang over for Thanksgiving dinner. Immediately, my mind began working: *Do we have space? Do we have enough china? I've only cooked a turkey once. What if it's no good? I'd better practice ahead of time.*

Despite my concerns, a tiny brave part of me wanted to volunteer. And, nervously, I did.

I got up at four o'clock on Thanksgiving morning to begin working through my list: Start the turkey, recheck the place cards, put pecans on the sweet potato soufflé and so on. I rearranged the refrigerator and cleaned the shelves in case one of the women took a peek.

At around eleven, I realized I couldn't find my husband Rick or our thirteen-year-old son Thomas. I trudged down to the basement and then circled outside the house, calling for them. *How, when there's so much to do, can they manage to avoid helping?*

Thirty minutes later, I heard them stomping their feet on the front doormat. They came in, bundled up and grinning.

"Mom, you've got to come see what Dad and I did!"

"Didn't you hear me calling you?" I asked.

"Just come look," Thomas begged.

We walked halfway down our winding driveway, where they had constructed a fourteen-foot wooden cross at the edge of our woods.

"I figured this might make the women feel welcome," Rick said.

I stood there with Rick and Thomas, gazing upward in humility and silence, giving thanks.

> *Father, forgive me. Often, I've forgotten about You,*
> *to Whom we give thanks on Thanksgiving Day.*
> —JULIE GARMON

In every thing give thanks.
—I THESSALONIANS 5:18

When I was a girl growing up in Weirton, West Virginia, Thanksgiving meant my mother ripping up soft slices of Wonder Bread for stuffing, getting out the big tin roasting pan and putting the turkey into the oven, and sliding cranberry sauce out of a can. One year she had to thaw the frozen turkey with a hair dryer; another year we all came to the table to find the cat curled up in the bowl meant for mashed potatoes.

My great-aunt Anne and her best friend Mary came for dinner; my father wielded an electric knife and said, "When Father carves the duck, potatoes fly amok." And before we ate, there was always the prayer that, to hungry children, seemed to go on and on. My father thanked God for our many blessings, asked God to bless just about every family member who was and wasn't at the table, and ended with "God bless little children everywhere."

After I moved to New York City, I would invite up to twenty people to Thanksgiving dinner in my one-bedroom apartment. How I cooked in a kitchen the size of what today would be considered a closet, using an oven barely big enough to hold an eighteen-pound turkey, I'll never know. Later I shared a weekend country house with friends. Bigger kitchen, more people, much merriment. And still always the prayers.

Today I usually spend Thanksgiving at my sister's cabin in the woods outside Seattle, where a whole new cast of wonderful characters gathers. I make the stuffing, ripping up crusty loaves of whole wheat and rye and adding apples and fresh-rubbed sage. My sister and I are the great-aunts now (emphasis, as we always say, on the great!). And as we bow our heads before the meal, the prayer still ends the same way:

Dear God, bless every family member who is and isn't at the table. And bless the little children everywhere.
—MARY ANN O'ROARK

Giving thanks always for all things....
—EPHESIANS 5:20

*O*ne day last spring, I found myself in a grouchy mood. I inflicted my grumbling on family and friends until at last someone at the office challenged me to spend one full day giving thanks to God for everything.

It should be easy to give God thanks, I thought. *Just do it!*

The next morning I got up, put on my bathrobe and started down for coffee. But what was that all over the window and on the walls in the foyer? Swirling...writhing....

Tiny insects—thousands of them. The front door had been left open a crack and the bugs swarmed in, attracted by the light we leave on at night. For two hours my wife Tib and I swept, shooed, swatted, vacuumed until the last bug vanished. But so had my morning. Remembering my promise, though, I said a shallow, "Thank You, God."

And that was just the beginning. The car battery was dead: *Thank You, God.* A story disappeared into the innards of my computer: *Thank You.* Tib got stuck in a massive traffic tie-up and missed the doctor's appointment she'd waited months for. *Thank You, God.* Each Thank You was a bit less spontaneous.

At least these were minor mishaps. Suppose they'd been serious. Could I thank God no matter what happened? When someone was sick? When a company folded? When relationships soured?

Perhaps so, because as the day went on, despite the hassles, I found I was immersed in an atmosphere of thanksgiving that was beginning—just beginning—to be independent of circumstances. How wonderful if I could live this way all the time!

Thanksgiving takes us beyond the circumstances to the Father Who stands beside us in the circumstances. I can always thank Him for being a loving God. A forgiving God. A guiding God...and even, I thought as I looked back over the annoying mishaps of the day, a God Whom I distinctly heard chuckling.

Thank You, Father, for all things.
—JOHN SHERRILL

God is our refuge and strength, a very present help in trouble.
—PSALM 46:1

*T*rouble had come at me from all sides, and I wondered how much more I could take. I needed help, so I went to see an elderly friend whose counsel I respected. "My husband's not getting any better," I began. "Every time I see him, he's worse."

My friend nodded. He'd seen my husband in the high-security ward at the provincial mental hospital in Riverview, British Columbia. After three years of aggressive treatment, he still showed no sign of improvement. Besides, other stresses had bombarded our family of seven: I had totaled our Volvo; a gasoline explosion had sent our thirteen-year-old son to the hospital with burns; my daughter, just out of high school, was leaving home for Europe; and illness had made me miss too many days at work, jeopardizing my nursing job.

My friend listened to my outpouring without interruption. Then he asked, "Helen, does God still love you?"

Stunned, I looked at his kind face. I wasn't prepared for this simple question. "Yes," I stammered. "Yes, I think so. The Bible says God's love is everlasting, so it's got to be the same whether my life is good or bad, doesn't it?"

He nodded. "You can stand on this fact: God loves you and will never leave you. Knowing that, you will cope." Then he smiled and said, "Now, before you go home, let's pray."

"Father," he prayed, "I thank You for my sister here. Thank You for Your great love for her. Thank You that You're with her now and always will be. Amen."

During the drive home, I reflected on our visit. My friend hadn't really answered my questions; he hadn't said very much. All he'd done was remind me that I have a refuge. And isn't that what a person lost in a raging storm needs most in life?

Father, thank You for Your welcoming embrace
when I come running to You. I feel safe in Your presence.
—HELEN GRACE LESCHEID

In his hand is the life of every creature and the breath of all mankind.
—Job 12:10 (NIV)

*I*t was another beautiful day in Italy. The sky was a rich blue, devoid of clouds, and once again I was taking in the breathless sights of Florence. We'd spent the morning wandering through ancient cloisters, lush gardens, and open markets where I bought fresh bread and bright tangerines. Now my friend and I walked above the city to a small white church on top of a hill. Both of us were tired and sat to rest for a while on the steps of the old building. We were overlooking the city, watching the sun's slow descent over the rust-colored rooftops.

A few steps in front of the church, a small cemetery caught my attention. I walked through the gate and wandered among the marble tombs, statues and colorful flowers. There were pictures encased in glass on most of the stones; one was an old photograph of a woman of thirty-six, her hair tied in a loose bun. I did my best to read the inscription and wondered about the life of this woman who now rested in this beautiful graveyard.

I didn't feel sadness or fear of death as I looked at these memorials. Rather, I found them strangely comforting. *Today I am alive,* I thought as I watched the sky turn pink and violet with the sunset. *One day, in God's good time, someone will come upon my tombstone and wonder about the life I once lived. But today, He's given me life.* And there, with the beauty of Italy before me, I'd never felt so deeply the richness of living it.

Thank You, Lord, for the gift of life and for this magnificent world You've given us to live in. And when the time comes, bring me peacefully home to You.

—Karen Valentin

Open the gates, so that the righteous nation that keeps faith
may enter in. Those of steadfast mind you keep in peace.
—ISAIAH 26:2–3 (NRSV)

*T*used to wonder how prayer could alter our minds and create a state of peace, until I stepped into Rome's Pantheon, a majestic, circular temple built to honor all the gods of Rome but rededicated as a Christian church in AD 607.

I approached the building slowly, admiring the sixteen high granite columns; then I slowly passed the bronze doors, which were ajar. I peeked in. Sunlight fell in a shaft, angling down from the high dome toward the place where I entered. I slipped in softly, barely breathing. A holy place.

Spellbound, I circled the interior, gazing past statues and paintings to the high, open dome and the spill of hushed sunlight. As I circled, I felt almost weightless, and I was not surprised to read later that the building was designed to create a sense of perfect equilibrium.

The startling subtlety was the architect's intent. He wanted all who entered his Pantheon to find a place of perfect balance. And so effective was his work that the roaring bustle of everyday Rome outside was silenced, and tourists and children fell quiet.

And now I know why prayer alters our state of mind. When we pray, we enter a holy place, uniquely designed by the Master, a place designed for perfect balance.

Father in heaven, when life is chaotic and noisy, help me
to remember that through prayer there is a place I can go for
equilibrium, relief from my burdens and perfect peace.
—BRENDA WILBEE

November 27

Enter his gates with thanksgiving and his courts with praise;
give thanks to him and praise his name.
—Psalm 100:4 (NIV)

*T*t was the only brand-new car I ever had—a bright red Toyota Tercel wagon, small enough to handle easily but big enough, with the seats down, to haul my son's drum set to band contests and to transport my kids and all their possessions to college dorms and apartments. I put 192,000 miles on that car and kept it for seventeen years.

Before I moved to Florida, my dad, brother and friends all said, "You have to get rid of it. The air-conditioning hasn't worked for ten years. You cannot take that car to Florida."

I argued, whined and cajoled, but finally gave in and sold it to a young man for 750 dollars. I took his picture standing next to my little red car, walked into the house and cried when he drove away.

When I flew down to Florida, the first thing I had to do was find a car. I prayed about it, knowing I had to find something very inexpensive.

"My son Joseph has a car for sale," my new friend Jack told me. He drove me over to see it.

There, in the driveway, was another little red car just like my old one, only this was a sports car, six years newer, with a CD player, a sun roof and air-conditioning! I climbed in and saw it was a stick shift. *Wow, I haven't driven a manual transmission in years! This'll be fun!*

I turned the key, drove it around the block and wrote Joseph a check.

I've learned that when I'm down and out about losing something I love, God comes through with something better, something I never even imagined. Who'd have thought God wanted me in a sports car...and a little red one to boot? With a sun roof, no less!

Father, You continue to amaze me with Your surprising goodness
in taking care of all my needs. Thank You for my little red car.
—Patricia Lorenz

November 28

Then Job answered the Lord: I know that you can do all things,
and that no purpose of yours can be thwarted.
—Job 42:1–2 (NRSV)

*W*hen you're faced with a decision or you need to do something you haven't done before—a new job or a new Bible study group or planning next week's menu—how do you approach it? My default mode is to be cautious. I want to know what other people's expectations are, the rules I need to follow. I don't want to make a mistake because I don't want people criticizing me. No criticism? Then all is well.

Shortly after I started my new job a couple of years ago, I had a cup of coffee with a colleague. I was telling him about my cautious approach to the new work. He got a quizzical look on his face and said, "Don't you believe the Bible?" My first thought was, *Oh no! The most brilliant Bible scholar I know is criticizing me. What have I done wrong?* Then he smiled and gave me a pat on the back. "The Bible is clear," he said. "God loves you, God has gifted you and God watches over you. If that doesn't give you the confidence to be creative and courageous, I don't know what will."

I'll probably never be a bold, caution-to-the-wind person. But since that day I've tried to be a more biblical person, trusting more in God and less in my own abilities. I must say, it's a great way to go.

Lord, give me the faith to stand up on my own and try something new.
—Jeff Japinga

NOVEMBER 29

Out of Zion, the perfection of beauty, God will shine forth.
—PSALM 50:2 (NKJV)

In the early 1970s, Bea Alexander told our churchwomen's group about the most beautiful tree she'd ever seen—a Chrismon tree. The pictures of exquisitely crafted white-and-gold ornaments on a stately balsam tree were breathtaking. Bea said Frances Kipps Spencer of Danville, Virginia, had created the ornaments, which were all symbols of the Christian faith, to remind people of the true meaning of Christmas.

We voted unanimously to replicate the tree in our small church and immediately ordered the pattern book and kits. Despite the fact that I'm all thumbs, I agreed to make three ornaments. Reality hit two weeks later when I received a bag of wire, pearls, foam and gold trim to make a Latin crosslet, the symbol for perfection.

I tried, but my ornament bore only a vague resemblance to the picture. "What a joke!" I lamented to the pastor's wife. "My crosslet is about as far from perfect as possible."

She examined the crosslet and then said, "It's a bit lopsided, and the beads aren't spaced right. But that's beside the point. The Chrismon tree isn't about perfect craftsmanship. It's about Jesus."

My crosslet was among the ornaments on our tree the first Sunday of Advent, along with my two less-than-perfect stars placed on the back of the tree. The flaws would hardly be noticeable to the people sitting in the pews. In fact, they made the tree more special. Our congregation of imperfect people entered the season of preparation with an imperfect but beautiful tree inviting us to a deeper faith in our perfect Savior.

Beautiful Savior, may every symbol of Your birth draw us closer to You.
—PENNEY SCHWAB

November 30

To every thing there is a season.
—Ecclesiastes 3:1

The field is fallow, the recently plowed moist soil turned to greet the sun. Tufts of dirty cotton blow across the clotted clay, remnants of the summer harvest from a neighbor's field. Autumn's colors now drape south Georgia, and the afternoon is chilled by the approaching winter. Bundled in denim and flannel, I slowly circle the field.

For years, my wife's grandfather farmed this land, and Beth's clan still gathers on the old farm for special occasions. When we assemble to feast, I always drift away to greet my old friend, the cotton patch. For me, walking around this large field has become a treasured ritual, a time to be alone with God and His creation. This afternoon as I walk, I ponder the future.

I'm slowly making peace with the fact that I'm no longer young. Early this morning the shaving mirror revealed wrinkles crinkling my eyes, and the stubble of my beard is turning gray. Our children are growing older, and I'm wondering what I will do with the next chapter of my life. Seasons change. Harvests demand new seeding. And time rolls on.

Stopping to stand quietly by a cedar fence post, I look down to see a butterfly land on the toe of my dusty boot. It's late in the year for butterflies. But there it is, the most ancient Christian symbol for the Resurrection of Jesus.

Slowly I break into a smile. In the silence of the cotton patch, it seems I can hear the voice of my resurrected Lord: "In the world, you have tribulation, but take courage; I have overcome the world" (John 16:33, NASB).

> *Lord, help me to believe that as I grow older, there will always be new life, new joy, new discoveries.*
> —Scott Walker

December

DECEMBER 1

For God so loved the world, that he gave his only begotten Son.
—JOHN 3:16

*I*t was December 1, and I hadn't even started on Christmas preparations. I hadn't picked out cards, bought a single gift, gotten ready for the houseguests arriving in two days. I'd come back the night before from a Thanksgiving trip to our son's home in Miami—an anxious time following his recent surgery.

As I waited for my computer to come to life, I thumbed through a stack of unanswered letters. My desktop appeared on the monitor; every icon seemed to scream overdue assignment! I was staring at a bottomless scroll of e-mails when first the phone rang and then the doorbell.

And so it went for two increasingly frantic hours as each thing I turned to meant not doing something else equally pressing. I was near tears when the printer suddenly gave a cough and a whir and flung a piece of blank paper onto the tray. I snatched the unasked-for sheet from the tray and slapped it back on the paper stack.

And as I did, something caught my eye. Way up in the far left corner was a tiny black mark. I picked it up and looked closer.

It was a heart.

Now the tears that had been building really did come. Anxiety, weariness, pressure—all of it poured out, released and relieved, at the sight of that small symbol appearing in a totally unexpected place. As unexpected as a stable for the birthplace of a king, as small as a baby born to save the world.

It's love, that little heart said. Love was the reason for the trip to Miami. Love is the reason for the cards and the gifts and the guests and the letters to answer and the work God has given you to do. The loving chores you've taken on are simply your response to the Love that came down at Christmas.

Faithful Lord, keep my focus this busy month on the reason for the season.
—ELIZABETH SHERRILL

December 2

Let your light so shine before men, that they may see your good works,
and glorify your Father which is in heaven.
—Matthew 5:16

*T*noticed them as I drove home that dark evening. Someone had wrapped strings of lights around all the tree trunks in their front yard. Round and round the twinkling colors went, but only about six feet up. After that, the trees ascended heavenward in darkness. *Odd,* I thought. But the next night, as I approached the lights, they didn't seem so odd. They seemed, well, pragmatic.

I had no idea why the lights stopped so abruptly. Perhaps the homeowners didn't have a ladder or weren't permitted to climb for some reason. Perhaps they had a limited number of lights and a limited budget to spend on them. Perhaps they didn't have much time to give to decorating but wanted to make the effort. Whatever the reason for this unusual display, it inspired me. They had done what they could with what they had.

Kind of like Mary and Joseph that night in the stable, with a manger for a crib and beds made of fresh straw. Perhaps that's all God ever requires of us: to do the best we can with what we have. It was a comforting thought to ponder while driving through December darkness.

In this season of hustle and bustle, Lord, let me set aside
the need to do things perfectly. Help me focus, instead,
on letting my light shine...perhaps in odd and pragmatic ways.
—Mary Lou Carney

*That...which we have seen with our eyes, which we have looked
at and our hands have touched—this we proclaim.*
—I JOHN 1:1 (NIV)

*T*t was December in that wall-less, dung-floored school in Uganda. In a
Kampala bookstore I found a slender paperbound collection of beloved
Christmas songs. All month long we learned and sang them. A "star of wonder,"
a "newborn King," a "lowly cattle shed"—all these things the students could
imagine. Other words were easy to explain: "Shepherds," I told them, "are
like goatherds."

An image in one hymn, though, was hard to get across. How, the students
asked, could water be "like a stone"? These kids were familiar with water! Every
day they lugged pails of it to their homes from Lake Victoria, shimmering at the
foot of the hill beneath the equatorial sun. Water poured; stones were hard and
stiff! My efforts at describing ice were met with silent stares. Young Ugandans
do not challenge adults, but it was clear that my claims were not believed.

Then I thought of the little ice cube unit in our refrigerator!

Next day I brought both trays to the school. Amid squeals and shouts, the
frozen cubes passed from hand to hand. In the sweltering heat beneath that iron
roof the frigid "stones" had not reached the end of a row before it was clear they
were indeed water.

Something was clear to me too: Why Christmas had to be.

The image of a loving, personal God was also hard to get across. For
centuries, the claims of seers and prophets were not believed either. This
unimaginable God had to come to us in a form we could see and hear and touch.
Christmas had to happen.

Show me Yourself today, Lord, in this physical world You came to live in.
—ELIZABETH SHERRILL

DECEMBER 4

Mine eyes have seen thy salvation, Which thou hast prepared before the face of all people; A light to lighten the Gentiles, and the glory of thy people Israel.
—LUKE 2:30–32

I retired after thirty-eight years with Guideposts, and Medicare hadn't processed my records. I was on the phone for hours trying to clear it up. After hanging up in frustration for the umpteenth time, I glanced out of the window to see our Christmas tree leaning forlornly against the garage and I winced. I'd meant to put it up days ago.

As I lugged a box of decorations across the living room floor, I kicked the morning newspaper aside and my eye caught the headline INTENSIFIED FIGHTING IN IRAQ. I thought of our soldiers there, put down the box and prayed for them. *When does the world ever make time for Christmas?*

It hadn't that first time, either, I thought. A poor carpenter and his about-to-deliver wife struggled hopelessly to find a room in a town teeming with visitors; a jealous king ordered a senseless massacre; a people trembled under the oppression of occupying troops. Yet through it all there radiated a hope and joy that would inspire a hundred generations.

I took a deep breath, put on my jacket and went out to get the tree. The world will always have its troubles, but this birthday will always be a celebration.

> *Lord, when things seem their darkest, let me*
> *always see the light from Your manger.*
> —RICHARD SCHNEIDER

December 5

The Word became flesh and lived among us.
—John 1:14 (NRSV)

*M*y aunt Elsie is a spunky, pint-sized widow in her eighties who keeps house, grows organic vegetables and fruit, and loves to fish. Every year I receive a hard-to-decipher handwritten Christmas letter from her, full of the details of her life. She tells me about getting her snowblower fixed just in time for the blizzard, the tasty blueberries in her freezer, the first spring robin in her yard, her repaired roof that's now "snug and good," her daughter-in-law's weight loss, her granddaughter's success in a Bible quiz, her grandson's soccer game, the fishing trip "on the beautiful Juniata River, so clear you could see the muskies looking like fence posts lying out there."

Why do I love these Christmas letters? Because Aunt Elsie spreads out the meat-and-potatoes of her days like a sumptuous feast. Her letters zing with the joy of the ordinary. She inspires me to savor the homey things that are the staples of my own life: the vacuum repaired in time for Christmas, the beads of rain on the window, my husband Whitney's arm around my shoulder, a daughter's phone call, the smell of clean laundry, a hug from a child, the punctual wail of the train whistle.

It's a healthy outlook that spices my days with gratitude. And it reminds me that in becoming one of us, our Lord forever made the ordinary rich beyond measure.

Lord Jesus, I adore You, the Holy One Who put
on our flesh and shared our garden-variety days.
—Shari Smyth

DECEMBER 6

But these are written that you may believe that Jesus is the Messiah,
the Son of God, and that by believing you may have life in his name.
—JOHN 20:31 (NIV)

hree years ago yesterday, following emergency surgery, I was diagnosed with stage-four ovarian cancer. Alone in my hospital room with the doctor, I asked, "Give it to me straight. What does this mean?" "About life expectancy?" she asked hesitantly. I nodded. "Two years, on average." So today, three years later, I'm celebrating a miracle. For a long time I resisted applying that word to my experience. Miracles are mysterious. And they happen to other people, like the people in the Bible—and Skylar, the baby boy whose picture I put on my refrigerator shortly after coming home from the hospital with my diagnosis. His mom is a friend.

Several weeks after his birth, Skylar was diagnosed with leukemia. He was put on life support, and finally the doctors told his parents to prepare for the worst. His mother tearfully asked the nurses to pull all the tubes when the end came near so she could hold him until he died. Meanwhile, across town at the family's church, a group gathered for prayer and someone reported that Skylar was dying. A pastor suddenly stood up and almost defiantly announced, "There are diagnoses and statistics—and then there's God!"

Back at the hospital, little Skylar drew a few breaths on his own, and then a few more, slowly at first but then more steadily.

The Bible tells us that miracles are made known to us so we might believe that God is real. Today I look at the words written across the bottom of Skylar's picture: "And then there's God." I believe.

Lord, thank You for still sprinkling miracles into our days.
—CAROL KUYKENDALL

DECEMBER 7

You lift me up on the wind, you make me ride on it,
and you toss me about in the roar of the storm.
—JOB 30:22 (NRSV)

*T*his is the captain speaking. There's a lot of weather around the Denver
airport, so you might want to buckle up early as we try to land."

Whoa! What was that? Try to land? I dutifully fastened my seat belt and
attempted another article in the in-flight magazine, but no chance. We were
beginning the roughest reentry since Orville at Kitty Hawk, bouncing around
like a Chihuahua on caffeine. Finally the runway came into sight. We were still
all a-jolt, but at least we were on the ground.

Wrong! The pilot aborted the landing at the last second and we went
screaming skyward. After a few minutes of top-notch roller-coaster action, the
pilot informed us we were going to Colorado Springs. Some people applauded.
No one complained about the abrupt delay; phone calls were made, plans
changed, meetings rescheduled. Once we were on terra firma, I was tempted to
kiss the ground.

I cannot tell how many times my life has met with rough weather and bumpy
rides, and usually without the warning to buckle up. Birth, death, joy, sorrow—
they pop up like a sudden thunderstorm. Sometimes you land. Sometimes
you try to land but then take off again. Sometimes you end up in a completely
different place, and there's nothing to do but call on the Almighty and ride it out.

Lord, when the storms of life are tossing me about, help me
to remember that only You can say, "Peace, be still" (MARK 4:39).
—MARK COLLINS

"Be still, and know that I am God!"
—PSALM 46:10 (NRSV)

*Y*ears ago I wanted to be a part of everything people were doing that appeared to be God's will. But before long I had made more commitments than my calendar could possibly hold. I cut down on sleep, exercise and playtime with my family. Things got more and more chaotic, until one night I woke up in a panic. I could see myself failing and being shamed by having to admit I couldn't do it all. Thoroughly revved up, I jumped up to another frantic day of jockeying appointments, meeting deadlines and shortchanging my family, promising that I was almost caught up. Something told me my frantic life was far from Jesus' "peace that passeth understanding" (Philippians 4:7, KJV), but I felt guilty giving up projects that seemed to serve God.

As I tossed up a "please help me" prayer and sat on the floor to do a few sit-ups, I recalled an old newspaper story. Before dawn on a cold December morning, three duck hunters in waist-high rubber waders were thrown into the icy black water of an unfamiliar lake when their small, flat-bottomed boat capsized. All three drowned trying to swim to shore. The accident was particularly tragic because the water was less than five feet deep. Had the men not panicked but simply put their feet down, they could have waded out.

I shook my head, smiling at my own blindness. I'd been struggling so frantically to take over Jesus' job and save the world that I'd almost gone under. All I had to do was stop, be still and let my full weight down on God.

Lord, thank You that You're always close enough to save me from my messes.
—KEITH MILLER

December 9

Put your hope in God.
—Psalm 42:5 (NIV)

An out-of-town friend was stopping in my area on business and we'd arranged to meet for coffee before she headed back home. I looked forward to seeing her, yet dreaded it at the same time.

Helen had lost her job several years back and now was losing her home. A brand-new Christian, she was facing her first real crisis of faith. "Every sermon I hear and every book I pick up says God is going to take care of me," she had challenged me the last time we spoke. "But where is He now, Roberta?" Every response that came to my mind seemed feeble in light of Helen's losses.

Fix her the nicest present you can think of. The idea came totally unbidden and seemed pointless. But I filled a gift bag shaped like an old-fashioned purse with a butter rum candle and a package of pansy-printed tissues and tied a miniature teacup on the handle of the gift bag. When I presented the gift to Helen, she didn't even make eye contact.

It was several days later that I heard from her. "That candle," she gushed, "is absolutely wonderful. I burn it a little each day, so it will last. And the tissues—at least now I cry pretty." I heard a smile in her voice. "Can you help me find some more of those itty-bitty cups? Wherever I end up living, I want to have a little Christmas tree filled with them. God's going to take care of me, Roberta, just like He says."

> *May I always listen, Lord, for Your urgings, like the ones that turn despair into Christmas hope.*
> —Roberta Messner

December 10

The Lord shall guide thee continually.
—Isaiah 58:11

*E*ach time New England enters a deep freeze, my thoughts race back to February 1934, the coldest month ever recorded in my hometown of Williamstown, Massachusetts. The temperature plunged to twenty-seven degrees below zero and then crept up to ten below, where it remained for days. Another force gripped our village then, the Great Depression. We constantly worried about money, jobs and the future, which squeezed the joy from our lives and discolored our outlook.

But there was a bright spot. Each Sunday evening I walked against the punishing wind and the biting cold to St. John's Church on Park Street. No matter how warmly I was dressed, I reached St. John's with chattering teeth and icy fingers. Once there I hurried downstairs, and as I opened the kitchen door, the warmth rushed out to greet me. This barren room contained a stove, a sink, a long table and folding chairs. Gathered at the table were our pastor, his wife, a nurse from the Williams College infirmary, a college professor and several students.

We were attending the Young People's Fellowship. As we sipped cocoa, the professor talked about his struggle to acquire an education. The nurse spoke of her joy when a patient was on the road to recovery. Students from the college shared their dreams. We left the kitchen feeling warmed and lifted. Outside, the wind seemed less troubling and the Great Depression less oppressive. We had each other and we had faith. That faith has guided and strengthened me all my life.

Blessed Jesus, the glow from that barren room glows in my life today.
—Oscar Greene

DECEMBER 11

So Rehoboam dwelt in Jerusalem, and built cities
for defense in Judah. And he built Bethlehem.
—II CHRONICLES 11:5–6 (NKJV)

To the casual eye, Bethlehem was an odd choice for the birthplace of a messiah. It was just another ho-hum dot on the map, yet it had a rich, romantic history that made it a shoo-in for a king's birth.

All my life has been spent in small towns. Only someone who has lived in these little villages can appreciate their genius. The city dude, passing through, doesn't "get" it, but a small town is a perfect slice of life. A small town has one of every kind of person. Most important, you actually know these people. You sit with them in the library and worship with them in church. You talk to them at the gas pump and in the hardware store.

Moberly, Missouri, where I live and work as a college teacher, is a town of thirteen thousand. "There's nothing to do here," my students complain, but that's the beauty of it. Here children learn to entertain themselves without pricey theme parks and museums. The more leisurely pace of the small town is conducive to reflection, and spiritual instincts are fed by close contact with nature. When I say my prayers, I can lie on the grass under a tree and breathe in a sweet breeze and listen to the sound of bees. Try that on Wall Street.

My wife Sharon has spent a lifetime reading about American presidents. "Did you know that most of our presidents came from small towns?" she points out. Maybe she's on to something, something God knew when He chose the little villages of Nazareth and Bethlehem to cradle His Deliverer.

Truth is, God can use me wherever I live, as long as I am available.

Lord, help me to be great right here, where You have planted me.
—DANIEL SCHANTZ

DECEMBER 12

Even the night shall be light about me.
—PSALM 139:11 (NKJV)

*I*t's not how I would have done it. If I had news as big as the Gospel, I would have called simultaneous news conferences at high noon, in Athens and Alexandria, in Jerusalem and Rome. But when God announced the birth of His Son, He did so at night, in a rural pasture. Jealous kings and picky Pharisees were slumbering then, but receptive shepherds were watching the sky when it exploded with the glory of God.

Darkness is not my favorite time. Since childhood I have needed a night-light to make it to sunrise. I also own thirty-eight flashlights. Everything seems to get worse at night: aches and pains, anxieties, regrets. At times I can't tell the difference between my nightmares and reality until my wife Sharon nudges me and asks, "Are you okay, hon?"

Yet, even I welcome darkness at Christmas. Without it, I could not enjoy the necklaces of light that grace the trees and homes of our neighborhood. Without darkness, I could not see the flickering candles of the carolers coming up our sidewalk. Without darkness, I couldn't enjoy our traditional candlelight Christmas supper.

Spiritual darkness can settle over a person at any season. Even at Christmas, things go wrong with marriage and health. Temptations sneak up on you, just when you're supposed to be singing "Joy to the World." At such times, it's good to step outdoors and look up at the stars. The night sky is filled with a trillion eyes, the eyes of angels, watching over us, longing to help us find our way back to the light.

Thank You, Father, for not leaving me in the dark.
—DANIEL SCHANTZ

DECEMBER 13

*Let us now go even unto Bethlehem,
and see this thing which is come to pass.*
—LUKE 2:15

*I*n a fit of madness this year, I decided the best way to teach four-year-old Maggie the Christmas story was to organize a neighborhood pageant. I made arrangements for space at the chapel around the corner and then sent an announcement to our community e-mail list to round up some kids.

I was so laid back about the project I completely forgot about the first of three rehearsals. On my second try, two dozen kids showed up, most of them preschoolers. Hearing my description of the adventurous rehearsal later, my husband Andrew looked at me oddly and commented that I seemed awfully mellow.

At the next rehearsal I remembered to bring the script for the narrator but forgot Baby Jesus. The kids were okay with that. So was I. What mattered to me was that the children got the basics of the Christmas story and learned a few carols. On the way out, one of the moms murmured, "Better you than me!"

The day of the pageant arrived. The chapel filled with shepherds in bathrobes and angels in oversized white T-shirts. I quieted the babbling horde and chatted with them briefly. "Remember, this is a real story. It's not a cartoon. We're not here to make people laugh, but to honor Baby Jesus and teach others about Him." They all nodded and looked remarkably serious.

Much to my delight, the angel Gabriel didn't gallop up to meet the Virgin Mary, the shepherds didn't bean each other with their crooks, the heavenly host came out on cue without trampling the shepherds, the Magi looked regal as they processed to the crib. Children sang, parents glowed, people applauded. Everyone asked if we could do it again next year.

I don't see why not. It's not as if it's stressful or anything.

*Jesus, help me to remember that Your birthday
isn't supposed to be about stress.*
—JULIA ATTAWAY

Trust in the Lord with all thine heart.
—PROVERBS 3:5

*I*t would be my first Christmas without him, and I felt as though my heart had been yanked out of my body. My husband John had died mercifully, gently, that October. We were having a cup of tea together when, without any warning, he went into cardiac arrest. Instantly, he was taken into the presence of our Lord.

"We need a Christmas tree we can carry," my daughter and I agreed. We tried our joint strength and found that even a four-footer was a struggle—a far cry from the six- to eight-foot pine John took pride in setting up.

"Yup, a big one," he'd insist. "Fill the end of the living room, it will."

After we'd brought the little tree home, I thought sadly of John's Christmas traditions: plum pudding, wassail laced with cinnamon sticks and cloves, and kippers for breakfast Christmas morning. Not only was I twisted up with grief, I was shaky, insecure and scared. "I know you're happy, darling," I whispered into the darkness of the night, "but I miss you most unbearably. What's heaven like? Can you send me a postcard?"

The next morning a nip was in the air as I trudged down our driveway to get the newspaper. Leaves crunched underfoot, each step breaking the silence with a rhythmic beat: *He's gone. He's gone.* Then I saw a bit of litter by the mailbox, smeared with dirt as though a car had run it over. As I picked it up to trash it, I turned it over. It was a sheet pulled from a stick-um pad, and across the top, printed in bold blue italic, was "Trust in the Lord with all your heart. Proverbs 3:5."

"A postcard from the gates of heaven!" I gasped.

I turned my eyes up to the brightness of the morning star. "Thank You, Lord. Thank you, darling. Merry Christmas!"

Your love is here beside me, Lord. Please take my hand
and guide me through today and each tomorrow.
—FAY ANGUS

Joseph also went from the town of Nazareth in Galilee
to Judea, to the city of David called Bethlehem.
—LUKE 2:4 (NRSV)

*O*ne year I found Christmas at a fast-food restaurant in the Orlando International Airport. Or perhaps more accurately, Christmas found me.

Actually, it was Hakim who found me—sort of. All he really wanted was a place to sit for himself and his wife, who was obviously tired and even more obviously pregnant. I was occupying one seat of a four-person booth, nursing the last of my onion rings and feeling enormously sorry for myself because I was missing a Christmas program back home.

"May we sit down here?"

"Of course." Feeling awkward in the silence, I ventured, "Going home?"

Hakim nodded and then, looking at his wife, added, "To have the baby. And raise him."

"Where is home?" I asked. And he might as well have said the moon, so taken aback I was with his reply.

"Bethlehem," he said, eyeing me seriously. "Do you know of it?"

Do I know of Bethlehem? I did, I told him, but as we talked I learned about the real Bethlehem—how dangerous a place it was in Jesus' day and how dangerous it remains today. And yet Hakim said, "The God of the universe continues to touch a most ordinary place of our world in a most extraordinary way—and through it touches us all."

Once, a baby born in Bethlehem changed the world. That year, in a fast-food restaurant, a baby about to be born in Bethlehem changed me.

Grant me, O God, ears to hear and eyes to see the wonder of Your presence
this holiday season, in the ordinary places of my life.
—JEFF JAPINGA

December 16

*The Spirit of the Lord will come powerfully upon you, and you will prophesy
with them; and you will be changed into a different person.*

—I Samuel 10:6 (NIV)

I was packing my bags for a weekend retreat when I heard my wife calling me. "Pablo, it's Denise from Boston on the telephone."

I picked up the phone. "I'm calling you about my brother Charlie," Denise said, her voice low and withdrawn.

It seemed like yesterday when Charlie walked into the Boston church where I ministered on Sunday mornings. He was a thin young man, not much older than I was, nervous, fragile and distraught. He was addicted to drugs and was struggling to get his life on the right track. I prayed with him, asking God to help him break his addiction and give him the courage to start a new life.

In the weeks and months that followed, I helped Charlie through rehab and recovery. We developed a special bond, but we lost touch with each other when I moved to the West Coast. We had reconnected a few months before Denise's phone call, and I'd learned that he was fighting lung cancer.

"Charlie is dying," Denise said. "He's only got a few days. I called you because Charlie loved you and you meant a lot to him. You were always his pastor."

Denise put the telephone by Charlie's ear so I could say good-bye to him. I took a deep breath and said, "Charlie, I love you. I'll see you soon, my friend. Thank you for your friendship." Two days later, Charlie died.

Whatever I'd been able to do for Charlie was nothing compared to what he had done for me. His victorious struggle with drug and alcohol addiction taught me the power of making the most of a second chance in life through faith in God.

*Lord, thank You for putting Charlie in my life. Give me the faith
to lend my hand and heart to those who need a second chance.*

—Pablo Diaz

December 17

"Do not fear, for I have redeemed you; I have
summoned you by name; you are mine."
—ISAIAH 43:1 (NIV)

*B*ecause of my work schedule, waking up at home on a Saturday with nothing to do is rare. On one of those mornings, my wife Rosie and I sat and talked, and she said, "Dolphus, there are days that I feel like God is far away and I am all alone."

I realized this was not a time to talk but a time to listen, and that Rosie was not looking for a solution but a place to share deep feelings. So I listened, which, I have to confess, is hard for me to do.

Rosie told me that a few days earlier she had been feeling lonely and low. She wondered how she could go on in such darkness. Then an amazing thing happened: God brought a song to her heart, "Walking in the Light, Jesus Is the Light." In that moment God gave her strength to move on.

A Scripture also came to mind, Isaiah 43:1. "Dolphus," she said, "as I remembered that beautiful, reassuring verse, my heart felt joyful."

I praise God for songs of remembering and Scriptures of comfort—and for that rare Saturday morning when I had nothing to do but listen to the woman I love.

Lord, when I feel as Rosie did and have my questions,
lead me to those things that will enable me to rejoice.
—DOLPHUS WEARY

DECEMBER 18

May you rejoice in the wife of your youth.
—Proverbs 5:18 (NIV)

*G*od willing, Carol and I will celebrate our fiftieth wedding anniversary this year. As I write, I find myself mulling over a verse I just read as part of my daily Bible reading: "You have stolen my heart...my bride; you have stolen my heart" (Song of Songs 4:9, updated NIV). Coincidence? More like a divine reminder.

On a snowy afternoon, two days before Christmas 1961, Carol and I stood together before the altar of Pittsburgh's First Presbyterian Church as the pastor, Dr. Robert Lamont, pronounced us husband and wife. I remember looking into Carol's sparkling brown eyes at that moment and being struck by the thought, *We're not here by chance!* Back then I was too spiritually ignorant to understand the significance of that moment. Now I do.

Although I'd never been particularly religious, Carol had a real hunger for God. Eleven years later, in 1972, at her urging, we attended a Methodist Lay Witness Mission where I was transformed by an encounter with the living God. That new reality of Jesus in our lives has cemented our relationship as nothing else could. He has carried us through illnesses and tough economic times, and on occasion has lifted us to spiritual heights we couldn't have dreamed of before. Together, we've raised two beautiful daughters who have followed us in faith. We've encouraged, taught and prayed with others and witnessed some real miracles.

So today, Carol and I, our daughters, son-in-law and three grandchildren will be singing praises to the One Who arranged it all. For He will be there too—and that's no coincidence.

Father, who knew? You certainly did. And Carol and I will be forever grateful.
—Harold Hostetler

DECEMBER 19

In all thy ways acknowledge him, and he shall direct thy paths.
—PROVERBS 3:6

I am not very good at directions. Okay, the truth is I'm terrible at directions. I get lost in airport terminals and mall parking lots. I shudder every time I stop to ask directions and someone says, "Oh, it's easy. You can't miss it." Because that's exactly what I almost always do: miss it.

So last year, when we bought a new car, my husband asked if I'd like to have a Global Positioning System (GPS) included that would help me navigate. Now I have an electronic pal who speaks to me, telling me where to turn and what lane I need to be in for exits. I have a colorful digital map with a small arrow that is "me," so I can watch as I progress down highways and toward intersections. But before any of this marvelous assistance can take place, I have a screen full of text that comes up every time I start my car. It contains a promise that I must make to drive carefully, obey traffic rules—and not stare too much at the navigational screen. And until I hit the AGREE button, I get no help or guidance.

I thought of that GPS last night when I opened my Bible. It, too, wants to give me direction as I travel the road of life. But first I have to agree to take time to read its words, to apply its wisdom, to surrender to its Author.

I'll probably always be "directionally challenged," but I know that if I use both my GPS and my Bible wisely, I'll be making more right turns in life.

Lead me, Father, down the road that will take me closer to You.
—MARY LOU CARNEY

Jesus saith unto him, I am the way, the truth, and the life:
no man cometh unto the Father, but by me.
—JOHN 14:6

One day, after my husband Alex and I had lived in Oxford, England, for several months, I was walking across town to my favorite college garden, through medieval stone archways and winding passageways. I encountered a tour guide telling her group they would soon enter Christ Church College. Flabbergasted, I watched as she led them the wrong way, down an alley with no access to the college.

When I was in college, I found myself like those tourists, naively heading down a wrong path. In desperation, I prayed, "God, if You exist, please show me." That winter, I impulsively registered to go on a church ski trip. Suddenly Michigan was hit with unseasonably warm weather, and I received a call informing me that the ski trip was being replaced by a "Weekend in Christian Living" at a nearby camp. Eager for any chance to get off campus, I went.

Instead of skiing, we walked in the woods and sat by the fire discussing who Christ was and what it meant to be a Christian. After listening to my doubts all weekend, my group leader finally looked at me and said, "Mary, Jesus Christ is the Son of God. This is the truth. He wants you to follow Him and have His life within you. Will you accept it?" That evening I knelt in the chapel and said, "Yes, Lord."

Lord, on this holy night I say yes to You again.
Please be the Way for me, the Truth and the Life.
—MARY BROWN

December 21

They shall call his name Emmanuel.
—Matthew 1:23

The Christmas season was here once again and, as usual, I was running behind. It would be hours before I could leave the office. Then I'd have to fight the crowds in an effort to get my last-minute shopping done.

"Your mother is on line one," my assistant said. I already knew why she was calling.

"Mom, I don't have time to go to church," I said without even a "hello." It was Wednesday, so church was tonight and it was the last thing I had time for.

"Now, Brock, tonight's the live nativity scene, and if you don't go, I think you'll regret it." Most sons are familiar with the dreaded "you'll regret it" line. I had no choice now.

"Okay, Mom," I said, sighing, trying my best to let her actually hear me rolling my eyes. "I'll see you there." Even though I'm now thirty-six years old, I still find myself listening to my mother. As I sat in the pew, next to my smiling mom, the children's choir sang "Happy Birthday, Jesus" a cappella in their sweet voices. I took a deep breath and felt a calm coming over me that I hadn't felt in some time. "Silent night, holy night," my little winged-and-haloed niece Abby was singing. I looked around at my church family as she and the other children sang, "All is calm, all is bright." Then I could feel it coming: Christmas, headed straight for my heart.

Dear God, Christmas calls. Let me be smart enough to stop and listen.
—Brock Kidd

Come and hear, all you who fear God, and
I will tell you what he has done for me.
—PSALM 66:16 (NRSV)

Last December I had open-heart surgery and that meant Christmas was mostly a time of recovery. No parties, no singing, no traveling, no shopping. One day, scarcely home from the hospital, I walked very slowly to the corner to get a gift certificate for my wife Carol. That was about it. On Christmas Eve, with the help of a few painkillers, I made it to church and then went to bed early.

Carol would just as well forget last Christmas. She took pictures of our celebration around the tree, but she's never let me see them. She says it's because I look bad. It wasn't much fun for her to have the holidays with a half-functioning husband. Last Christmas is something she could just skip.

But there's stuff I vividly remember and want to hold on to: all the cards, all the food that people dropped off, all the visits and phone calls, all the prayers and e-mails. It's funny, I don't remember much about the pain in my chest and being tired a lot and never feeling warm enough and running a low-grade fever. What I recall is feeling loved and appreciated.

Please don't get me wrong; I hope your Christmas is full of abundance and good health. But if you're having a hard time, if you're worried about your health or your job or a loved one, let me tell you there will still be something to treasure. The good stuff shimmers in the dark like tinsel in candlelight. Think of that first Christmas. It was one of the hardest on record. Look what came of it.

Even in the struggles, Lord, I know You are there.
—RICK HAMLIN

DECEMBER 23

What shall I render unto the Lord for all his benefits toward me?
—PSALM 116:12

*C*hristmas Eve came almost three weeks after my heart surgery. I was thrilled to be back at church, delighted to see so many dear friends after the rigors of hospitalization. The minister even announced that I was present. I rose to my feet, my hands in my pockets and a scarf wrapped around my neck to keep me warm, and received a round of applause. I waved to my cohorts in the balcony where for countless Christmas Eves I'd sung with the choir. It sounded like they were managing fine without me.

Sharing a hymnal with my son, I was having a little trouble singing. No doctor had warned me about this. They said it would take a while before I would be walking at a quick pace or running or going to the gym, but they didn't tell me my breath for singing would go wonky on every other note. I'd sing a phrase and then have to rest to sing the next one. One venerable carol after another, and I was only half present, if that. Usually we like to divide parts as a family and harmonize together. Well, I was pretty useless. *How can I celebrate Christmas if I can't sing?*

Then we came to one of my favorite carols, "In the Bleak Midwinter," and I wanted to throw down the book at the ugly croaking I was making. But there in the last verse was the message I needed to hear: "What can I give him, poor as I am?" The answer from Christina Rossetti, the lyricist: "Give him my heart." Nothing more, nothing less. I didn't have to sing a stirring tenor descant from the loft. All I needed to do was love and be loved.

What I can give, Lord, I give: my heart, my self.
—RICK HAMLIN

December 24

I am the bread of life: he that cometh to me shall never hunger.
—John 6:35

In our family, as in so many across the world, Christmas Eve is a time filled with laughter and the joy of giving. There will be homemade goodies—Tennessee cheese and my grandmother's "nuts and bolts" party mix—laid out in my parents' kitchen and piles of presents waiting under the tree. But all this comes later. We start this night at the six o'clock Communion service at Hillsboro Presbyterian, where my father has been minister all my life. The church is candlelit, and my father waits at the altar as small groups of people come forward.

I close my eyes and see myself as a little boy standing beside his grandfather. With his huge hand laid gently on my shoulder, we wait in a holy silence as my dad passes out the sacrament. Every Christmas Eve of my life has been the same. And even as the years have flown by, even with my hand laid on my son Harrison's shoulder, I become a child again. Somehow, in the candle glow, I can sense all those I've loved—grandparents, aunts, uncles, dear friends—gathered near, and as my father looks into my eyes and says, "This is the body of Christ, Brock, broken for you," my heart is filled with enough hope to sustain me through the year.

And so on this Christmas Eve, I will come again to the candlelit church. On this night of miracles, I'll join the great crowd of people all around the world—whoever is coming now, whoever has come in the past and whoever will come in the future—all His children, all His church. "This is the body of Christ broken for you."

Father, on this holy night, I wait as a child in faith and hope.
—Brock Kidd

"I am the true vine, and my Father is the vinedresser.... I am the vine,
you are the branches. He who abides in Me, and I in him,
bears much fruit; for without Me you can do nothing."
—JOHN 15:1, 5 (NKJV)

*S*everal years ago our family spent Christmas Day in South Africa. On our way home from church in Cape Town, we stopped at a restaurant overlooking a vineyard. On this hot day (December in the Southern Hemisphere is summer), we sat on a shaded balcony, enjoying the lovely view: rows of lush grapevines well-staked, weeded and cultivated. The vinedresser had planted a rosebush at the end of each row to attract pests away from his precious fruit. Not ripe enough yet for harvest, grapes hung from the vines in clusters of pale green pearls, luminous in the sunlight.

It occurs to me now that this unusual setting for our Christmas lunch holds more meaning than the sentimental snowy landscapes back home, which I'd missed as "really Christmas." Before the coming of Christ, the image of the vineyard symbolized Israel as God's cherished inheritance. Now the vine is Christ Himself with us as His branches. Today, Jesus reveals how all His "I am" promises can be fulfilled in our lives: Simply remain in Him as a branch on a vine. How wonderful for each of us to be a living branch of this vine! And what encouragement! The vine does the work, holding on to the branches, pouring nourishment and life through them to bear fruit. All the branches need to do is abide.

Dear God, what a precious gift You've given me, to be a branch
in Your beloved vineyard. Please help me remember, especially
during trials and struggles, that You are holding on to me.
—MARY BROWN

*"You are to go into all the world and preach
the Good News to everyone, everywhere."*
—MARK 16:15 (TLB)

Christmas morning with my son Michael's family began like most family Christmases. Two-year-old Caden was thrilled with a toy train and tracks. His older cousins were delighted with gift cards for food, clothes and movies.

But after breakfast, the day took a different turn. We tuned up our singing voices and headed to join our "team" at a nearby care facility. All over town, members of Michael's church were doing the same thing. On Christmas morning, pastors and laypeople visit every nursing and long-term care home in the city as part of their mission to share Christ's love.

About thirty residents were waiting. We sang "O Little Town of Bethlehem," "Joy to the World" and all five verses of "We Three Kings." Someone read the Christmas story. We gave candy and gifts—lovingly chosen and paid for by church members—to every resident. Then it was time for tea, cookies and sharing.

One man had rows of military ribbons and medals pinned to his bathrobe. "I'll be rejoining my unit in England tomorrow," he told me. "The war's not won, you know." A woman in her seventies was worried about her ninety-plus-year-old mother: "I don't think she can cope if I go first." A young man receiving wound care was effusive in thanks for his gift of socks. Later, I learned it was the only package he would open and our group would be his only visitors.

As I closed my eyes for the prayer before we left, I pictured one particular ornament from the Chrismon tree at my church: the cross of Christ on top of the world. I opened my eyes and looked at the residents, and I knew that on this Christmas, we were where we were supposed to be, doing what the Lord of all called us to do.

*Lord and lover of the world, let this day be
the beginning of my own loving outreach.*
—PENNEY SCHWAB

DECEMBER 27

*"See, I am sending an angel ahead of you to guard you
along the way and to bring you to the place I have prepared."*
—EXODUS 23:20 (NIV)

*M*y father was dying, and I was called home from Indiana to North Carolina. The first night at the hospital, my twin sister Debbie and I sat by Daddy's bed, holding vigil as we listened to his raspy breathing.

In the early hours of the morning, I awoke from a fitful sleep. Deb was sitting by the only window in the room. "Come here, Lib," she said. "I want to show you something."

I went around Daddy's bed, and Deb pointed to a framed picture hanging on the wall over the sink. "Can you see the angel in that picture?" she asked.

I had stared at that picture over and over, but until now had noticed nothing unusual. In fact, Deb and I agreed we didn't particularly like the picture, a wooded scene with red poppies at the bottom and a bird sitting on a branch to one side.

But now, as I glanced at the picture from the angle by the window, I immediately spotted the angel. The sculptured wings and body were clearly made up of the light between the trees and the poppies. The shape was unmistakable.

"I asked God to give me a sign that Daddy would be okay, that he would be at peace," Deb said. "When I looked up, there was the angel. And I thought, That angel is overlooking red…and I was going to say poppies, but then it occurred to me that it was overlooking Red." "Red" was our father's nickname. With a head full of bright red hair, he had been called nothing else since childhood.

Suddenly that picture became the most beautiful thing in the room for all of us, a sign of God's love and divine protection for our father.

*Lord, I thank You for signs that assure me that You
are present and active in every aspect of my life.*
—LIBBIE ADAMS

DECEMBER 28

"Follow me," Jesus told him, and Levi got up and followed him.
—MARK 2:14 (NIV)

I used to wonder how Jesus could have had such an impact on the lives of His disciples in the few years He spent with them. But that was before I met Bill, the pastor of the church I attend at college. Young men from my college have been attending Bill's Friday afternoon Bible study for more than two decades—longer than I've been alive.

When I came to the Bible study, I was full of doubts and worries. One Friday afternoon I talked about my struggles, half expecting a stern reprimand from Bill.

"What's the opposite of faith?" Bill asked.

"Doubt," someone said.

"No," said Bill. "The Bible tells us to walk by faith and not by sight, remember? The opposite of faith is sight. Doubt is just a natural part of growing in your faith."

I wrote down those words in a journal in which I've written hundreds of other things Bill has taught me over these past few years. And it's not just me. On his birthday, at homecoming and during other times throughout the year, men ranging in age from their early twenties to almost forty can be found in Bill's living room, spending time with the man who helped their faith grow roots.

Jesus had a great impact on His disciples. As Bill has shown me, all it takes is the willingness to share your life and your love—and your Friday afternoons.

Lord, thank You for the mentors who have helped me along my spiritual journey.
—JOSHUA SUNDQUIST

DECEMBER 29

Get rid of the old yeast.
—I CORINTHIANS 5:7 (NIV)

"*I* meant to do my work today—"

That's the first line of a favorite poem by Richard Le Gallienne. Today I "meant to do my work," specifically, to set up my account books for the new year. But I got distracted by a plastic wastebasket I walk past several times a day. It's full of papers I've let pile up all year because I've been waiting for a spare minute to slip them through the shredder. I couldn't seem to turn my full attention to my new-year accounts until I'd properly disposed of last year's.

I rather mindlessly shredded the old accounts, until a twinge of anger welled up at the sight of an old work order. I had completed the job on time. Why had they waited three months before paying me? "Shred it," a small voice urged. As the machine slashed the paper and its print, my memory relinquished the experience. I picked up another paper—representing another grudge still intact, stashed away earlier in the year. A guest's tactless comment. A friend's neglectful slight. With each *zwip* of the blades, I let the Holy Spirit rip.

In a few days I'll be ready to turn to my new-year work, now that I've shredded the contents of two wastebaskets, only one of them made of plastic.

Lord, before I tackle the projects of the new year, distract me
with the task of shredding last year's resentments.
—EVELYN BENCE

DECEMBER 30

*So teach us to number our days, that we
may apply our hearts unto wisdom.*
—PSALM 90:12

*L*ast night I stopped at a restaurant for dinner. I was alone and brought my datebook to plan for the next day. After ordering, I gazed at the datebook and realized this year was almost over. I flipped slowly through the pages of past days and weeks and reviewed the past twelve months.

I was amazed to discover all that can happen in a year: I had accepted a new professional position and moved from Texas to Georgia. Beth and I had witnessed the wedding vows of our first child Drew and welcomed our daughter-in-law Katie Alice into our family. Our son Luke had entered the insurance industry, and our daughter Jodi had graduated from Furman University. Somewhere in the middle of all this, I counseled with dozens of students, preached sermons, conducted funerals and wrote a book.

These were just the major events; most of my hours were spent in the routines of living: sleeping, eating, exercising, repairing my car, mowing the lawn, preparing our income tax returns, going to movies, and all the other unremarkable events that fill everyone's days and nights. As my food arrived, I realized the real question confronting me wasn't *How did I spend last year?* but *How will I spend the next? How will I use the most precious of God's gifts—life and time?*

I can make long lists of things to accomplish and commit myself to New Year's resolutions. But I really need to do only two things: Love God with all that I am and love my neighbor as much as I love myself. This is all that matters.

*Lord, keep me from seeing my days as something
I own but rather as a gift that comes from You.*
—SCOTT WALKER

I will forgive their iniquity, and I will remember their sin no more.
—JEREMIAH 31:34

W hen my wife Shirley and I are in Florida, we go out our back door every evening and watch the sun set over the Gulf of Mexico. Some of our neighbors do the same, and they know all about my sunset rating system—ten for the most colorful, on down to one. Usually, I rate them midway on the scale, depending on the intensity of the red afterglows that cascade off the clouds. Tonight's was about a six, but it was special because it was the last day of the year. When the orange orb disappeared behind the sea, it marked the end of this year.

As the shadow of years grows longer, I have a tendency to look back (sometimes perhaps too much) on my wins and losses, my successes and failures. Tonight, after the sun had set, I studied the sandy shore and the gentle waves that caressed it. As I listened, I was reminded of something the late Anne Morrow Lindbergh wrote in her classic *Gift from the Sea* about the tide erasing everything it touches...all our scribbling, all our footprints. Like lost memories. Sometimes we forget things we'd like to remember, but it's also true that some baggage is best left behind.

That's why this is a good day to accept God's forgiving grace for mistakes and shortcomings of the year past and get on with life. He is indeed a God of second chances, and if I truly seek His pardon, He will wash away my sins like waves cleansing the beach. With His help, I can turn away from old sunsets—no matter how beautiful—and look to the redeeming dawn of the new year.

In the next year, Lord, help us aim high,
To heed our best angels—and upon You rely.
—FRED BAUER